p. 136- Conductors

# A COMPOSER'S WORLD

## HORIZONS AND LIMITATIONS

THE CHARLES ELIOT NORTON LECTURES
1949–1950

# A COMPOSER'S WORLD

## HORIZONS AND LIMITATIONS

PAUL HINDEMITH

HARVARD UNIVERSITY PRESS · CAMBRIDGE · 1952

DISTRIBUTED IN GREAT BRITAIN BY
GEOFFREY CUMBERLEGE · OXFORD UNIVERSITY PRESS · LONDON

LIBRARY OF CONGRESS CATALOG CARD NUMBER 52-5033

PRINTED IN THE UNITED STATES OF AMERICA

# PREFACE

IN Thomas Morley's *Plaine and Easie Introduction* (1597), among the important books dealing with the technique of musical composition an exceptionally pleasant one, there appears in the dialogue between the Master and his disciple Philomates a sentence of which I am particularly fond. It reads: "It is no maruayle to see a Snayle after a Rayne to creep out of his shell, and wander all about, seeking the moysture." We all know how sometimes such sentences cling to our memory, annoying and uninvited, sticking all the harder the more we try to remove them. Morley's molluscoid creeper proved to be of this insistent quality. During the period of my writing the present book it hunted me — if this expression may be used with regard to a snail — incessantly and without any reason. Can one be blamed if after many attempts to neglect or outstrip the persecutor, one not only tolerates it but actually feels it to be a part of the present circumstances of creation and construction? Something would be missing if suddenly we were left without such companionship.

Eventually the importunate sentence led me to ask: Is a composer writing a book not like that Snayle, creeping out of his abode of settled professionalism and solid experience, seeking what corresponds to the moysture, looking for readers instead of listeners and forfeiting musical security for doubtful successes in a field through which he can only roam unsupported by professional know-how but at the same time free of professional inhibitions?

After the Snayle and the moysture there still remains the Rayne to be accounted for in our sequence of equalizations. Its equiva-

lent which lured this writer out of his shelter was his being
honored with the appointment to the Charles Eliot Norton pro-
fessorship at Harvard University for the academic year 1949–
1950. The series of lectures given under the auspices of that illustrious Chair of Poetry provided the subject matter for the present
book, although the book form demanded varied modifications
and elaborations in content and structure.

Neither the lectures nor the book was intended to be a musician's professional report to his fellow musicians. Thus the ever-
menacing temptation to write a disguised form of textbook had
to be fought. On the other hand there was no intention to add to
the vast stock of lectures and books on the appreciation of some
phase of musical production or reproduction, all those glimpses
into workshops, those opinions on composers and compositions,
those noncommital aestheticisms, popularizations, and sugar-
coated banalities. Musicians producing words instead of notes are
too easily apt to fall into this sometimes enticing but mostly insipid kind of gossip with its strictly egotistic or pseudoprofound
attitude.

The book aims to be a guide through the little universe which
is the working place of the man who writes music. As such it talks
predominantly to the layman, although the expert composer may
also find some stimulation in it. The core of all the problems puz-
zling the composer — namely, the theoretical considerations concerning the nature and technical potentialities of chordal and tonal
progressions which are his material of construction — is demonstrated in a general way, so as to acquaint the reader with the gist
of the matter without bothering him with the subtleties of technique. Even so, the versed musician may find in that demonstration opinions somewhat different from our scholastic theory. (He
may be interested to know that I am preparing an elaborate textbook on the technique of composition, based on the theories presented in this book.) From the center of basic theory our
discussion will spread out into all the realms of experience which
border the technical aspect of composing, such as aesthetics, soci-
ology, philosophy, and so on. This will be done without the
faintest pretension of saying anything new. Every fact given
is derived from somewhere—even some ideas which I cherished

as the unique results of my own speculation turned out to have
come from predecessors, parallels, or similar formulations elsewhere. Thus the only merit of this survey seems to be its tendency to focus everything surrounding us on the one point: the
composer's work. This approach to a problem is magnanimously
comprehensive; it is at the same time stubbornly one-track. In
short, it is the typical artistic way of understanding the world. It
is entirely opposed to the approach of a scientific mind. To the
scientist our method — or, in his eyes, nonmethod — of looking at
everything without ever fundamentally comprehending it must
seem utterly amateurish. In fact, the artistic approach *is* essentially and inevitably amateurish, its distinction from the amateur's
point of view being merely a considerably wider panorama. We
must be grateful that with our art we have been placed halfway
between science and religion, enjoying equally the advantages of
exactitude in thinking — so far as the technical aspects in music
are concerned — and of the unlimited world of faith.

The tendency of maintaining, nay defending this position
against any nonartistic, nonscientific, and nonreligious attack by
the forces of brutal personal ambition, commercialism, low-grade
entertainment, and the like must inevitably lead to severe criticism
of certain prevailing conditions in the musical producer's orbit.
The reader, once convinced of the author's honest intentions, will
doubtless take this criticism not as an acid outpour of an ill-tem-
pered mind, but as a contribution towards the betterment of untenable and regrettable facts in our musical life, written by one
who has had the privilege of becoming an active factor in it
and by his inclination and vocation is profoundly devoted to the
task of making music maintain a state of integrity in the cultural
development of this continent.

A musician writing a nontechnical book is in an odd situation
compared with the real man of letters. Unless he wants to make
writing books a major part of his activities (which means neglecting composition, a necessity not aspired to by the present writer),
he will hardly ever have an opportunity of amending his statements, of showing further developments, of correcting his mistakes, or of defending himself against misinterpretation, all of
which the professional writer can do in his future books. The

musician-writer simply has to put up with this fact. Let me show you how harassing a situation may arise out of this ostensible incorrigibility of former statements. A quarter of a century ago, in a discussion with German choral conductors, I pointed out the danger of an esoteric isolationism in music by using the term *Gebrauchsmusik*. Apart from the ugliness of the word — in German it is as hideous as its English equivalents workaday music, music for use, utility music, and similar verbal beauties — nobody found anything remarkable in it, since quite obviously music for which no use can be found, that is to say, useless music, is not entitled to public consideration anyway and consequently the *Gebrauch* is taken for granted. Whatever else I had written or said at that time remained deservedly unknown, and of my music very few pieces had reached this country; but that ugly term showed a power of penetration and a vigor that would be desirable for worthier formulations. Some busybody had written a report on that totally unimportant discussion, and when, years after, I first came to this country, I felt like the sorcerer's apprentice who had become the victim of his own conjurations: the slogan *Gebrauchsmusik* hit me wherever I went, it had grown to be as abundant, useless, and disturbing as thousands of dandelions in a lawn. Apparently it met perfectly the common desire for a verbal label which classifies objects, persons, and problems, thus exempting anyone from opinions based on knowledge. Up to this day it has been impossible to kill the silly term and the unscrupulous classification that goes with it. However, this book might accomplish what a lifelong devotion to serious music could not, although one may assume that again some clever classifier will deposit it in the *Gebrauchsmusik* drawer without really knowing what he has stored away. Doubtless the book aims to be useful, but certainly not in the sense that has become synonymous with our term, that is: relying on the tritest relationship of cause and effect in music. Music that has nothing else as its purpose should neither be written nor be used, and the same is true with books on music.

The people of the Harvard University Press have been more than helpful in the preparation of this work. They unflaggingly encouraged a side-line literate who rather preferred writing music; they were patient with an author whose only reliability was his never being on time with his installments; and they had a most generous understanding for his literary and linguistic weaknesses. It is a pleasure to assure them of my heartfelt gratitude.

Paul Hindemith

New Haven, Connecticut
June 1951

# CONTENTS

# A COMPOSER'S WORLD

## HORIZONS AND LIMITATIONS

# 1·

## THE PHILOSOPHICAL APPROACH

A COMPOSITION of everlasting value" — we know of quite a number of musical creations upon which in humility and admiration we bestow this title of reverence. It is our belief in the stability of musical facts that leads us to this and to similar statements. But which musical facts are stable? Certainly not the external body of music in its audible form, although for many people sound seems to be the only factor of importance, perhaps of exclusive validity in their musical experience. An individual piece of music, being many times reborn and going through ever renewed circles of resonant life, through repeated performances, *magic bird —* dies as many deaths at the end of each of its phoenixlike resur- *resurrec. from* rections: no stability here, but a stumbling progression from per- *own ashes* formance to performance. And the totality of this kaleidoscopic *variegated* picture, all the way from a composition's conception to ultimate *changing* death in its last performance is not a stable curve either. Periods *pattern* of appreciation alternate with periods of neglect; false interpreta- tions, overrating, suppression, nonmusical evaluation — all such uncontrollable circumstances influence the total course of the life of a composition; they shorten, darken, brighten, or lengthen it as they do a human being's life on earth.

Sound, the ever present ingredient of music, is the frailest of its qualities. The sound of a Beethoven symphony, performed by our players on modern instruments, in modern concert halls, is different from the audible form the piece assumed in a perform- ance in Beethoven's time. Attempts to reconstruct the sound which was the ideal of Bach and his contemporaries still encoun- ter many obstacles (and probably always will); and access to the world of musical sound in the Gothic era is almost entirely ob- scured and obstructed.

It is partly man's own frailty and his unstable conditions of life that forces each new generation to modify its musical aspects and with them the evaluation of compositions; and it is partly the frailty of the musical form itself, which, because it is not built to withstand continual wear and tear, is subject to the musical equivalent of oxidation and decay. Our modern orchestral repertoire rarely includes pieces more than two hundred years old and most likely never will include much music written before 1750, so long as we maintain our manners and places of performance. The more complex the means of reproduction are, the less time-resistant are the pieces they help to represent. Solo pieces, ensemble and choral works of the sixteenth and even the fifteenth century may occasionally appear on programs, and courageous explorers are sometimes apt to dive down to the very beginnings of organized harmonious music.

All this shows that the "everlasting" value of compositions and their potentialities of performance are by no means eternal, and the majesty of the term "everlasting" dims even further when we compare the vigorousness of a musical composition with the thousands of years an architectural creation may last, or with the periods of development in general history and geology.

And yet, there are in music certain values that are not subject to instability. If we want to recognize and understand such values, we must perceive music not as a mere succession of reasonably arranged acoustical facts; we must extricate it from the sphere of amorphous sound, we must in some way participate, beyond the mere sensual perception of music, in its realization as sound; we must transform our musical impressions into a meaningful possession of our own. How we can do this will be investigated in the following chapters. For the present we will deal merely with philosophical values, the objective of such efforts.

These values, not being tied to the instability of sound or to any other external quality of musical creations, are domiciled in the more esoteric realms of our musical nature. We have to turn to the immaterial, the spiritual aspects of music in order to find them. In our dealings with the ingredients that go into the making of a composition, these values will be of the foremost importance: they will determine the human quality of our music. A musician of culture can hardly be thought of as lacking a strong feeling for, an innate devotion to these values; yet it cannot be the task of a composer untrained in philosophy to analyze them thoroughly. He is not called upon to develop a musical-philosophical system; nor need he, in looking for confirmations of his home-grown philosophy, go systematically through every statement on music ever made in the philosophers' works. Since in venturing into the realm of philosophy we all enjoy freedom of choice, we may concentrate on the works of certain writers and entirely neglect others. We can exercise our prerogative of emphasis or bias without forgetting that our primary concern is, after all, not philosophy, but music.

## II

Let me first refer to a book which, more than fifteen hundred years ago, pronounced remarkable postulates concerning eternal musical values; postulates which have only in the most recent de- *axioms* velopment of music philosophy and music psychology regained importance — obviously without due consideration of the earlier appearance. I am talking about Saint Augustine's *De musica libri sex*. In five of these six books the subject of discussion is meter as used in poetry — for us, whose concept of music differs in many respects from that of the ancients, a musically rather unproductive investigation.

In the sixth book, however, the work develops into a most intelligent analysis of musical perception and understanding. According to Augustine, musical impressions are by no means simple reactions to external stimuli. They are, rather, a complex mixture of diverse occurrences. First, there is the mere physical fact of sound. Although sound can exist independent of any listener, it is indispensable as a basic experience before the perception and mental absorption of music can take place. Second, there is our faculty of hearing: the physiological fact that sound waves act upon our ear and by muscular and nervous transmission release reactions in the brain's center of hearing. Third, there is our ability to imagine music mentally without the stimulus of music actually sounded or without recollective reference to a definite former impression. Fourth, there is our ability to uncover previous musical experiences stored in our memory like old keepsakes, to draw them out of their hiding places, revive them mentally, and allow them to impress us with the same intensity as actual music would do, after which they may again be put to rest in the storage chests of our soul. In all these musical happenings both our corporeal and mental nature participate, with the emphasis constantly shifting from one to the other. Fifth, our mental activity must rise to predominance; we must in the moment of actual perception or of soundless concept subject the musical substance to an intellectual examination and judge its musical shape and grade. Thus the mere activity of perceiving or imagining music is combined with the satisfaction we derive from classifying and evaluating it. But we must not become slaves of this enjoyable satisfaction; it deserves as little confidence as a wooden board carrying us through a river's rapids: although we know its ability to float, we would not trust it without reservation. Musical order, as recognized and evaluated by our mind, is not an end in itself. It is an image of a higher order which we are permitted to perceive if we proceed one step further to the sixth degree on our scale of musical assimilation: if we put our enjoyment of such knowledge ("enjoyment, the weight of the soul!") into the side of the balance that tends towards the order of the heavens and towards the unification of our soul with the divine principle.

This sober abstract of an extensive and erudite dialogue cannot give an idea of its truly modern analysis of our faculty of hearing, nor of the profound and enthusiastic treatment of the subject and the conclusions drawn therefrom. Yet these few excerpts will show the lofty heights of psychological and moral clarity reached by musical comprehension in that period. Practical music in the declining Roman Empire had degenerated from a science into a form of agreeable pastime. It impressed people mostly with its entertaining, sensuous qualities, as it does the overwhelming majority of modern listeners. A work like Augustine's De musica must, in such circumstances, have appeared as a voice of admonition, and as such cannot have enjoyed a great dissemination. On the other hand, such a musical-philosophical treatise was certainly not the individualistic formulation of an isolated philosopher. It must have expressed the thoughts, feelings, and desires of many a person dissatisfied with the state of music in his time.

Books one to five of the work readily confirm this impression, since they deal with a portion of the classical intellectual heritage that was familiar to any cultured person as part of his education. But the abhorrence of everything pertaining to entertainment, even to professional musicianship is evident in the sixth book; and the conclusions of its final chapters transgress the inherited body of knowledge to a hitherto unexpected degree. However, in their serious attempt to coördinate music with the theses of the Christian creed — thus reinstating this form of art in an elevated community of sciences, a position it had enjoyed in the times of ancient philosophy — the consent of believers who saw in music more than a pleasant play of sounds was assured. They recognized in Augustine's conclusions the best moral, musical, and theological foundation for the development of religious music. True, religious music shows us most clearly the direct effect of the Augustinian attitude, but our secular music also can profit from those venerable ideas — in fact, it cannot exist without their support if it is to be more than entertainment. The tenor of that doctrine is: music has to be converted into moral power. We receive its sounds and forms, but they remain meaningless unless we include them in our own mental activity and use their fermenting quality to turn our soul towards everything noble, superhuman, and ideal. It is our own mind that brings about this conversion; music is but a catalytic agent to this end. The betterment of our soul must be our own achievement, although music is one of those factors which, like religious belief, creates in us most easily a state of willingness towards this betterment. In short, we have to be active; music, like humus in a garden soil, must be dug under in order to become fertile. Composers, performers, teachers, listeners — they all must outgrow the mere registration of musical impressions, the superficial and sentimental attachment to sound.

### III

Acknowledging the moral values of the Augustinian attitude and observing its honest scientific foundation, for centuries left unrecognized, we nevertheless may ask whether the serious emphasis on spiritual and even religious aspects is not so grave a burden that its general application will forever remain an unrealizable ideal. Many participants, despite their best intentions, will not have the strength or the knowledge to develop their musical morality above a mediocre level. Can their genuine efforts be considered equal to the experts' more perfect achievements? Can we, furthermore, give full credit to those who after such perfect achievements relapse into periods of idleness? Even the most cultured mind sometimes feels a desire for distracting entertainment, and, as a principle, music for all possible degrees of entertainment ought to be provided. No music philosophy should overlook this fact. There are many methods of creating, distributing, and receiving music, none of which must be excluded from its theses so long as the slightest effort towards stimulating the receiving mind into moral activity is perceptible. The only musical activities to be condemned are those that do not aim at fulfilling such requirements.

Admittedly the dividing line between a devaluated or basically worthless music and a light-weight music of some moral value may not be clearly discernible. Moreover, our Augustinian theorems may not be lenient enough to serve as a guide through this moral-musical no man's land, and there may exist other cases of doubtful musical value in which rigorous decisions may lead to unjust or even entirely false judgments. No wonder, therefore, that many people try to approach the problem of musical responsibility from another angle. Already in medieval times we encounter musical philosophies and theories which oppose Augustinian severity with a more liberal attitude. If on examination we find that these philosophies deal with the problem of musical comprehension with the same devotion and seriousness exhibited in Augustine's work, they will also be accepted as valuable support in our search for clarity.

The most helpful indications of this type can be gathered from Boethius' work *De institutione musica*. It was written in the early sixth century, about one hundred years later than Augustine's *De musica*. Unlike the latter work, it was a well-known book, which throughout the following centuries exerted a strong influence on European musical education. Without this influence the organized technique of composition and its underlying theories, up to about 1700, would probably have taken a course different from the one it actually followed.

The first sentence in Boethius' work can be regarded as the principal thesis of his philosophy. It says: "Music is a part of our human nature; it has the power either to improve or to debase our character." In the relationship of music and the human mind the position of forces has now changed: music has become the active partner; our mind is a passive receiver and is impressed and influenced by the power music exerts. No wonder, then, that music abandons its role as a modest aid to moral growth and assumes gubernatorial rights.

Music itself exists in three different forms, one of which, the so-called *musica humana*, is the principle which unifies the immateriality of our faculty of reasoning with our corporeal existence; which keeps the conscious and rational part of our soul aligned with its instinctive and animalistic feelings; and which brings about the harmonious coherence of our body's members and their smooth and well-tuned synchronization.

The second form of music is *musica instrumentalis*, music as executed by human voices or with the aid of instruments. This meaning of the term "music" coincides with our own modern definition.

The third form, however, acquaints us with the term's most comprehensive meaning. It is *musica mundana*, which governs the heavens, time, and the earth. It causes the planets to revolve in their orbits; it moves the celestial spheres. Without such organizing harmony how would the cohesion of the entire universe be possible?

This definition of music strangely widens the limits of this art, limits which, according to our own concept, are drawn by nothing but the possibilities of the musical material and the intellectual abilities of the producing and reproducing participants. It would lose its strangeness if we could, as did the ancients, classify music as part of the quadrivium, that group of four sciences dealing with measurement. Here we would find music united with geometry, which is concerned with the measurement of nonmoving planes and bodies; with astronomy, as the measurer of moving entities; and with arithmetic, in which measurement is sublimated and concentrated into the operation with abstract numbers. The science of music deals with the proportions objects assume in their quantitative and spatial, but also in their biological and spiritual relations. There is no doubt about the existence of these measurements and the importance of their recognition. The only disturbing element to us seems to be the fact that it is music which rules in this field, and that so many great minds clung tenaciously to this concept. They did not doubt the correctness and reliability of music as a science of measurement. The fact that we see so many scientific heroes contribute to the evolution of music theory seems to provide strong justification for this attitude. The great second-century astronomer Ptolemy, whose concept of the planetary system was generally accepted until the Copernican theory dethroned it some thirteen hundred years later, wrote the major work on Greek music theory; a work that served as a fundamental source of information for many similar books of a later time, including Boethius' *De institutione*. Or we may think of the geometrician Euclid, the physicist Huygens, the mathematician Euler — to mention only one representative of each related science — all of whom wrote on musical-theoretical subjects; or Kepler, whose three basic laws of planetary motion, expounded at the beginning of the seventeenth century, could perhaps not have been discovered, without a serious backing of music theory. It may well be that the last word concerning the interdependence of music and the exact sciences has not been spoken.

IV

The emphasis Boethius placed on the scientific part of musical experience led him quite naturally to judgments which sometimes sound strange to us. Whereas today we evaluate musicians exclusively with regard to their artistic activities, Boethius classified them according to their intellectual and scientific abilities. For Boethius (as for Augustine before him), singing and playing, especially for the purpose of earning a livelihood, is a low-grade, rather contemptible pursuit. Even a performer of highest vocal or instrumental perfection is far removed from musical in-

sight, is not gifted with scientific enlightenment. How could he
be, since all his efforts must be directed towards his technical improvement? Somewhat more elevated than these most sordid of
all musicians are those who are given to composing without being
totally conscious of the technical and intellectual premises of
their actions. They may do their work with talent and conviction,
but with them musical instinct is more important than knowledge.
It is knowledge — knowledge beyond all craftsmanship and intuition — that dictates the actions of the musician belonging to
the third and highest class; "they have the gift of judging everything pertaining to music according to scientific rules," as Boethius says. Let us assume that to the members of this most exalted
caste of musicians it was a duty of honor to combine the craft
of the two lower classes with their own wisdom. Without this
combined insight they could scarcely have possessed the all-em-
bracing power of artistic judgment, as demanded by Boethius,
unless we conjecture that even at that time uninformed music
judges were already existent. Critics ?!

In his *De institutione* Boethius is by no means an independent
author with original ideas. We have already mentioned Ptolemy
as his authority, and as further sources for his music theory he
frankly adds the names of Aristoxenus, Nicomachus, Archytas,
and others. He is, so far as the mere subject matter of his book is
concerned, one of numerous compilers of classical learning. Even
his book's first sentence, already quoted, which depicts music as
the force that influences our souls for good or for evil, is not the
result of his own contemplation. This sentence, the intellectual
meaning of which is the tenor of the entire work, expresses the
idea of musical ethos, so frequently dealt with in Plato's Dia-
logues. In a social order, as envisaged by Plato, music is neither
entertainment nor a stimulus for the moral improvement of the
soul. Music's purpose is to aid the government in its attempt at
educating its citizens to be better citizens: it is music's ethical
power that is summoned up.

Fortunately, Plato's Republic has remained theory. During the
past few decades, in which, for the first time in history, governments have influenced the practice of the arts in a grand
dictatorial manner, our experiences have been rather discourag-

(Stalin)

Prokof.

Shostak.

ing. Theoretically the dictatorship of the philosopher-king and the royal philosopher is demanded, but practically it is without doubt always the greatest musical nitwit with the greatest non-musical power in whose hands rests the decision on both life and style of a musician.

The idea of musical ethos in its extreme Platonic form is in strict opposition to Augustine's musical attitude. To be sure, they agree in strictly refuting an autocracy of music in the form of shallow and narcotizing entertainment, but Augustine would never grant any worldly power the right to block the individual's musical and spiritual evolution and thus prevent his intellectual apprehension of a supreme divine law. Opponents of the Platonic idea also appeared from the opposite direction. To them it seemed quite inadmissible to couple such sober concepts as state, government, philosophy, and mathematics with music, which in its audible form seemed to be eternally elusive and irrational, and accordingly suspect.

v

A glimpse at the writings of the Roman philosopher Sextus Empiricus (ca. 200 A.D.) will confirm this statement. As a convinced skeptic, inventing arguments against all the sciences practiced during his time, he also scrutinizes music (in Book VI of his treatise *Against the Mathematicians*). He does not believe in any ethical effect of music. Music, as a mere play with tones and forms, can express nothing. It is always our own sentiment that ascribes to the ever-changing combination of tones qualities which correspond with certain trends in our mental disposition. Consequently, music cannot be used as a means of education, and all the stories which are told about the ethical power of music are plain bunk. There is the well-known anecdote of the flute player who plays for a drunk a tune in a certain mode, in order to prevent him from doing mischief. It merely proves that flute players are sometimes more successful educators than are philosophers. Spartan soldiers enter a battle to the accompaniment of music — certainly not because of the exciting effect the tunes have on them, but because of their need of some doping influence which blots out the fear of the horrors to come. Frequently music's salutary effect on animals is mentioned; but have we ever seen a horse react to music the same way an audience does in the theater? Although Sextus' attacks are spiced with similar tidbits, his argumentations are not to be taken too lightly. They contain many sound notions which are important as a regulative against a superemotional or superspiritual evaluation of music. His philosophical system is so well founded that it could serve as a pretty strong justification for our lowest-grade modern entertainment music! Only towards the end of his brisk arguments does one hesitate to follow him. Here he tries to disprove other philosophers with their own logic and demonstrates rather convincingly the nonexistence of melodies and rhythm, and consequently of music altogether.

If Sextus' maxims became our sole guide in the search for musical enlightenment, we would soon be relieved of any worries concerning our musical behavior, for sooner or later music would disappear from our lives. Also Plato's ethos, as recommended and regulated by the government, would be no source of satisfaction, because we do not want to be deprived of our self-determination in respect to music; and so long as no brown, red, or other colored dictatorship sterilizes any individual impulse, we want to be free to produce music, perform it, and listen to it in our own personal ways and to assimilate and interpret it likewise.

It seems that of the different attitudes towards music, as discussed in these pages, our best choice would be either the Augustinian or the Boethian philosophy. Both grant us our own personal and uninhibited decision. There is even, in principle, no third position. The ethos of Plato, the skepticism of Sextus, and many other attitudes, no matter how unrelated they may appear at first sight, are only deviations from, or variations of, our two main trends; or they may represent one of the innumerable middle positions between the two extremes.

Extremes they really are! The Augustinian precept, in which our mind absorbs music and transforms it into moral strength; and the Boethian precept, in which the power of music, its ethos, is brought into action upon our mind. Truly these are basic and unalterable musical values. Either of these philosophies can lead us to the loftiest goals; either enjoys the protectorship of the sci-

ences. Great composers may apply their talent in either direction;
the listener may in either way find his most sublime satisfaction.
Each individual participant (author, performer, and listener
alike) has to decide — and does so, mostly unconsciously —
whether he wants to turn to the one side or the other; whether he
prefers a half-and-half enjoyment of advantages; or whether
eventually, as an unstable wreck without any motion of his own,
he merely suffers himself to be tossed around in the ocean of
sound.

## VI

The ideal conduct would be not a weak compromise of extremes, but their forceful unification in one single act of will
power. In other words, although the Augustinian doctrine is
silent in respect to the merely technical aspects of music, so that
theoretically the highest moral effect could be achieved with
music of lowest technical quality, we may assume that music of
high quality will at least not be felt to disturb the moral effect.
Thus we can imagine that the participant of a high culture, due
to his musical taste wants his moral activity incited by only the
most perfect music — music that answers the strictest Boethian
demands. On the other hand, if we understand the ethical power
of music and know how to apply it with maximum efficacy, performers and listeners conscientiously desiring to appreciate such
music can do so only by profound devotion to the cause; and
once they reach this point of unselfish penetration, the step to the
Augustinian ideal of moral assimilation is a slight one. To see the
fusion of both doctrines in one single piece of music and its perfect appreciation by performers and listeners who in their noble
and understanding fervor do justice to both, we will have to wait
for a better world. Here on earth we can do nothing better than
strive for the closest possible approach to this ideal.

Augustine's musical philosophy, with its decided renunciation
of external effects, its inclination towards superhumanity, is never
threatened by the danger of degeneration. To many, even to
those *bonae voluntatis*, the path to perfection will be too steep;
they may feel forced to be satisfied with whatever level they can
reach, and some may give up in desperation. Still others, in their

craving for the utmost sublimation, may escape the realm of physical music entirely and dwell in a sphere of purest musical spirituality. Boethius' musical philosophy, however, demanding a submission to the ethic power of music (hence implicitly to its sensual allurements as well) easily becomes the subject of degeneration. Its strongly intellectual trend may produce music that in its utter aridity is unpalatable; it may transform the listener into the frequently occurring snob. The emphasis on all facts technical may end in meaningless sound that runs along self-sufficiently without moving the listener's soul. The stress laid upon the outward qualities of the musical material — on sound and form — may in megalomaniacal hypertrophy explode into unartistic noise. The essentially active function of music may force the listener into such a state of passivity that his faculty of musical perception will crave only pieces which offer no resistance whatever, which in every respect satisfy his basest instincts — music which is nothing but a cheap and trashy amenity, an opiate always and everywhere available. Our present era, in which the majority of listeners is constantly subject to this kind of music, has, in my opinion, reached a point below which a further degeneration of the Boethian attitude is impossible.

In spite of this gloomy statement, I do not mean that the situation is hopeless. There still are, and always will be, composers who are more than mere arrangers of sounds. Among the multitudes of listeners there exist large groups who demand more from music than a permanent lulling accompaniment to their most banal activities. And not all performers are as godforsaken as many of our virtuosi with their limited repertoire of circus tricks. Finally, in that science which deals with the essence, the effects, and the history of music, one observes a growing tendency to replace the predominantly materialistic methods of the past with ways of research and communication the impulses of which stem from a closer inclination towards an Augustinian interpretation of music and its functions. The durable values of music are not forgotten; they are as alive as they were thousands of years ago, and we as musicians can do nothing better than to accept them as the guiding principles for our work.

# 2·

## PERCEIVING MUSIC INTELLECTUALLY

A PLAIN listener who wants nothing but musical enjoyment; the ordinary performer, eager to display his dexterity; the simple-minded composer who writes his music in a
kind of harmless bewitchment — what do they care for the philosophical approach to music! They say: let the philosophers pile
up obstacles between the music and its appreciation, we want
our music in its natural state, and we shall not spoil our uninhibited receptivity with cerebral extravagance. A clever member of
this group, who has read our first chapter, may find the justification for his endeavors in our own words: what else is he doing
but experiencing music in the Boethian sense, which did not preclude low-level, unresisting surrender to the charms of music?
We may ask: if he is that clever, could he not have seen his plain
so-called musical enjoyment as one of many simple reactions
to music which had to be established before any Boethian or
Augustinian — or any intermediate — method of evaluation could
be assumed? Augustine acquainted us with the necessity of perceiving music first before any qualitative comprehension could
result.

Before we investigate further, we must agree on one point:
music, whatever sound and structure it may assume, remains
meaningless noise unless it touches a receiving mind. But the mere
fact that it is heard is not enough: the receiving mind must be
active in a certain way if a transmutation from a mere acoustical
perception into a genuine musical experience is to be accomplished. The following pages will be devoted to an inquiry into
this transmutation.

The first step, the initial detachment of music from its sounding
medium and its approach to our inner ear, seems to be what is

usually called a musical impression. Only too willingly are we inclined, whenever we listen to music, to interpret the word "impression" literally and think of something being pressed upon us. If musical impressions were exclusively of this kind, however, it would be impossible to build up musical structures in our memory, independent of music actually sounded; and it would be equally impossible to imagine musical structures independent of any recollection, or structures that have no connection with actual music and perhaps not with sound at all. As everybody knows, such imaginary structures can evoke in one's mind the same feeling of musical satisfaction, of artistic fulfillment that is released by the perception of music actually sounded. They may not only be far removed from sound, they may even appear without being supported by any musical knowledge or regulated musical experience of the fanciful mind. Are there not many among us who scarcely can read musical notes, to whom the daily influx of musical sounds has no significance as something conceived and constructed, and yet who in some moments feel within themselves, neither prompted nor lured, a ringing and singing, a vague musical impulse? There is no clearly circumscribed vision, let alone an organized form. Yet these vague feelings may provide more valuable musical sensations than any overwhelming actual musical manifestation ever could. Certainly those moments of inner ringing and singing are but minute chemical and electrical transformations in the cells of our brain, but we nevertheless have to understand them as the very origin of musical composition, as the conceptional sparks out of which may grow a musical masterpiece. Although they may occur frequently and in great number in anyone's imagination, most of them will remain without any creative consequence, for it is only with all the technical implements, with all the experience of a versatile composer, that those vague phantoms can be converted into real music.

II

Perhaps one may doubt the practical applicability of such considerations. For a composer the dimness of the inner ringing and singing is most frequently superseded by more prominent steps in the course of musical creation. In the performer's mind sensations of the kind described will almost inevitably be buried under percepts closely tied to his usual means of expression. And for the listener, the average consumer of music, hardly ever will music as he hears it be confronted with music as it appeared in his dreamlike musical phantoms; nor will he, haunted by some musical inferiority complex, have any confidence in his musical vision. If in exceptional cases his creative inner voice should begin its mysterious ringing while he is listening to the sound of actual music, he probably will immediately and unconsciously concentrate his entire attention on the audible reality, and his yet unborn ideas will again drown in the flood of the unconscious, whence they rose palely and timidly. He is what he wants to be, and in that role he is the musicians' most preferred customer: the fully devoted listener, the absorbed recipient of music.

Did we not mention an activity instrumental in the transformation of sounded music into percepts? Our recipient is not as inert as his attitude suggests. His efforts are not noticeable, though, as they do not cross the limits of their mental dwelling. His activity can be described as follows. While listening to the musical structure, as it unfolds before his ears, he is mentally constructing parallel to it and simultaneously with it a mirrored image. Registering the composition's components as they reach him he tries to match them with their corresponding parts of his mental construction. Or he merely surmises the composition's presumable course and compares it with the image of a musical structure which after a former experience he had stored away in his memory. In both cases the more closely the external musical impression approaches a perfect coincidence with his mental expectation of the composition, the greater will be his aesthetic satisfaction. This sensation, consisting of the sounding stimulus which reaches the listener's ear and his active transformation of it into musical meaning by matching it with a known musical image, may be compared to the optical impression caused by two differently colored lantern slides projected simultaneously from a single luminous source: an imperfect concurrence of their contours has a dissatisfactory, perhaps even disturbing or revolting effect on the spectator. Only their perfect coincidence ensures the ful-

fillment of aesthetic expectations the picture is supposed to release.

Doubtless this ability of parallel mental construction will be
considered natural for a musician who by his professional experience ought to be used to all sorts of creative or recollective
imaginations of a musical nature. Also a skilled listener of long
standing and musical intelligence may easily be seen to possess
such ability. But how can a listener without musical education
and with only a modest auditive experience accomplish this seem-
ingly complicated task of mental coconstruction? He is ignorant
of both its possibility and necessity, and probably would never
like to be made conscious of its existence, since to him conscious
knowledge seems to be the deadly antagonist of the emotions
which apparently are the immediate and undisturbed effect of an
active perception. Why, after all, should be dragged into consciousness something which, with even a slight amount of experience in listening, operates almost automatically? The answer is:
Everyone who wants to listen understandingly to musical structures builds up within his mind his own technique — the musical
specialist as well as the unsophisticated recipient. The difference
between their actions is one of degree rather than of quality.
Courses in music appreciation, like other equally well-meant but
silly educational devices which intend to help the man of little experience, will aid just as little in his accumulation of analytical
knowledge beyond the crudest outlines as any instruction in fiddle playing can tell the pupil what his subtlest muscular adjustments at any given moment ought to be. Vague indications
can be given, nothing else. The innermost physical and mental
adaptation is the individual's own personal achievement.

Seen from this angle, our way of listening to music or imagining music is based on previous audibly-musical or imaginary-
musical experiences. A judgment of a most recent musical
impression depends for its establishment on such antecedent experience, and serious musical enjoyment in turn depends on the
preceding judgment. Enjoyment of this kind arises only if the recipient of music, guided by his judgment, knows at each moment
which part of a musical development is entering into the focus of
his conscious attention, and what the value and function of this

part is within the entire structure. He is in the same position as a hiker in a landscape, who knows his bearings in relation to the surrounding hills and valleys by conclusions derived from former excursions, descriptions, or imaginations, and who distributes his required efforts according to this very scale of measurement. The difference between the naïve hiker, on the one hand, and the professional geometrician or the native fully acquainted with the countryside, on the other, is merely the greater experience of the latter two and their knowledge of short cuts that permits a more rational distribution of their efforts — again a difference in degree instead of quality. Furthermore, in the case of the experienced connoisseurs, the element of surprise is felt as less disturbing than with the less informed judges, so that deviations from or additions to their former experiences are not shunned as blurrings of the present enjoyment, but are appreciated as an increase in knowledge.

If all evaluating perception of music or an equally appreciative manner of performing can always be traced back to preceding experiences, there must have been in each human being's life a moment when a first conscious apperception of a musical impression did not permit any reference to former ones. Consequently there exists a primordial musical experience of a very primitive nature, and we must assume that it comes into existence in the undeveloped being's mind by perceiving a fact of life that is common both to him and to music, namely motion. The novice in his earliest encounter with music seeks for sensations corresponding to those that he knows as being caused by his own acts of motility. Their organization according to space, duration, and intensity, the feeling of which is already well established in his emotional experience, serves as measurement for the penetrating audible impressions and soon he finds in them also a motion the course of which can be felt as being short or long, energetic or sluggish, as going to and fro.

### III

Two different conclusions can be drawn from our considerations. First, it is a long way from a primitive participation in music founded on mere associations of motion to a simultaneous and parallel mental construction of a musical form's sounding entity with all its ballast of temporal proportions, harmonic-tonal implications, and melodic lines. Many listeners progress but slightly on this path. Their ability of simultaneous mental reconstruction of sounding successions does not rise too far above the aforementioned sensation of a simple correspondence between motions. If they are to participate in musical experiences and in the enjoyment of musical structures, they must be given a kind of music which makes use of obtrusive (if not importunate) meters, brief and symmetric phrases, and simplest harmonic-tonal and melodic constructions. Thus kept in close proximity to the most primitive impulses of motion, this music permits them to activate coconstructively even the scant recollections of their inarticulate musical practice. Our present-day composers of marches, dances, and songs see to it that this group of participants in music be not in want of substance for their analytical and reconstructive activity. But even the more experienced and more pretentious participants will not always be able or in the mood to construct simultaneously their own images of complex musical compositions. A composer must take into account such periods of slackening energy. In his calculations he must include the inevitable fact of instability in quantity, intensity, and duration of the perceptive energy a listener is able to muster and he must avoid weakening the listener's attention by a constant demand for a high-tensioned collaboration.

Secondly, we recognize as a requisite for the listener's active coconstruction the essential possibility of foreseeing and anticipating the musical structure as it arises in the performance, or at least, if the composition is utterly new to the recipient, his being given a chance to conjecture with a high degree of probability its presumable course. A musical structure which due to its extreme novelty does not in the listener's mind summon up any recollections of former experiences, or which incessantly disappoints his constructive expectations, will prevent his creative coöperation. He cannot adjust his sense of proportion to the unfolding structure, he loses the feeling for his position in the sounding terrain, he does not recognize the significance of the single structural members in reference to the entity, he even loses the feeling for the coherence of these members. For him music goes astray, disappears in chaos; it deteriorates into the mere amorphous assembly of sound it was before it entered the zone of active coöperation in the listener's mind.

In view of all this, we may conclude that there is — strange as it may sound in the face of countless attempts at modernization of the musical means of expression — in principle never anything new in the general order, shape, and mutual relationship of musical successions. We may even go so far as to say that basically nothing new can ever be introduced into such successions, if we do not want to see the participant in music degraded to a dull, apathetic receptacle, an absorbent sponge reaching the point of saturation without showing any sign of reaction.

IV

Once we agree to this statement, our opinion in respect to musical facts will undergo significant changes. What then remains of the importance which we customarily ascribe to all questions of a composer's style? We prefer to think of his tone-combining craft as possessing an infinite variability, even power of eternal regeneration; but it merely permits a limited number of variations within the given limitations of its sounding ingredients. The building material cannot be removed very far away from certain structural, harmonic-tonal, and melodic prototypes, so that the listener can assume an active part in the process of musical realization.

Furthermore, the continual accumulation of experiences in a listener's mind should not be overrated. Once he reaches a certain point of versatility in his power of musical coconstruction, no further progress seems to be possible. Thus his experience, rising from primordial feelings of comparative motion to a climax of lateral cocreation, can be likened to an arc which surges up as part of a tremendous circle and then slows down and flattens into a parabolic curve. From now on, all musical structures that stand entirely without his previous experience will have to exert their impact many times on his physical and mental receptivity if they are to be added to his stock of accumulated knowledge. We know how the more performances a listener needs for the comprehension of music complex in texture, the less chance he seems to be given of a sufficient number of hearings. Even if he were to have such hearings, the final effect would not be a sensation of constantly accumulating novel experiences. Rather, the more familiar he became with the piece, the more he would continue to discover in it similarities to compositions previously heard.

However, we must admit that the amassment of many listeners' experiences in the course of decades and centuries causes some kind of so-called progress, which expresses itself in the acknowledgment of hitherto unknown stylistic patterns or technical novelties. This progress does not greatly exceed the very banal but ever newly experienced and always overrated fact that Ockeghem's style is different from Schönberg's, and that a production of tones with the aid of lever-works or valved tubes provides other technical possibilities than strings or human vocal chords afford. Beyond the ever-changing aspects of stylistic and technical evaluation this "progress" does not affect the essential qualities of music, its meaning and its emotional effects on the recipient, its everlasting values. Although the recipient may derive certain advantages from the accumulated experiences of generations, just as in turn these generations profit from individual contributions, the music of our day cannot touch other regions of our intellectual and emotional life than those touched in participants of the past by their own contemporary music. In this respect a modern symphony concert is neither more advanced nor better than the simple tune a stone-age man created musingly on his bone flute.

This fact seems to emerge from our investigation: we are not omnipotent in the field of musical creation. We must be grateful if within the narrow domain that is marked out by the participants' mental abilities and by the limited number of technical possibilities, we can move about to some extent without encountering too many obstacles. Beyond the aforementioned "progress" there is no continous advancement. If in our incessant onward march we can avoid a repetitious circling around, we shall have achieved a good deal. Transforming the circle, with all our energy, into a spiral on which at a higher or lower level we repeatedly come close to what in music others before us have constructed, felt, and experienced — more we cannot do. All this sounds, at least to many musicians and music lovers, very pessimistic. It disturbs their *Weltansicht*, which generally is the musical equivalent of a stockbroker's: it is bright as long as business is lively, and collapses with a train wreck, a strike, or the appearance of the boll weevil. The importance of these facts is gone once we begin to understand our world as a tiny spot in the universe, its life of a moment's duration, its matter a particle of dust. Again the musical equivalent: how unimportant is a composer's personal ambition, a performer's craving for success, the listeners' craze for enjoyment.

This is, of course, no invitation to a negligence of the highest quality in music. On the contrary. How could a man creating music overcome his personal ambition, if the achievement of a perfect technique did not enable him to develop his gift to its limits? A performer must earn his successes with his musical superiority, and the listener must be brought to artistic satisfaction. But they must not become the victims of such tyrants as technique, success, and pleasure. If they recognize in their greatest achievements the vanity of all earthly efforts, only then are they worthy to contribute with the full weight of their conviction to the eternal values of music. This is their genuine intellectual approach.

# 3·

## PERCEIVING MUSIC EMOTIONALLY

MANY medieval writers on musical subjects open their statements with an impressive flourish which is intended to put the reader in the right mood. Sometimes such openings are hardly more than rhetorical fanfares, but there is one that has a more profound signification. It is the sentence *Musica est scientia bene modulandi* — a definition as clear, well-coined, and fitting as any ever given. We first encounter it in Augustine's *De musica*, we see it again in the *Institutiones musicae* of Cassidorus, a contemporary of Boethius, and we find it in its original or in slightly changed form in many another treatise.

According to this statement music is a science, not an art, and like science, is governed by laws derived by reasoning from accurate natural facts. It is not an activity subject to the caprices of our moods, it forbids arbitrariness. In Boethius' classification of musicians, already mentioned in Chapter I, we became acquainted with this attitude towards music. Further confirmation can be found in an amendment to that classification by Regino of Prüm (ca. 900), who states that a musician "with deliberate calculation learned the science of musicianship, not by the practice of the craft but by the power of reasoning."

Going back to our sentence *Musica est scientia bene modulandi*, we may read the adverb *bene* with particular stress, since it brings the scholastic definition into closest relation to our previous statements. Music being a science, doing it *bene* not only means the achievement of a high perfection, fulfilling the Boethian ideal of flawless composition and performance; it means that this perfection be used for a moral end, with conviction, without any disturbing external brilliance or other inessential factors, in short: in Augustinian spirit.

This science of *modulandum* is not concerned with modulation in the modern sense. We have to interpret the word in the original meaning of modeling, assembling, shaping; in a more specific sense: constructing, composing rationally; or, emphasizing its basic and most profound signification: fitting something pliable into a concave mold. The pliable matter in this case is sound with all its possibilities of *modulandum* in Boethius' interpretation, the mold being the performers' and listeners' minds, into which this material is cast and through which it gets its meaning and its moral significance — provided the performer and the listener know their Augustinian obligations.

Has all this any bearing on our modern activities as composers, musicians in general, and listeners? Yes. First of all, that old sentence has a healthy prophylactic power which always reminds us that music is not something nebulous, is not created out of nothing by the artist's unconscious furor, is not a hazy utterance, hazily perceived. It tells us: in producing and perceiving music you must keep your feet on the solid ground of our earth, although with your imagination you may rove through the universe. Once you lose this firm stand on solid ground, music loses its characteristics as an artistic manifestation, it becomes an individualistic vagary and as such has no validity except for the composer himself and his bewitched devotees. The *scientia* of music gives us this firm stand.

Generally a musician is not too fond of sciences, especially of those that in his opinion have no connection with music. Physics he perhaps allows to have its say, since he is well aware of the acoustical conditions of his art. At mathematics, however, he looks with scorn, because in his opinion the obvious exactitude of this science cannot be reconciled with the artistic liberty of musical creation. Yet in former times the scientific roots of music were embedded in mathematics. With the continous increase of technical knowledge in music, notably the widening aspects of harmony and tonality, mathematics proved insufficient as a foundation. Physical facts became a more reliable scientific basis, and nowadays we are on the verge of entering with our research that innermost field in which the very actions of music take place: the human mind. Thus psychology, supplementing — in due time perhaps replacing — former mathematical, physical, and physiological *scientiae*, will become the science that eventually illuminates the background before which the musical figures move in a state of meaningful clarity. But this science is, as a foundation for musical speculation and technique, even more suspect to the musician than was mathematics. Now it is not only the sounding form of music that is violated by nonmusical intrusion, it is the musician's own artistic self that is attacked. The sacred circle which he himself does not dare penetrate, save in a state of divine delirium, seems to be blasphemed by rude-minded ignoramuses. Something has been touched that only music itself can touch: his most personal musical feelings.

II

The term "musical feeling" is vague and ambiguous: it may have completely different meanings to different persons. If we replace it with "emotional reactions," we know more precisely what is meant: musical structures impress us; we receive them, either submitting our minds to the ethical power of music, or transforming the impression into moral strength, as shown before; but besides that, we are touched emotionally. Some structures are sad, sound sad, express sadness, or make us sad — or whatever commonplace expressions may be used to describe this fact. Gaiety and an infinite number of other emotional hues are likewise connected with musical impressions.

If we want to apply the term *scientia bene modulandi* to our modern state of musical activities, we shall have to divide this *scientia* into two branches. One will be concerned with all facts technical, namely the qualities of the sounding material; how to put this material together into audible structures; questions of performance — in short, with music as it appears until the moment it steps over the threshold between our outer and inner ear. This branch corresponds essentially with *scientia* in its ancient sense, the difference being the many times greater number of modern technical possibilities. The second branch tries to discover what happens to music when the transformed audible impression reaches our cerebral center of hearing, where it is removed from the directive influence of conscious action and acts

autonomically and automatically; in short, the second branch
deals with emotional reactions. Technical questions will be discussed in a later chapter; here and now I want to concentrate on
the discussion of emotional reactions only.

The listener cannot avoid having emotional reactions; the musician must not attempt to neglect them. The more our *scientia*
brings them into the musician's power, preventing them from degeneration, the more justified and esteemed is music. If the emotions did not respond to music, musical sounds would be as senseless as a gramophone playing on an uninhabited island. Listeners
usually do not want to be bothered with an analysis of their emotional reactions. They feel clearly that they are touched emotionally by musical impressions and sometimes try to formulate in
words what they feel. Beyond that they do not progress, because
as listeners they want to derive the greatest amount of pleasure
possible from their participation in music, and any attempts at
reflection and analysis are apt to disturb their enjoyment. From
musicians we could expect a more profound penetration of the
subject, but alas, they are almost more opposed to enlightenment
than are the listeners. Of course, they know by experience that
the forms of sound they erect release matching responses in the
listeners' minds, and they trust their own unconscious ability of
selection which doubtless will lead them to find the right patterns. Can we blame them, after the kind of education they have
gone through? Usually they were made to believe that too clear
a knowledge of physiological and psychological facts had distracting effects on musical production and reproduction, and
their daily work with musical building material and tools made
them accept emotional reactions as foregone conclusions which
did not need to be subjected to further questioning.

Scientists, working in the field of musical research — philosophers, psychologists, musicologists — could have done much to
clarify this muddled situation. Instead of asking hecatombs of
average-minded *Versuchspersonen* how they listened to music
and what their feelings were while perceiving it, would it not
have been more instructive to ask the musician, particularly the
creative musician, how he obtained this or that emotional reaction and what kind of stimulus he used? It seems that the scien-

tist, in a kind of fear, shuns the music of the real musician, just as much as the musician shuns science, as disturbing his familiar hunting grounds. Perhaps we demand too much. This branch of our *scientia* is still so young that to expect definite answers to even a few of all the burning questions would be unwise. These answers will be forthcoming when excellent scientists, interested in music instead of collecting mere data about music (almost exclusively music of the past at that!), come into close collaboration with excellent musicians interested in science. In the meantime a musician who wants to make his artistic activity more efficient by recognizing more clearly the definite relations between musical causes and emotional reactions, can do nothing but struggle along unaided. In his capacity as a musician he can handle musical causes with authority, since all the musical experience possible can be his. As a scientist his labor necessarily remains that of an amateur, lacking the support of both scientific erudition and scientific methods of research.

III

I would like to see all following statements in this chapter evaluated on this basis. No harm is being done if our discussion leads to false conclusions. On the other hand, even this dilettantism may within the framework of our modest project produce some valuable results. Let us, with the amateur's uninhibited courage, pick out the most crucial of all questions and try to find an answer to it, trusting that the solution of one riddle may spur the reader to proceed on his own account with further explorations. This question is: What really are the emotional reactions music releases? For an answer let us turn to the most significant member in the group of participants in music, the composer. He faces the problem of musico-emotional relations with utter directness; he is always forced to solve it technically in some way or other, consciously or instinctively. The performers' and listeners' experiences are not essentially different from the composer's. They repeat what he anticipated, in a weakened, diluted, less concentrated manner. Thus his individual answer may, in spite of its inevitable exaggerations, be regarded as generally valid for all participants. Having obtained his answer we shall ask him to amend it with a second statement. After his answer to our question we shall know about emotional reactions, but we still shall be ignorant about what could be done musically with such knowledge. We shall therefore ask him what conclusions a composer draws in respect to his craft, once he has entered the obviously somewhat dangerous field of psychological curiosity.

Let us approach the answer to our first question — the question "What are emotional reactions?" — in a rather roundabout way. This will acquaint us with many different facets of our problem. Let us first question one of those composers who insist that his listeners are not supposed to "feel" anything while listening to his compositions. They are merely to perceive, to understand, and possibly to admire the form of appearance of his musical work and its performance, nothing else. Even if his listeners want to please him and try hard to act as he wants, can they really do so? Does not the step from merely perceiving a musical structure to a very rudimentary understanding of it (which would have to be achieved by way of our mental parallel construction) already cause some feeling of aesthetic satisfaction in the listener's mind? Does not the next step, which the composer wanted to have taken, from this satisfaction to admiration cause an even higher feeling of satisfaction? These feelings of satisfaction, which inevitably are accompanied by some feeling of enjoyment, are due to this very feeling of enjoyment already contrary to the composer's sober intentions. But matters are getting worse. Beyond the primitive enjoyment derived from a mere perceiving, understanding, and admiring, some phrases of the piece which according to the composer's intentions were to remain unconnected with the listener's emotions, will have, merely by their individual form of appearance, a more pleasing effect than other phrases. Their comparatively high sensual appeal will distinguish them from their environment. They are felt as being more beautiful and are appreciated accordingly. A purely sentimental evaluation, deranging our composer's plans, has sneaked in through the back door, has been smuggled in illegally as contraband. Moreover, one listener's sentimental evaluation will be different from another listener's, and this individualistic behavior is of course a hard blow to the composer's unsentimental demands, the more so, since neither he nor the listener can prevent it.

Let us assume that this composer, in order to block his listeners' relapse into sentimentality, announces: "This piece which I wrote for a group of string instruments, has to be played to sound like a riveting machine and the listener has to take it as he would take a riveting machine's rattling." As advice to the players on how to reproduce the acoustical part of a piece of music by playing it, this statement is admissible. We may understand it as a metaphorical remark of an artist about his work, which as in all such cases is a rather uncontrolled utterance born out of the impulse of the moment. As a statement concerning the emotional reaction of the listener it does not take into account the real facts.

How does the listener react after being told about the relation between the piece and the machine? If he is a listener of some musical culture, his reasoning will probably run as follows: "This piece reminds me very faintly of the rattling of a riveting machine, but it is not like the rattling of a riveting machine, since it lacks the incessant regularity of it. If the composer wants me to have the same feeling a riveter's rattling releases in me, he is wrong. Although the comparison of the piece's rattling with the machine's gives me some aesthetic pleasure which is somewhat on the humoristic side, I do not feel satisfied. If he wanted to produce a rattling effect similar to the machine's, his rattling is only a weak reproduction, it does not rattle enough, and it is too much 'stylized away' from the original. If, on the other hand, he wanted to impress me on a purely musical basis, my musical judgment, conditioned by my experience and the taste derived therefrom, tells me that it rattles too much and that it does so at the expense of the string instruments' sound, which here is very much removed from their intrinsic sonority."

We are convinced that the composer should not have told the listener of the similarity with the riveting machine. If he wanted the rattling effect to impress the listener, he could have produced it without referring to the machine. Then the listener would perhaps have drawn the conclusion "it sounds similar to a riveter's rattling," although he would have had a choice of other rattlings in describing his impression, such as: the clattering of a railroad on the tracks, the chirping of a cricket, or the constant dripping of rain on a metal roof. Or he might detest the reference to any nonmusical rattling altogether and want to hear it just as rattling *an sich*. If the listener of his own free will decides that, in spite of the similarity to the noises of railroads, crickets, and rain, it reminds him of a riveting machine's rattling, he may do so if he pleases, but he should not be directed verbally.

If the composer was wrong in leading the listener astray, he is doubly wrong because he deceives himself. If a riveting machine's rattling had to be produced, the simplest way would have been to use this instrument. But he avoided this. Instead he went to a great deal of trouble to invent, construct, write down, and have performed a highly stylized form of rattling — a rattling the production of which is so expensive, compared to the cost of the original rattling, that with the money spent in paying the cost of engraving, printing, and publishing the piece, the honorarium of the composer (if any), and the players' fees, five or six riveting machines of the best quality could have been bought. If he went to all this trouble merely to have the same effect the more rational and cheaper-working machine produces, he puts the value of his work on a low level indeed. If, furthermore, he thinks he is awfully modern with his reference to a riveter, we have to tell him that he is a romantic with all the trimmings, for only a composer of the romantic type can deceive himself to such a degree as to believe: (1) I am actually demonstrating a riveting machine's rattling — which he is not, since he is using a group of string players. (2) The effect of my piece is that of a riveting machine's rattling — which it is not, since it rattles musically. (3) The listener takes this rattling for a riveting machine's — he does not, no listener is that naïve. (4) Music has to portray the spirit of our time and consequently make use of impersonal, unsentimental, nonseducing, antiromantic sounds.

It is particularly the last-mentioned "spirit of the time" which is the reason for much confusion in composers' minds. How can a man who seriously believes in this powerful spirit adhere to our manner of writing music? He believes in mechanization, but he himself uses the most old-fashioned ways of manufacturing. His methods of production, that is, writing scores by hand, copying parts, practicing with players, are so obsolete, that the man who uses a whirling wooden rod instead of switching on the electric current in order to produce fire seems to be rather modern. And our composer is telling us about modernism in art!

Only in one case would this romantic enthusiast have been fully justified in doing what he did, namely if his artistic objective actually was to puzzle the listener with the conflict of interpreting the instruments' playing mechanistically or the riveting machine's rattling musically. However, we may doubt whether this result is worth the relatively great musical effort, and whether the element of surprise which doubtless was the hidden motive of this procedure could not have been served more effectively by just putting the riveting machine on the stage before a non-expecting concert audience.

All this shows that an artist's remark about one of his pieces, whether made casually or meant as a serious statement, is not to be taken as an artistic confession, as is too often done. On the other hand, nothing is in principle said against rattling effects in music, against musicians who like to write them, or even against riveting machines (this is the last time in this context that riveting machines are mentioned).

IV

In the preceding example it was the similarity of a rattling in music to a certain natural rattling which was supposed to strike the listener. It is the well-known technique of program music which counts heavily on this principle of imitation — imitation of noises not always in a naturalistic but sometimes in a stylized form, in which only a remote connection with mere noise remains. Plain confrontation of sounding structures provided by nature (as, for instance, the recorded voices of nightingales) with a composition's sounds as part of the artistic effect, seems to be the most primitive application of a programmatic technique. Musical descriptions of railroad locomotives, football games, and steel mills need a higher degree of transformation, and once we are served music which is supposed to tell us about Lelio's opium dreams, the domestic life of the Strauss family, or the fruitless siege of a city, we can assume that program music has climbed to the highest peaks of its possibilities.

The value of all this onomatopoetic tone juggling would not amount to much, if beyond it (and sometimes despite it) the composer did not tie it to music which impresses the listener in a purely musical fashion. The listener's reaction to this kind of music is: "What I am hearing now is supposed to be the sigh of relief that the whale emitted when Jonah took his leave. But since I know that it is the tuba that produces it and not a whale, there must be some musical reason for it. If the none too happy personal relations of Jonah and the fish lead me to the understanding of the music I am hearing, I shall agree and take the tuba's sigh for the whale's." This reaction certainly is burdened with much nonmusical recognizing and reasoning, and although program music occupies an important place in composition throughout musical history, we could, in a discussion of *scientia bene modulandi* discard the problem of program music altogether as a factor of minor importance, were it not for the tendency of some philosophers, psychologists, and musicologists to see in onomatopoetic imitation the source of all composition — in fact, of all organized music. If it is emotional reaction that is placed at the end of music's path from the composer's imagination to the listener's, would onomatopoeia not be the most convincing manner of fostering it? Would not the similarity of musical sounds to those that are a part of our everyday nonmusical acoustical experiences, facilitate the evaluation of musical sounds? Melody, even in its most developed form, could, according to those theories, always be traced back to some primitive melodic model in free nature, such as the song of birds, the murmuring of water, the melodious dripping of falling drops, and it would be up to the composer to decide how far away from these natural sources he wanted to remove his melody. Harmony would be derived from natural harmonies, such as the chordal howling of the storm, the simultaneous chirping of many birds or crickets. And for rhythmical forms in music there would be many models in nature: anything pounding, beating, and ringing with a certain steadiness, such as the noises of primitive craftsmen at work, the beat of tribal dance rhythms, or the pecking of woodpeckers.

For a musician this theory of the origin of organized music is not too satisfactory. Although it is possible that even in a very early state of musical experience many stimulations came from such natural sources and prompted simple-minded musicians to imitate them, it is more likely that music stems from the bodily experiences of each individual human being. The baby's own crying, whining, and playful crowing is probably the primordial material which according to our former statements assumes a very primitive musical meaning after comparison with the already experienced feeling of general motion. Thus he bursts out spontaneously, without models, into simplest songlike utterances, and with his growing experiences and a desire to self-expression develops them into audible forms of a slightly higher degree of musical significance. From here on it is a question of further experience and education, how — and how soon — these basic phenomena can be developed into organized music.

But even as a mere stimulus in an advanced musical technique the value of onomatopoeia is greatly overrated. Had its advocates asked the musicians about their methods instead of dealing with the listeners and their impressions, they probably would have abandoned their theory; for every observant musician knows that the effect upon a listener, caused by onomatopoetic imitation, even if extremely stylized, is always a secondary effect that accompanies the specifically and exclusively musical coherence of the melodic, harmonic, and rhythmic material. All kinds of effects may be helpful in intensifying the primary musical effect, but they can never be used in its stead. After deduction of the onomatopoetic part of a musical structure, the purely musical substance of the melodic, harmonic, and rhythmic material must still be strong and convincing, otherwise no musical satisfaction can be raised in the listener. All this shows that as an explanation of emotional reactions released by music the importance of programmatic references seems to be, to say the least, exaggerated. In my opinion the conditions are reversed: musical experiences must be established before any onomatopoetic references to music can be understood, not vice versa. This means that instead of saying "audible forms produced in nature release certain emotional reactions, therefore music that uses similar-sounding pat-

terns releases the same reactions," we would have to say, "if a musical structure of a certain type releases through the arrangement
of its melodic, harmonic, and rhythmic components a certain
emotional reaction, audible forms in nature that in a primitive
way bear a certain similarity to such artistic structures, will remind us of music and thus will release reactions close to those
released by organized music." Of course, this opinion depends on
the answer to our yet unanswered question: what the emotional
reactions are and how they are produced.

v

Other analysts, in explaining the effects of music on the listener, see in music a kind of language which by its peculiar means
of expression conveys some meaning, whatever this meaning may
be. But the difference is, that in a spoken or written language
each verbal expression used has unchangeable connotations, while
in music each component of an audible form can be understood
and interpreted emotionally in many different ways. The word
"river" always means a stream of flowing water, but a certain
phrase in C minor may cause one listener to experience some feeling of sadness, while to another listener the same phrase means
something entirely different. This discrepancy in interpretation
will be particularly obvious in the case of music that is unfamiliar
to the recipient. Those who have had some experience with oriental people and their music will confirm this observation. In
hearing oriental music for the first time, the Western listener usually cannot detect any musical significance in it — which it would
have, if music was an internationally recognized and understandable language. The strangeness of its sounds will strike him as
funny, even ridiculous, and the only emotional urge he will feel
will be a desire to laugh heartily. But this same piece may induce
the initiated to feel sad, pathetic, heroic, or whatnot. We do not
even need to go so far away into foreign regions; sometimes in
southern countries church music can be heard which for the visitor from the North has the most exhilarating effect, although it
may be intended as funeral music and will have the proper effect
of such on the native listener. On the other hand, there are people

in whom Gilbert and Sullivan operettas arouse only feelings of boundless desolation and despair.

A composer who wanted to use music in the same sense a language is used could do so only by preparing a voluminous dictionary, in which each particle of a musical form corresponded with a verbal equivalent. But apart from the fact that he never would find a strict definition of the term "particle of a musical form," he would have to come to an agreement with other composers as to the exact meaning of the entries in the musical-verbal vocabulary. Knowing what musicians are like, we can be sure that there will be as many different versions of the dictionary as there are musicians interested in the project; and even if through some supernatural influence the ideas of two or more musicians could be unified, the listeners would never want to get acquainted with the fixed symbolism of a musical language. This means that music, due to the absence of any stable connotations in its messages of sound, does not have the properties of a language and cannot be used in the same sense verbal communications are used.

VI

There will always be a tendency for all participants in music to trust their musical equivalent of the prosaic but helpful horse sense: to believe that an inspired composition will inevitably release in the minds of all concerned one and the same kind of emotional reaction. But quite apart from the fact that inspiration is not a plain artistic phenomenon to be taken for granted (as our next chapter will disclose), the following more careful examination of our emotional reactions to musical impressions will disprove so simple a supposition.

The most generally accepted explanation of the effect music has upon a listener is: it expresses feelings. Whose are the feelings it expresses? Those of the composer, the performer, the individual listener, or the audience? Or does it express feelings of a general character, the specification of which is left to the members of any of these groups?

Music cannot express the composer's feelings. Let us assume a composer is writing an extremely funereal piece, which may require three months of intensive work. Is he, during this three-months period, thinking of nothing but funerals? Or can he, in those hours that are not devoted to his work because of his desire to eat and to sleep, put his grief on ice, so to speak, and be gay until the moment when he resumes his somber activity? If he really expressed his feelings accurately as they occur during the time of composing and writing, we would be presented with a horrible motley of expressions, among which the grievous part would necessarily occupy but a small place.

Perhaps we are to believe that the composer need have the feeling of grief only once at the beginning of his work, in order to drench the opus with somberness, notwithstanding his own feelings of hilarity, jocularity, and whatever else he is going to experience during the time of incubation? This idea is even more ridiculous than the preceding one, because there is no reason why in a series of feelings just the first one, due to its position, should be of greater importance. If the feelings of the series occur with equal intensity, it is most likely that the latest one, as the most recent experience, has the greatest importance, while the first has already lost its significance; and if the intensity is variable, then it will be the points of greatest intensity that are predominant.

If the composer himself thinks he is expressing his own feelings, we have to accuse him of a lack of observation. Here is what he really does: he knows by experience that certain patterns of tone-setting correspond with certain emotional reactions on the listener's part. Writing these patterns frequently and finding his observations confirmed, in anticipating the listener's reaction he believes himself to be in the same mental situation. From here it is a very small step to the further conviction that he himself is not only reproducing the feelings of other individuals, but is actually having these same feelings, being obsessed by them whenever he thinks he needs them, and being urged to express them with each stroke of his ever-ready pen. He believes that he feels what he believes the listener feels; he tries to construct musically the ultimate ring of this strange chain of thought — and consequently he does not express his own feelings in his music.

Can music express the feelings of the performer? Even if performers of any kind — singers, players, conductors — were actually the demigods that many of them want us to think they are and some of them believe themselves to be, in reality they are, in respect to the current that flows from the composer's brain to the listener's mind, nothing but an intermediate station, a roadside stop, a transformer house, and their duty is to pass along what they received from the generating mind. Although our system of notation can give them no more than approximations of the composer's intentions, they are supposed to understand his written symbolism and by means of their own interpretational liberties and changes add merely what is the minimum requirement for a realization of the composition in sound. The ideal performer will never try to express his own feelings — if ever he thinks that feelings are to be expressed — but the composer's, or what he thinks the composer's feelings were. Covering a piece with a thick layer of the performer's so-called feelings means distorting, counterfeiting it. A performer, in doing this, changes his function from that of a transformer to a competing generator — and the shocks received from the clashing of two different currents always hit the innocent listener. Whether the performer trusts he is adding a minimum of his own feelings to a piece he performs, or whether he soaks it thoroughly in these feelings like a piece of pot roast in brown gravy, he is in the same state of self-deception as was the above-mentioned composer. What he thinks are his feelings is again the series of conclusions mentioned before: observed correspondence of music and emotional effect on the listener — confirmation by frequent recurrence — identification of himself with those effects — the belief that he himself "feels" them.

The case is somewhat more involved with the feelings of the individual listener or the collective feeling of an entire audience. All listeners, individually or collectively, are also the victims of the treacherous chain of thought, although their unconscious reasoning enters at another point of its course. The composers' and performers' unconscious starting point was the listeners' emotional reaction, intellectually anticipated. The listeners, having these emotional reactions as the final result of the musical process do not actually start with the intellectual anticipation of them.

Their chain of reasoning is: (1) The composer expresses his feelings in his music — which opinion, although wrong, is excusable, since the listener is unaware of the composer's previous miscalculations. (2) The performer expresses the composer's or his own feelings (equally wrong, as we have seen). (3) The composer's and performer's feelings, expressed in their musical production, prompt me to have the same feelings.

Since the listeners' conclusions are based on the composers' and the performers' false suppositions, they cannot contain any truth, and we can also state that the listeners' individual or collective feelings are not expressed in music.

### VII

If music does not express feelings, how then does it affect the listener's emotions? There is no doubt that listeners, performers, and composers alike can be profoundly moved by perceiving, performing, or imagining music, and consequently music must touch on something in their emotional life that brings them into this state of excitation. But if these mental reactions were feelings, they could not change as rapidly as they do, and they would not begin and end precisely with the musical stimulus that aroused them. If we experience a real feeling of grief — that is, grief not caused or released by music — it is not possible to replace it at a moment's notice and without any plausible reason with the feeling of wild gaiety; and gaiety, in turn, cannot be replaced by complacency after a fraction of a second. Real feelings need a certain interval of time to develop, to reach a climax, and to fade out again; but reactions to music may change as fast as musical phrases do, they may spring up in full intensity at any given moment and disappear entirely when the musical pattern that provoked them ends or changes. Thus these reactions may within a few instants skip from the most profound degree of grief to utter hilarity and on to complacency without causing any discomfort to the mind experiencing them, which would be the case with a rapid succession of real feelings. In fact, if it happened with real feelings, we could be sure that it could be only in the event of slight insanity. The reactions music evokes are not feelings, but they are the images, memories of feelings. We can compare these memories of feelings to the memories we have of a country in which we have traveled. The original journey may have taken several weeks or months, but in conjuring up in our memory the events of it, we may go through the entire adventure in a few seconds and still have the sensation of a very complete mental reconstruction of its course. It is the same trick dreams play on us. They, too, compress the reproductions of events that in reality would need long intervals of time for their development into fractions of a second, and yet they seem to the dreamer as real as adventures he has when he is wide awake. In some cases these dream-events may even be the "real" life of the individual, while the facts they reflect, distort, or rearrange are nothing but an inconsequential and sober succession of trifles.

Dreams, memories, musical reactions — all three are made of the same stuff. We cannot have musical reactions of any considerable intensity if we do not have dreams of some intensity, for musical reactions build up, like dreams, a phantasmagoric structure of feelings that hits us with the full impact of real feeling. Furthermore we cannot have any musical reactions of emotional significance, unless we have once had real feelings the memory of which is revived by the musical impression. (The importance of recollection in respect to musical perception has been mentioned in the second chapter.) Reactions of a grievous nature can be aroused by music only if a former experience of real grief was stored up in our memory and is now again portrayed in a dreamlike fashion. "Musical" gaiety can be felt only if a feeling of real gaiety is already known to us; "musical" complacency arises in our memory only if complacency felt before without musical prompting was already part of our experience. It is only with the memory of feelings in our mind that we can have any feelinglike reaction caused by music. This can be proved. If, for example, we assume that music is able to arouse a reaction, which in the mind of a mass murderer uncovers the memory of the satisfaction he felt after having slaughtered a row of twenty victims, that feeling cannot be reproduced in our own minds unless we do as he did — murder twenty people and then listen to the adequate music. Certainly we can imagine what this fellow felt and we can direct our reactions to music so that in their dreamlike way they make us feel as if we had the mass murderer's experience and the memories thereof, released by music. But these reactions can never be like the genuine ones of the mass murderer, as we do not have the actual experience that left its imprints in his mind; they can be nothing but reactions of a similar — never identical — nature; reactions based on the feeling of satisfaction we had after other cruelties we committed. These are now substituted by us for the lacking experience of greater cruelty, and are rather artificially brought into contact with a musical impression.

If music did not instigate us to supply memories out of our mental storage rooms, it would remain meaningless, it would merely have a certain tickling effect on our ears. We cannot keep music from uncovering the memory of former feelings and it is not in our power to avoid them, because the only way to "have" — to possess — music, is to connect it with those images, shadows, dreamy reproductions of actual feelings, no matter how realistic and crude or, on the contrary, how denatured, stylized, and sublimated they may be. If music we hear is of a kind that does not easily lend itself or does not lend itself at all to this connection, we still do our best to find in our memory some feeling that would correspond with the audible impression we have. If we find nothing that serves this purpose, we resort to hilarity — as in the case of oriental music, mentioned above — and have a "funny feeling," but even this funny feeling is merely the image of some real funny feeling we had with some former nonmusical experience, and which is now drawn out of its storage place, to substitute for the memory of a more suitable feeling.

This theory gives us a reasonable explanation for the fact that one given piece of music may cause remarkably diversified reactions with different listeners. As an illustration of this statement I like to mention the second movement of Beethoven's Seventh Symphony, which I have found leads some people into a pseudo feeling of profound melancholy, while another group takes it for a kind of scurrilous scherzo, and a third for a subdued pastorale. Each group is justified in judging as it does. The difference in interpretation stems from the difference in memory-images the listeners provide, and the unconscious selection is made on the basis of the sentimental value or the degree of importance each image has: the listener chooses the one which is dearest and closest to his mental disposition, or which represents a most common, most easily accessible feeling.

We may ask: what is the relation of the reaction to music as described here to the form of perceiving or imagining music, discussed in the second chapter? The intellectual act of building up in our mind a parallel structure of a piece heard or imagined, simultaneously with its performance or with its imagination, is not to be confused with the emotional reaction to music as described now. Although the presence of both is the indispensable condition for our mental absorption of musical impressions, they are not interdependent. They are independent, and their independence may go so far, that a piece which we relish emotionally may have a very discomforting, even disgusting effect on us while we are producing its parallel form mentally; and a piece which gives us the highest satisfaction intellectually may have only a minor effect on our emotions. Examples for the first category can be found in many of Tchaikovsky's, Dvořák's, Grieg's, and other composers' pieces, in which the audible structure frequently is enchanting and is apt to release easily and pleasantly all the images of feelings as mentioned before, but intellectually sometimes makes us ask: "Do these fellows really assume that we are so naïve as to take their jesting for serious creation?" For the second category we find examples in many supercontrapuntal or otherwise overconstructed compositions, when our intellectual faculty of understanding may be carried to very high spheres, but emotionally we are left with dissatisfaction, because these structures are so involved or overburdened or unpredictable, that our activity of reconstructing them intellectually absorbs all our attention and prohibits emotional enjoyment.

### VIII

Let us recapitulate. Music touches both the intellectual and the emotional parts of our mental life. Intellectually we build up structures parallel to actual musical ones, and these mental structures receive weight and moral meaning through the attitude we assume towards their audible or imaginary originals: either we consciously allow music to impress us with its ethic power, or we transform it into moral strength. Emotionally we simply are the slaves of musical impressions and react to their stimulus, inevitably and independent of our own will power, with memories of former actual feelings.

If we agree that music does not express feelings but merely releases images of feelings, we are justified in asking: What is the physiologic or psychologic connection between music and those images? There must be some factor common to both which serves as the connecting link between the outward world of sound and the cerebral activity of sound interpretation. The basis on which they can be brought together may be expressed by the equation: actual motion on the one side equals feeling of motion on the other side. This is on an infinitely higher mental level the same equation the baby drew when for the first time in his life he absorbed a musical impression, and in spite of the tremendous mental burden of memories and transformations we are adding to this equation, it still preserves its original primitivity. This can be seen by observing a very simple musical structure and analyzing the emotional reaction it evokes in our mind. The simplest structure that is already organized music and yet remains as close as possible to the basic sounding material used in music is a short melodic line without addition of simultaneous harmony, containing mostly stepwise progressions, moderately interspersed with leaps not larger than a fourth. The most natural way of absorbing the musical contents of such structures is to compare the speed of the underlying meter, which is felt in its tone successions, with the tempo of our heartbeat. If the metric units of progression in our melodic line correspond with our heartbeat tempo, we feel that it progresses without causing any excitement. This immediately reminds us of moods, feelings, and situations, in which our heart and with it our general mental disposition was equally at ease. The image of a complacent mood will change in the same degree as we change the speed of metric-temporal succession in the melodic tone progressions, accelerating or retarding, so that it deviates from the heart's "normal" tempo. (Note that we are talking about deviations, that is, arrangements in which only after the occurrence of a considerable number of temporal units a coincidence of a heartbeat and a melodic temporal unit takes place. This is quite different from the mere subdivision of beats, by which a heartbeat's duration is broken up into a number of melodic tones.) If in our melodic succession the metric units are felt as being slower than the heartbeat, we feel that they evoke memories of quieter and gloomier moods, developing into sadness, dejection, and finally desperation, whereby the deviation from our normal heartbeat tempo determines the degree of somberness in these images of moods. Or, what amounts to the same result, we are reminded of mental situations of the described kind caused by a heart beating more slowly than normal. On the other hand, if the temporal units of the melody are felt as being accelerated against the heartbeat, we will be reminded of moods of alertness, serenity, mirth, and frolicking, the degree of merriness again being determined by the degree of deviation from the heart's natural metronome.

As long as we adhere to the most primitive structural material which even neglects the rhythmic or metric subdivision of temporal units in a melodic line, we can be fairly sure of its emotional effects. But adding to these basic facts all other ingredients music uses, such as melodic elaboration, harmony, meter, tempo, dynamics, tone color, et cetera, the range of simple mood images will, between the extremes of utter sadness and utter gaiety, be filled up with an endless number of variations and deviations, each conditioned by the groupment of the musical material at any given moment. With this gradual addition of material to the simple melodic original we may intensify its effects, so that, for instance, sadness will be more profound; if harmony and dynamics are added to our melody, we are further broadening its possibilities. If with our most modest melody the listener was hit by a single bullet at a time — the coincidence of metrical unit and heartbeat, or the mental measuring of their degree of discrepancy — he now is hit by a hail of bullets, consisting of the countless variety of musical ingredients just mentioned. These bullets are now scattered over a larger surface and thus the listener is able to draw each moment on many images of moods instead of only one or two. Different listeners will experience different images, and even one and the same listener will not react uniformly to reappearing musical stimuli. Thus a composer can never be absolutely sure of the emotional effect of his music on the listener when using complex material, but by experience and clever distribution of this material, moreover with frequent references to those musical progressions that evoke the uncomplicated feeling-images of sadness or gaiety in an unambiguous form, he can reach a fairly close approximation to unanimity of all listeners' reactions.

IX

When we began to discuss the modern *scientia*, we wanted to find an answer to the question: "What are the emotional reactions music releases?" The conclusions drawn from our elaborate inquiry have given us an answer that seems to be sufficiently satisfactory. We can now turn to the second part of our question and ask: "What is the practical value of all this in respect to a composer's actual work?" If his mind is filled with philosophical and psychological considerations, how can he possibly write any musical successions without constantly being puzzled and diverted? Whenever a musical idea turns up in his mind, how can it break through this barricade of mental obstacles? Can it ever reach the point of crystallization into a musical form?

No answer of general validity can be given. The fates of musical ideas on their journey from the place of origin to the fixed form in the written score are as numerous and manifold as the composers' personalities themselves. Some composers may not feel bothered by those mental hurdles, may perhaps even not feel them. Others may suffer terribly in bringing their ideas through alive. To yet others these obstacles are just what they need to kindle their imagination; and finally there are those who simply like to shut their eyes and do their composing in a lunatic fashion: without knowing what they are doing.

We cannot establish laws which govern the way a creative mind works. Each individual has to develop his own procedure. Nevertheless people have their notions about a composer's activities. To most of them — and strangely enough to many professionals, too — factual knowledge and imaginative composition seem to be two irreconcilable opponents. To them the ideal composer is the simple-minded instrument of a superior will, a kind of mystic loud-speaker that proclaims messages the sense of which he himself does not understand. In times past he was a philosopher, a scientist, an educator. When he lost this extramusical esteem, he still was the great craftsman who in the public's opinion ranked highest among the musicians. Nowadays it is the performer who has conquered this position, and the composer more or less dwells in one and the same class with the medicine man of a savage tribe, who exorcizes instead of reasoning, who emanates superstition instead of wisdom. Certainly those people are right who look at a perfect composer's craft as something that for the average man is strange and inapproachable. But why this strangeness should preclude consciousness, exactitude, and rational working methods is a mystery. In music, as in all other human pursuits, rational knowledge is not a burden but a necessity, and it ought to be recognized as such by all.

To be sure, we must not confuse a certain light-handed technical and spiritual facility with a lack of knowledge, any more than we are to take diffuse pompousness for profundity. Those creative geniuses of the past who in our imagination are the dearest examples of a most gracious human mind, of serene lightness in both imagination and construction — Machaut, Dufay, Josquin, and Mozart, for example — are they representatives of a light-hearted manner of composing, undisturbed by intellectual overweight? How then could Machaut combine his eloquently charming style with the formalistic technicalities of the isorhythmic motet? Dufay's and Josquin's examples of trickiest contrapuntal intricacies — how do they fit into this picture of easygoing unconcern? And Mozart — is one not led to believe that he had to die in his youth because he knew too much? He started to draw away the covering curtain from harmonic and tonal secrets that were to appear decades later — in the works of Wagner, Reger, or even more recent musicians. A composer's horizon cannot be far-reaching enough; his desire to know, to comprehend must incite, inspire, and drench every phase of his work. Storming the heavens with artistic wisdom and practical skill must be his least ambition.

Although we found that the musician who in his person unites the highest form of Augustinian insight with Boethian perfection will always remain an unattainable ideal, we are justified in look-ing at him who works in the sense here described as the man who comes closest to this ideal. For him it is knowledge that is the foundation of his art, just as it was for his early predecessor, the Boethian musician. This knowledge is not solely confined within the narrow limitations of his tone-combining craft; it also em-braces the human abilities, both spiritual and emotional, which lead one to the understanding of music; and thus this knowledge will be the driving power in his work. And even if he succumbs to the dangers hidden in the Boethian approach to music — that is, to fall into doubts and desperation because he loses confidence in his work and his gift — even then he will never be completely lost! He will turn his doubts into creative power, and will always be able to do so, for he is held, supported, and carried by his solidly founded *scientia bene modulandi*.

# 4.

## MUSICAL INSPIRATION

F MUSIC influences the intellectual and emotional realms of our mental activities, there must exist for each effect achieved in these realms a corresponding cause. The material of musical construction — successions of differently shaped sounds in their infinite number of combinations — provides these causes. It is the composer who is supposed to know about the intimate relation of musical causes and intellectual-emotional effects, and to steer the successions of sound consciously and skillfully to the point where they exert their expected influence. There is no doubt that in weighing and comparing causes and effects he must have, beyond all craftsmanship, an innate gift of measuring the relationship in manner and intensity of these two components of musical impressions. A certain divination is necessary to lift such an evaluating process beyond the primitive level of materialistic calculation or simple empiricism. Recognizing such loftiness in a composer's endeavors, we are readily inclined to attribute to him what seems to be the most characteristic quality of the composing mind which differentiates him from the sober, non-composing crowd: the possession of creative ideas, of musical inspiration.

Although we must admit that musical inspiration is, in its ultimate profundity, as unexplainable as our capacity of thinking in general, we must not think of it as an irrational, entirely uncontrollable mental manifestation. After all, musical inspiration, like any other kind of artistic or scientific inspiration is not without bounds. It operates within the limitations drawn by both the material qualities of the artistic medium that causes the aforesaid effects and the state of mental erudition and preparedness in the mind of the individual who experiences them.

Recognizing these limitations will help us to understand more clearly the possibilities of an artist's imagination. Thus, if we know the specific limitations a poet encounters in using a certain language with its characteristic features, we shall not expect him to force his material into realms of expression that are alien to its qualities; we shall not confuse the poet's inspiration with the composer's, which in turn is limited materially by the entirely different properties of his working stuff, the succession of sounds. And what is true with the poet's and the musician's constructive materials is likewise true with respect to those of the painter, the architect, the sculptor, and other artists.

Beyond the specific limitations prescribed by each single art's material of construction, the composer seems to be limited in a way peculiar to his craft and unknown to the other creative artists. This craft, although through the immateriality and meaninglessness of its building stuff it is forced to dwell technically on a very high level of sublimation and abstraction, seems, with respect to its immediate impression on the recipient, of a lower value than all the other arts. Since music relies so much on our emotions, which come and go as they choose, unchecked and undirected by our reason, it occupies a place at the border line between the arts and mere sensual impressions. Its effects seem to be similar to those exerted upon the uncontrollable senses of smell and taste. In all other arts it is our power of reasoning that has to be satisfied first, before an aesthetic enjoyment of an artist's creation can be had: the words of a poem must be understood in their verbal meaning before its structural beauty or spiritual loftiness can be appreciated; the subject of a painting or its abstract lineations must enter our consciousness before any emotional reaction can take place. With music it is different. It touches our emotions first and we are the helpless victims of its attacks. Only after the emotional reaction has been released by the sounds of music can our power of reasoning take possession of the artistic impression and transform it into aesthetic satisfaction — by way of mental coconstruction, as we know. This reverse mode of action in the impressional stimulation of a musical composition is the reason for the comparatively low level on which music makes its initial appeal, as has just been mentioned.

Of course we know that music compensates its recipients in a manner not accessible to other arts. The range of emotions it can touch is infinitely larger, the variety within this range is unlimited, the tempo of consecutive emotions is unbelievably fast. We know the reason for this: the emotions released by music are no real emotions, they are mere images of emotions that have been experienced before, and we know about our unconscious technique of uncovering them in their mental hiding places. Paintings, poems, sculptures, works of architecture, after having impressed us consciously in the manner mentioned, do not — contrary to music — release images of feelings; instead they speak to the real, untransformed, and unmodified feelings. (Of course, additional memories of previous feelings may always participate in enhancing the artistic effect.) Gaiety released by examples of these arts is real gaiety, not a stored-away recollection of a formerly experienced gaiety; sadness is real sadness. This is proved by the fact that these real feelings lack entirely the range, variety, and speed of the images of feelings evoked by music, with their delirious, almost insane manner of appearance. Unlike these images of feelings, they are relatively uncomplicated, need time to develop and to fade out, and cannot appear in rapid succession.

II

One kind of limitation is common to all the arts: they are subject to the boundaries circumscribed by our common human and terrestrial sensual experiences of time and space. No artist, no craftsman was ever able to transgress these limitations, notwithstanding the commonplace usage of metaphorical, vague, and exaggerating terms in artistic discussions which to the uninitiated could easily suggest that such results have been attained or at least attempted. Neither could he suggest immeasurable largeness, as seen in the scientific field of astronomy, nor could he create an image of infinite smallness, as known in physics. The arts in this respect are, in spite of their great suggestive power, truly and immovably earth-bound.

The effects of an art on our receptive capacity may employ the element of space only, as do architecture, sculpture, and painting; or the element of time only, as does poetry; or it may operate

in both, as do the drama and the moving pictures. It is again the
art of music that cannot be caught in a net of temporal and spatial
relations as easily as the other arts. We cannot deny that musical
progressions evoke in our mind sensations of both a temporal
and a spatial nature, but the following investigation will show
that the sensations of musical time and musical space are not
identical with time and space as felt in our everyday life or in
the aesthetic effects of nonmusical works of art.

Musical time in its effect on our feelings is easily comprehensible as long as it uses temporal arrangements that are not essentially different from "normal" time. This is the case when it is
totally or predominantly expressed in a metrical succession of
temporal units, whose principal property is regular recurrence.
Here as in actual time a row of one hundred beats is nothing but
a row of one hundred beats, and its sum total is counted and felt
as such. Doubts may arise only with respect to the beginning of
the row, and the abatement of our attention may result in some
other irregularities of judgment. If our place of observation is at
the end of this row — meaning that we have heard it in its entirety up to its last beat — and we are looking back at its course,
we feel that this series of one hundred beats, in spite of some
more or less important subdivisions, could have ended earlier or
have been continued to any temporal point further on without
suffering an essential change in its structure and our evaluation
of it.

But there is another form of musical time whose effects are
quite different from those of normal time or of musical time as
expressed in metrical successions. Here, in contrast to meter,
irregularity in duration is the essential condition, irregularity
which possibly is heightened to incommensurability. This is musical time expressed in forms of rhythm. The term "rhythm" is
here used in its widest sense and includes everything irregular
from the smallest nonmetrical motif to what is usually covered
by the term "musical form." Music theory generally is not inclined to recognize in metrical and rhythmical forms two essentially different temporal orders of musical material. In fact, in
our music in which melody and harmony are linked together
mainly with the aid of meter, it is not wholly easy to separate

meter from rhythm. But experimentally, in the music theorist's laboratory, so to speak, the basic dissimilarity of meter and rhythm can be proved. We can understand this dissimilarity by comparing our everyday actions as a series of temporally irrational successions of time intervals with the metrically organized time intervals as measured by watches, clocks, and other time-dividing devices. In musical time, as expressed in rhythmical forms, the time interval, covered by our row of one hundred beats contains many rhythmical motifs which, although usually they can be measured by these beats, have just as little in common with them as have our temporally irrational actions with the clock's ticking. To understand such a succession as a rhythmic structure and not merely as a metrically organized row, we have to wait until it reaches its end. Then the complete form will appear to our analyzing mind as a new unit and not, as it appeared in meter, as an accumulation of single units. All the nonmetrical constituent parts of this new unit, although in their own rhythmic form clearly circumscribed, have now lost their individual meaning and are nothing but subordinate parts of this new entity. Now our place of observation has changed. We are no longer looking back on the past course of the row; we are above it, so to speak, and are looking down and can take in with one single glance the temporal form in its totality — indivisible, unrepeatable, unchangeable. We may say that musical time in this moment produced an effect which in normal time is nonexistent. This effect of comprehending as a new superunit what in the course of its development was built up by smaller units is borrowed from our spatial experiences, where this comprehensive judgment is a most commonplace fact — and yet it was the result of a strictly temporal operation.

III

Musical space is at least as far removed from our normal spatial concepts as was musical time in its rhythmic form of appearance from our temporal experiences. This seems strange, for even laymen without any musical training use the expression "ascending" for tone successions in which the second component has a higher number of vibrations per second, and conversely name "descending" any succession moving in the opposite direction. Actually there are in music no such spatial distinctions as high and low, near and far, right and left that correspond with the same definitions in real nonmusical space. Yet it is undeniable that successions of tones bring about effects of spatial feelings which in their obviousness are convincing even to the entirely untrained mind. Since neither the loudness nor the color of tones can produce or influence this effect, it must be the pitch relation among tones that is the reason for it.

To understand the connection between the movement from tone to tone in music on the one hand and the feeling of spatial movement on the other, we must again, as we did in our discussion of the emotional effects of music, find the common denominator of both factors. This time the equation is: the physical effort which we know is necessary to change from one tone position to another equals the physical effort we imagine when we think of a change of position in our common physical experience. Going from one given tone up to a tone with a higher vibration frequency is accomplished, in human voices and in string and wind instruments, with an increase in the energy of tone production. The amount of energy involved in such movement may be almost undiscernible (as in a violinist's progressing from the tone *a* of the open string to the next *c*), or it may be a tremendous physical effort, as when a tenor sings the same progression with full voice. But the absolute amount of energy involved counts only so far as our nonmusical interest in the performer himself or our sentimental reactions derived from his performance are concerned. It is the relative amount of energy that counts for our evaluation of musical space. Going to a tone of a higher frequency number means some effort, no matter how great or how small this effort in single cases may be. The recognition of this effort leads us to the comparison: Lifting some physical object from its place to a higher place means some effort; going from a tone of lower frequency to a tone of higher frequency means some effort; consequently one effort reminds me of the other, and since the lifting of the physical object took place in real space, the musical effect also reminds me of space. Going from a given tone to a tone of lower vibration frequency again reminds me of a change in position of a physical object, this time from a higher to a lower place, and again a spatial feeling connected with music is established by comparison.

This all is true without limitation in respect to singers' voices; it holds with wind instruments and, to a high degree, with string instruments, too, since the close relationship of all these instruments to the singing voice is always recognizable. But in keyboards this natural equalization of spatial height with musical height has dwindled to almost nothing, and the mere horizontal change of the hand's position does not distinguish between ascending and descending. That even with these highly artificial arrangements we still feel the correspondences strain-up and relax-down, is explainable only through our previous experiences with singing voices and string and wind instruments.

When we talked about the emotional effects of music, we found that no image of a feeling could be evoked in our mind, unless a real feeling, suffered earlier, could be recalled. With the recognition of musical space we again see that only in reference to our experiences in real space can we have an analogous image of space in our mind, evoked by music. If this is true we can go one step further.

Musical space is felt — again by analogy with our experiences in real space — as three-dimensional. If we describe movements proceeding in a three-dimensional space as going up and down, right and left, forth and back, we can easily see their equivalents in musical space. A spatial up and down corresponds with the musical straining and releasing of vibrational tensions (as mentioned); right and left has its correspondence in the harmonic and melodic relations that exist between the successive components of each musical progression; and the feeling of spatial depth, as expressed by the motion forth and back, is symbolized musically similar to the construction which produces the effect of perspective in painting. In painting the impression of visual depth is created by so drawing all receding lines of the picture's objects that their prolongations meet in one single point — the vanishing point; and in musical perspective, all harmonies, whether resulting from the vertical (up and down) distance between tones, or by the summing-up effect of consecutive tones in melodies, will by our analytic capacity be understood as in close relationship to tones which, by frequent recurrence, or by favorable position in the structure, or finally by support received from other tones, will be felt as tones superior to the others; tones that occupy the place of fundamentals, of tonics.

IV

Is it necessary to operate with the concept of musical space? Can we not conceive music that exists without reference to any real or imagined space? It seems that it is not possible to think of music as of something completely removed from any spatial conception, so long as we believe that music is supposed to touch our emotional life and to prompt us into the activity of simultaneous reconstruction. Since music revives in our minds the images of feelings which are inevitably connected with memories of spaces in which the originals of these images occurred to us, imaginary spaces will always show up simultaneously with the images of feelings.

If it is not possible to conceive music without any reference to images of spatial feelings, must we necessarily project all our three-dimensional experiences into our musical space? Could we not restrict ourselves to an image of a two-dimensional space by omitting the reference of harmonies to fundamental tones, to tonics, to the effect similar to perspective in painting? Do not many works of the pictorial arts renounce this effect? There was in musical history a time when these effects of perspective — or of tonality, as the technical term goes — were unknown to musicians. This was at a time before harmonies were used consciously and when music consisted only of melodic lines. Even nowadays in many countries and cultures that are not under the domination of Western musical techniques and habits, harmony is either unknown or flatly rejected as an unwelcome addition to the native material of music, and people with this exclusively melodic conception of music cannot have any effect of sounding perspective, of tonality, as expressed by harmonic reference to tonal fundamentals (although of course other means of tonal organization are applied). With harmony it seems to go as with the tree of the knowledge of good and evil: once you have tasted its fruits, you have lost your innocent approach to the facts of life. For us, after our musical development has gone through about a thousand years of musical knowledge that consisted exclusively of harmonized musical structures, it is quite impossible to understand melodic lines without harmonic and tonal implications. The intervals produced by the successive tones of melodies have, in addition to their melodic function, harmonic significance, and we cannot fail to perceive it. These harmonies, again without our active interpretational participation, assemble around fundamental tones, as did the vertical harmonies, and thus again produce the effect of tonal perspective. In painting it is up to the painter to decide whether he wants to have perspective as a part of the pictorial effect or not. In music we cannot escape the analogous effect of tonal unification, of tonality. The intervals which constitute the building material of melodies and harmonies fall into tonal groupments, necessitated by their own physical structure and without our consent.

Have we not heard many times of tendencies in modern music to avoid these tonal effects? It seems to me that attempts at avoiding them are as promising as attempts at avoiding the effects of gravitation. Of course, we can use airplanes to fly away from the center of gravitation, but is not an airplane the best evidence for our incapacity to escape gravitation? Tonality doubtless is a very subtle form of gravitation, and in order to feel it in action we do not even need to take our usual musical detour from actual experience via the image of it, released by music. It suffices to sing in a chorus or a madrigal group to experience the strength of tonal gravitation: to sense how a synoptic tonal order has a healthy, refreshing effect on our moods and how structures that in their obscurity reach the point of impracticability lead to real physical pain.

Certainly, there is a way to escape the effects of earthly gravitation, by using a powerful rocket that overshoots the critical point of terrestrial attraction, but I cannot see how music's less harmful projectiles could ever reach this point or its imaginary equivalent. And yet, some composers who have the ambition to eliminate tonality, succeed to a certain degree in depriving the listener of the benefits of gravitation. To be sure they do not, contrary to their conviction, eliminate tonality: they rather avail themselves of the same trick as those sickeningly wonderful merry-go-rounds on fair grounds and in amusement parks, in which the pleasure-seeking visitor is tossed around simultaneously in circles, and up and down, and sideways, in such fashion that even the innocent onlooker feels his inside turned into a pretzel-shaped distortion. The idea is, of course, to disturb the customer's feeling of gravitational attraction by combining at any given moment so many different forms of attraction that his sense of location cannot adjust itself fast enough. So-called atonal music, music which pretends to work without acknowledging the relationships of harmonies to tonics, acts just the same as those devilish gadgets; harmonies both in vertical and in horizontal form are arranged so that the tonics to which they refer change too rapidly. Thus we cannot adjust ourselves, cannot satisfy our desire for gravitational orientation. Again spatial dizziness is the result, this time in the sublimated realm of spatial images in our mind.

I personally do not see why we should use music to produce the effect of seasickness, which can be provided more convincingly by our amusement industry. Future ages will probably never understand why music ever went into competition with so powerful an adversary.

There is one strange fact about the feeling of musical space that has no equivalent in our ordinary spatial experiences: one of its imaginary, but nevertheless strongly felt dimensions coincides with the effects of musical time. What we feel as the spatial effect of moving sidewards, is accomplished musically by moving horizontally from one sounding unit to another, and this is exactly what produces the effect of musical time. The two different functions of one and the same factor do not have any disturbing effect on our interpretation of musical facts; musical time and musical space are felt as two clearly distinctive facts in musical progressions, and yet we know and feel that at some points they are interlocked, in a way that is unknown to normal time and normal space. We have already seen how musical time usurped a typical spatial effect with the fact that the cumulative single temporal units of a musical form produce a new entity, in which the total effect is not equal to the sum total of the single effects. Now we see that musical space in turn penetrates the realm of musical time.

I said before that no artist or craftsman could in his work suggest immeasurable largeness nor infinite smallness. Even less can he give in a work of art an idea of the relativity of normal time and normal space by means that are perceptible to our senses. Although this concept can be expressed in numbers and words, we can never experience it actually, as it is too far removed from our terrestrial sphere of knowledge. Yet music seems to be the only earthly form of expression which in the properties of its constructive material permits us to have sensations that are a very faint allusion to the feeling of beings to whom the universal concept of the relativity and interchangeability of time and space is an ordinary experience.

### V

Within the framework of musical time and musical space the musical action takes place, in which the composer's ideas are the actors who by harmonic, melodic, and rhythmic circumstances are turned into tragic or comic characters, their tragedies and comedies being of the kind that lives in the stored-away world of the listener's images of emotions.

The word "idea" is a very vague term for what we really mean when we talk of the composer's creative imagination. The German word *Einfall* is the perfect expression needed in our situation. *Einfall*, from the verb *einfallen*, to drop in, describes beautifully the strange spontaneity that we associate with artistic ideas in general and with musical creation in particular. Something — you know not what — drops into your mind — you know not whence — and there it grows — you know not how — into some form — you know not why. This seems to be the general opinion, and we cannot blame the layman if he is unable to find rational explanations for so strange an occurrence.

Even many composers, although the rather prosaic labor of writing musical symbols on paper absorbs about ninety-nine per cent of their work, look at the apparently unprompted appearance of their own ideas with amazement. They are in a permanent state of artistic narcissism, compared with which the harmless self-admiration of the original Narcissus is but child's play. They will tell you about their creations as they would about natural phenomena or heavenly revelations. You have the impression, not that they themselves did their composing, but that "it" composed within them almost in spite of their own existence. It is admirable how people can throughout a lifetime maintain this naïve self-confidence. We can merely envy them, that in spite of all professed temporary doubts in their craftsmanship they constantly think of themselves as exceptional examples of mankind, as incarnations of some supernatural being.

Let us look with a somewhat more temperate attitude at the ideas, the *Einfälle* that populate our stage set up by musical space and musical time. When we talk about *Einfälle* we usually mean little motifs, consisting of a few tones — tones often not even felt as tones but felt merely as a vague curve of sound. They are common to all people, professionals and laymen alike; but while in the layman's mind they die away unused in their earliest infancy, as said before, the creative musician knows how to catch them and subject them to further treatment. I know a scientist who said: "Everybody can have — and has — scientific ideas, but it takes a scientist to know what to do with them." I am very much inclined to include musical ideas in this statement. Who can be sure that the inner singing and ringing that any Mr. or Mrs. X feels bubbling up in a musically uncultivated mind — we talked about it in the first chapter — is not, in its unshaped authenticity, at least as beautiful and satisfactory as — and perhaps even better than — the greatest composer's unshaped inner singing and ringing? It is exciting to know how primitive, commonplace, colorless, and insignificant the first ideas, the primordial *Einfälle*, of even extraordinary musical masters are. But it seems almost more exciting to recognize the specific talent with which those masters keep their ideas fresh and, despite all mutations, basically intact, during the sometimes considerably long interval of time required for the treatment of these ideas. In this they are led by tradition, by the presumptive conditions of performance of the future piece, by its purpose and style, and, to a minor degree, by personal whims and fancies that may add certain flavors to the final form. Sometimes a composer may drive his musical material, on its way from the *Einfall* to its completion in a piece, through a tremendous barrier of frustrations which may suppress most of the aforesaid considerations and lead, even with the very first attempts at treating the basic material, to formulations of utter strangeness.

Although it is not possible to watch the source of the singing and ringing in other peoples' minds — it is not wholly easy even to analyze one's own mind far back into those remote regions of origin and creation — we can in some cases get glimpses of the early fate of musical ideas. To be sure, in order to be observable they must already have crossed the limitations of their first specterlike appearance and have gained some primordial form, either mentally by addition of the results of constructive conclusions, or even visibly in some jotted-down notes on paper. For the most part, only the mental form will exist, until a more extensive treatment brings the rudimentary material into some musically organized, yet still very primitive shape. Jotted-down notes can be regarded as the first steps away from the source, only if a composer's experience of many years has taught him to reduce the normally very long route from his brain to his writing hand. It is in the rare cases, when composers of this kind have left us some of these first-step sketches, that we can imaginatively trace these embryonic structures back to their still more elemental form, the original inner singing and ringing. Fortunately for our argument, one great composer left us a good many of these first-step sketches. I am referring to the sketch books of Beethoven.

In them we find many of the well-known themes which we are accustomed to think of as the most nearly perfect, the most convincing, the most suitable thematic creations: themes so homogeneous, so integrated, that they must have sprung up like the fully armed Minerva out of Jupiter's head. And yet we see them go through a process of transformation and conversion which sometimes gives us five or more intermediate steps from the first structural treatment to the final version. Some of the first versions are in quality so far below the final form, that we would be inclined any time to attribute their invention to Mr. X. And to watch the plodding through those many stages of development is oftentimes rather depressing: if that is the way a genius works, chiseling and molding desperately in order to produce a convincing form, what then is the fate of the smaller fellows? Perhaps it is always true that in working from the tiniest and almost imperceptible spark of structural invention up to an intelligible musical form, a petty composer is very much like Beethoven. If only the work involved in reaching this goal really counted, there would be many a genius. The petty composer could do the same, technically, as the real genius did, and he would almost be justified in feeling godlike — as so many authors did and do — because he was able to turn his bubbling inner singing and ringing into music, which Mr. and Mrs. X could never do.

Does all this mean that the genius and the average producer of music are of the same stuff; that in reality there are no such things as musical imagination, ideas, *Einfälle;* and that by mere accident one individual happens to develop into a Beethoven while the other just as accidentally remains an unknown sixth-rate musician? No. It merely means that if we want to understand the power that animates the ideational personages on our scene of musical time and space, we must not ramble through the mental regions that are common to Mr. X, the untalented composer, and the genius. It means that the regions of genuine musical creation are so far beyond our everyday experiences, that Mr. X will never know what they are and the untalented composer will never enter their inner secrets. Mr. X may always have all the wonderful ideas necessary for an excellent work of art; the little fellow may possess the acutest technique, which permits him to develop the most rudimentary ideas into forms of sound. But what the genius has — and what is far beyond their reach — is vision.

VI

What is musical vision?

We all know the impression of a very heavy flash of lightning in the night. Within a second's time we see a broad landscape, not only in its general outlines but with every detail. Although we could never describe each single component of the picture, we feel that not even the smallest leaf of grass escapes our attention.

We experience a view, immensely comprehensive and at the same time immensely detailed, that we never could have under normal daylight conditions, and perhaps not during the night either, if our senses and nerves were not strained by the extraordinary suddenness of the event.

Compositions must be conceived the same way. If we cannot, in the flash of a single moment, see a composition in its absolute entirety, with every pertinent detail in its proper place, we are not genuine creators. The musical creator, like any other creative individual, is permitted to share with the demiurge the possession of vitalizing visions; but it is the privilege of the demiurge to transform them into concrete existence without any interfering technical obstacle, whereas the creative musician, by reason of his earthly heritage, has to overcome many hurdles between them and their realization. If he is a genuine creator he will not feel disturbed or discouraged by this fact. Not only will he have the gift of seeing — illuminated in his mind's eye as if by a flash of lightning — a complete musical form (though its subsequent realization in a performance may take three hours or more); he will have the energy, persistence, and skill to bring this envisioned form into existence, so that even after months of work not one of its details will be lost or fail to fit into his photomental picture. This does not mean that any f sharp in the six hundred and twelfth measure of the final piece would have been determined in the very first flash of cognition. If the seer should in this first flash concentrate his attention on any particular detail of the whole, he would never conceive the totality; but if the conception of this totality strikes his mind like lightning, this f sharp and all the other thousands of notes and other means of expression will fall into line almost without his knowing it. In working out his material he will always have before his mental eye the entire picture. In writing melodies or harmonic progressions he does not have to select them arbitrarily, he merely has to fulfill what the conceived totality demands. This is the true reason for Beethoven's apparently more than philistine bickering with his material: a desire not to improve or to change any *Einfall* but to accommodate it to the unalterable necessities of an envisioned totality, even if with all his technical skill and experience he has to press it through five or more versions that distort it past recognition.

The man of average talent may have visions too; but instead of seeing them in the clarity of lightning, he perceives dark contours which he has not the divination to fill out appropriately. He may have lots of exciting and wonderful single ideas which he patches together in order to get a musical form that corresponds with his shadowy idea, after the formula: the greater the number of beautiful details, the more beautiful the over-all picture must be. For those gifted with flashlike visions, this hunting for beautiful details seems to be useless, since in fulfilling the demands of the vision they have no choice as to the kind and shape of building material; they can only try to obey these demands and find the sole suitable solution. If they should disregard them completely and consider a search for beautiful details justifiable, they would not be creative artists, any more than a philatelist is — or any other assembler of valuables, who with all his efforts succeeds merely in getting together a collection, never in creating an organism.

It is obvious that a composer, during the long period the notation of his work requires, is always in danger of losing the original vision of it. The flashlike picture may fade out, the outlines may dissolve, many details may disappear in darkness. One of the characteristics of the talent of a creative genius seems to be the ability to retain the keenness of the first vision until its embodiment in the finished piece is achieved. There is no doubt that this embodiment, if it is to appear as a true realization of the vision, can come to life only with the assistance of a great amount of technical skill. Skill can never make up for lack of vision, but on the other hand a vision will never receive its true materialization if a composer's technique does not provide every means towards this end. Yet, compositional technique can be acquired even by noncomposers, while clear visions are the privilege of real creative talent.

To acquire a decent technique in composition seems not to be too difficult. After all, there are a restricted number of rules of thumb concerning voice leading, harmonic progressions, tonal arrangements, and so forth, which are basically valid in all kinds

of musical settings, regardless of style and purpose. The fact that
after four or five years of study many so-called composers are
leaving our schools with sufficient practical knowledge in the
craft of putting tones together seems to prove this point. But the
technique of composition, like the technique of any other art, is
a deceptive thing. You may manage the few basic rules of construction with all their combinative possibilities pretty well, and
yet the highest degree of subtlety, in which each technical item
is in congruence with the respective part of the vision, again may
be attained by no one but the genius. There are relatively few
masterworks in which this ultimate congruence can be felt. Even
in our stockpile of classical music which by common agreement
consists of works written by superior composers not many pieces
fulfill those highest requirements. True, there are many other
great and excellent works, which in their artistic value are by no
means less important. They may in their ability to speak as human
creations to human beings be closest to our hearts, but it is in
those few uncontested masterpieces that we feel the breath of
universality and eternity, because their particular kind of perfection, the absolute coincidence of intention and realization, is almost superhuman.

The fact that very few masterworks display this congruence of
vision and materialization shows us that even the individual possessing the greatest gift and the highest technical skill is not
always able to reach this goal. A tremendous effort is necessary
in order to work towards it; not merely a technical effort, but
a moral effort, too — the effort to subject all considerations of
technique, style, and purpose to this one ideal: congruence.
Again, it is the aspiration towards the ideal unity of the Augustinian and the Boethian attitude towards music which must en-
noble our endeavors and which on the other hand pushes, as we
know, the final goal into an utter remoteness close to inaccessi-
bility.

### VII

Many composers will never feel an urge to exert efforts of this
kind, others may not want to have their pleasant musical microcosm disturbed by such artistic obligations, and those who have

the intuitive knowledge will not always summon the moral energy to force themselves very far forward on this thorny path. As for the listeners, the consumers, their feeling that in a composition the moral effort has been made at all, will be a sign that this composition has the hallmark of a work of art, and the perceptible amount of this effort will be considered the measurement for its artistic value. The more the composer feels impelled by his moral determination to drive the technical part of his work as close as possible to the goal of congruence, the higher seems to us the work's convincing quality. Other works, in which the composer's moral effort cannot be perceived, need not be bad music. They may have a pleasant, entertaining, touching effect. As mere technical mechanisms they may be without flaw. They may evoke wonderful emotional images in our mind, they may readily lead us to mentally reconstruct their forms; yet they may not impress us as works of art.

In addition to those composers who in their indolence or ignorance do not want to be bothered with the kind of problems discussed in this book, there are others who flatly deny the ethic power of music, nor do they admit any moral obligation on the part of those writing music. For them music is essentially a play with tones, and although they spend a considerable amount of intelligence and craftsmanship to make it look important, their composition can be of no greater value, as a sociological factor, than bowling or skating, and its intellectual or philosophical importance must necessarily be counted in the same class with the doings of snake worshipers and similar fetishistic isolationists. Nevertheless, there must in the minds of these creators exist some driving power that makes up for the lack of moral compulsion, at least dynamically, and keeps their writing apparatus well greased.

For some of them musical composition is identical with the problem of finding extramusical rules of tone distribution. The lack of any reasonable physical or psychological basis does not prevent their establishing such systems of organization; nor are they discouraged by the general impracticability of their creations and by the unresponsiveness of their audiences. It must be a peculiar satisfaction to follow laws of one's own invention, possibly laws that have no validity — or almost none — for other composers.

Others see in composition a safety valve for the mental over-pressure from which they suffer. Like people who have the ir-resistible urge to talk, they need some mental activity that gives them relief. Writing music is just the thing. It is preferable to incessant talking, since even the lowest grade of chatter must make some sense, whereas writing music is not subject to so rigid a requirement. Besides this amenity it gives its producer an air of sophistication and fortifies his ego.

Still another group, in an attempt to replace with an apparent rationality what is lacking morally, develops an oversublimated technique which produces images of emotions that are far re-moved from any emotional experiences a relatively normal hu-man being ever has. In doing so they advocate an esoteric *art pour l'art*, the followers of which can only be emotional imps, mon-sters, or snobs.

All these composers forget one important fact: music, as we practice it, is, in spite of its trend towards abstraction, a form of communication between the author and the consumer of his music. If with the method just described we try to push the lis-tener into the background, the picture will be filled with some-thing that is less pleasant than the dullest ignorance of a dumb group of listeners: our own selfishness. William H. Vanderbilt's maxim "the public be damned" would seem to be one of those composers' working rules; or else they claim that audiences have to rubber-stamp whatever they deem necessary to dump upon them; or, finally, they may say: "The present world does not understand my music, but in two hundred years people will be mature enough to follow me." Even if in exceptional cases it may happen that composers are discovered who were never heard in their lifetime two hundred years previous, this attitude is utterly unartistic, since it neglects one of the main reasons for artistic communication: the altruistic desire to present something of one's own to one's fellow men. An artist would be justified in retiring into this unproductive resignation only if he were con-vinced that he had done everything in his power to make himself understood by his contemporaries. If he cannot succeed in doing so, in one form or another, there will be very slight chance that posterity will recognize him as a great genius. It is more likely, however, that his composing is, except for himself, of no value to anyone living either now or two hundred years hence.

There are also many other producers of music who turn their backs on our ideals: those to whom music is nothing but a business proposition; those whose composing is a pleasant pastime without any reason or aim; those who compose just because they cannot stop; and those who are merely public entertainers. We need not discuss their activities, since we know that they add nothing to the great treasury of useful music and that many of them do not have the least ambition to be counted among those contributing to this noble objective. Nor need we tarry with the man who has all the necessary ambition but no talent whatsoever.

# 5·

## MEANS OF PRODUCTION

MUSICIANS having visions, knowing all about the effects of their artistic endeavors, being acquainted with both the emotional and the intellectual approach in perceiving musical creations, using their experience in the historical, pedagogic, and concert fields as a stimulus to further enhancement of their activities—what could they do with all this cleverness, talent, and ardor, if they did not have at their disposal a well-ordered tonal system which permitted them to transform their ideas into sound? A system, that is, which regulates all conceivable successions and relations of sounds: a system arising not out of the speculations of a single genius, but out of the collective thinking and laboring of many generations of musical producers and reproducers.

Usually musicians do not bother with an analysis of the material they work with. They do not question its excellence; nor do they doubt its natural soundness and permanent validity. In ages past, their forefathers received this material as a benevolent gift from a gracious deity — this seems to be the general opinion — and ever since, the musical world is the happy possessor of an unrestricted means of expression which, unlike the material used by the sculptor, the architect, the painter, and the poet, is lofty, mysterious, and always close to the fertile dimness of divine procreation.

Let us replace this somewhat sultry rapture with the brand of cooler enthusiasm (or rather, of sober eagerness) which has led us through our inquiries up to this point. Let us examine this material and the methods of its application as an impartial investigator, an intelligent layman would do, disregarding the musicians' own professional considerations. We shall act as if we had to provide the material for the musician to work with, unguided by previous experience — out of nothing, so to speak.

What, then, is to direct us? There are certain infallible guides: the inherent qualities and possibilities of sound; the purposes the material has to serve; and finally, our plain and reliable musical common sense. Disregarding the musicians' considerations means freeing ourselves from their ties to traditional thinking, their personal preferences, their stylistic rigidity, and last but not least their unconscious defense of everything that they have incorporated into their body of knowledge through study, deduction, and speculation. We may even use our freedom to have a critical look at those traditions and professional considerations; and we may even find more convincing and more dependable methods of applying the musical material.

The fundamental question of where to find this material seems hardly worth answering, since it is so obvious that we can pick out of the range of sound audible to the human ear any tones useful in forming musical creations. Nothing appears to prevent us from selecting as we wish; and in enjoying our freedom of action we feel urged to deplore all those who in their compositions or in their thoughts about music ever followed the rules of short-sighted lawmakers, theorists, and other music-alienated doctrinaires whose only purpose seemed to be to curb one's wonderful imaginative spirit.

Alas, this method, apparently so simple and so sound, produces nothing useful. It is not tone which, according to the deceiving French proverb, *fait la musique*. Singling out tones, entertaining as it may seem for hobby-seekers, leaves the musician without building stones. This sounds paradoxical, since tones, selected out of an unlimited supply of sounds, seem to remain single entities and can be apprehended as such no matter how many there are in succession. The truth is that as single tones they are mere acoustical facts which do not evoke any genuine musical reaction. No musical effect can be obtained unless the tension between at least two different single tones has been perceived. This tension may exist either between the two adjacent tones of melodic progressions or in the harmonic minimum of two tones sounded simultaneously. (We cannot doubt the truth of this statement, since we have already established that musical ideas live in the mentally conceived medium of musical space and musical time.) Since this tension is demonstrated by imagined distances in space and lapses of time, that is, intervals, considered both as spatial distances and as temporal stretches, we may take such intervals as the basic musical material.

Would this not mean that our quest for the source of musical material has merely receded one step? Instead of separating single tones out of the infinity of sound, we are now searching for intervals; and there seems to be no reason why their selection should meet with any greater obstacle than in the case of single tones.

We must find out if there is any truth in this assumption. Let us first talk about the intervals of musical space and deal later with the intervals of musical time.

As there are many different distances between the tones of spatial intervals, some way must be found of measuring them. Fortunately, our race is endowed by nature with a somewhat limited but nevertheless rather reliable scale of measurement: the human voice. Some intervals can be produced easily by our singing voice, others need relatively strong effort. Even in well-developed vocal technique this gradation of effort is ever-present. Practice can facilitate its partial conquest but cannot do away with the fact itself. In this respect the abilities of the untrained voice are not very different from those of the professional. With all this in mind, it is no problem for lawmakers and theorists to classify intervals according to the degree of ease with which they can be produced vocally. In a slightly more advanced state of research this kind of judgment would have to be expanded and improved by some method of measurement that relies on better criteria than the mere feeling of strain in the vocal cords. Such methods were known as early as 600 B.C. and they had the double advantage that they could express the size of intervals in numbers, and that these numbers, in turn, could be demonstrated in visible and therefore easily comprehensible form.

It was a simple wire or gut string — called the monochord — that served as the yardstick for the measurement of intervals. At first it was applied to the intervals known to be produced most easily by the singing voice. The interval most easily produced is the octave. In fact, it is produced with so little effort that perfectly uncultured people sing it, believing that they sing in unison. Reproducing this interval on the measuring string means comparing the tone sounded by the open string with the tone produced by dividing the string into two equal parts. Numerically, one part compared with two parts, or the ratio one to two (1:2), is the accurate measurement of the octave. The fifth, which next to the octave is the interval most easily produced, based on singing experience, is verified on the string by comparing the tone produced by one-half of the string (the octave, as we know) with the tone representing one-third. Thus the numerical ratio for the fifth is 2:3, which means one-half (two parts) compared with one-third (three parts), if we count the lower tone of the interval first; or, if we count the upper tone first, the ratio is 3:2. With this method we obtain for each interval the corresponding division of the string and the ratio that expresses this division. Thus not only could intervals be classified according to ease of vocal production and verified on a measuring string: it was further discovered that the degree of difficulty in singing an interval is in direct proportion to its numerical ratio, in the sense that the more easily an interval is produced, the smaller are the numbers in the ratio that measures it. Thus the octave, as the easiest interval, is represented by the two lowest numbers possible, 1 and 2. The fifth, demanding a slightly greater effort for its production, is expressed by 2 and 3. The next interval would be the one having the ratio 3:4 (which is the fourth), followed by 4:5 (major third) and 5:6 (minor third). Intervals like 8:9 or 15:16 are comparatively far away from the open string (1:1) and consequently are relatively difficult to produce. This is most obvious when the two tones are produced simultaneously, as their complex structure is felt by the singers as dissonant sound. Singing the two tones of such an interval as a melodic succession — that is, not simultaneously — reduces this hurdle, but still the complexity of the intervals makes it difficult always to produce them reliably in one and the same size, an obstacle not present with octaves and fifths. The interval 8:9 is a whole tone or major second; and 15:16 is a half tone or minor second.

The division of the string could be continued and the result would be small intervals which, although they cannot be produced accurately by singing voices, are clearly discernible when sounded mechanically on suitable instruments. Intervals of this kind, well known to theorists, are the half tone 24:25 (which is considerably smaller than the half tone 15:16) and the so-called syntonic comma with a size of about one-ninth of a whole tone (80:81). Other complications arise with intervals expressed by nonsuccessive numbers, such as 1:3 (the tenth); likewise with intervals using the simple proportions in inverted forms — 3:5 (the major sixth as inversion of the minor third 5:6) and 5:8 (the minor sixth as inversion of the major third 4:5); and finally, with intervals using prime numbers — 4:7 (a seventh, which is appreciably smaller than the "normal" seventh 5:9). I might go on to give a complete demonstration of the construction of a tonal system, but these few examples based on the division of a string will suffice to indicate the musician's primary musical material.

## III

The operations described, although desirable and valuable as a demonstration of basic measurements, cannot be performed on the monochord string beyond certain limitations dictated by the thickness and texture of the string, its distance from the sounding board, the size of the player's fingers or of dividing and plucking implements. Therefore the question may arise whether, after more than two thousand years, no other methods of measurement have been developed which can be applied with a high degree of precision even to very small intervals. Such methods are indeed known, and since the end of the seventeenth century they have been used in place of, or in addition to, the old method. The rather clumsy procedure of translating a mechanical operation into numerical symbols can be replaced by a simple comparison of sung intervals with intervals provided by such natural facts as the overtone series.

Overtones are faint-sounding higher additions to practically every tone produced vocally or instrumentally. Though they form an infinite ascending series, only sections of it appear in varied admixtures to the tone originally sounded, their number, pitch, and intensity being determining factors in the timbre or color of the tone as heard. The series grows from the octave of the fundamental upwards in intervals of ever decreasing size, and it is the gradation of this decrease that makes the series so valuable to us as a yardstick for the measurement of spatial intervals. The tones of the series follow each other in the same order as those making up the sung intervals earlier described. There the octave as the easiest, simplest interval was succeeded by the fifth, after which came the fourth, the major third, and the minor third; here ease of production corresponds to the proximity to the fundamental, and again the octave is followed by the fifth, the fourth, et cetera. As the intervals of this series are of the absolute purity nature provides in some of her more fortunate creations (that is, their number of vibrations per second expressing precisely the ratios 1:2, 2:3, 3:4, et cetera), we can compare our sung or played intervals with them instead of referring to the divisions of strings. The results, however, are in no way different from those obtained by the old method. Even if in the future after many years of further research we should be able to use methods of measurement that are based directly on our auditive faculty, following purely psychological considerations, still no change in the original evaluation would be observed: then also a fifth would be an interval of a simpler structure and an easier manner of production than is a half tone.

Now we are acquainted with the basic fact that the building stones of musical space, the intervals, are measurable. We know, furthermore, how to measure them. With the next step in our investigation of musical space we must ask: What are the results when intervals are put on top of each other so as to build chords, and how can these new arrangements be measured? A chord is by no means a mere agglomeration of intervals. It is a new unit which, although dependent on the formative power of the single interval, is felt as being self-existent and as giving to the constituent intervals meanings and functions which they otherwise would not have. Factors that now count are: the number of intervals involved; the position of an interval within the chord; the width of the interval (whether, for example, its two tones lie within one octave or are separated by one or more octaves); the importance of the bass tone; the so-called roots of the intervals; the accumulation of these roots; and finally, the root tone of the chord and the root tone's position.

What are root tones? In all harmonic units, intervals, or chords, the constituent tones seem to have unequal harmonic values. Some seem to us to be more important and to dominate the rest of the sounding entity. These roots, as they are called, are the carriers of the unit's potentialities in respect to its membership in a row of successive harmonies. Overtones, although providing excellent measurements for the size of the intervals, do not explain this fact. The way in which the overtones determine the qualities of intervals resembles the entries in those columns of a doctor's file that describe the patient's physical appearance, his age, his size, his complexion, revealing nothing of his inner constitution, his mental capacities, and his potentialities as a citizen. The data in other columns must supply this information. Concerning intervals one would think that the one gradation, according to vocal difficulty, would make superfluous the additional measurement of the harmonic value, the weight, the quality of their succession potentialities, expressed in roots and their relation to the coöperating tones, since in fact the intervals most easily produced are those of the highest harmonic quality. In simple configurations this coincidence is evident, but in more involved cases it becomes clear that these two factors are of a different nature. A fifth, for instance, the interval of the highest harmonic quality and the one most easily producible (next to the octave), may in certain chordal structures be more difficult to sing than the two simultaneously sounded tones of a second.

The harmonic importance of an interval is determined by its content of combination tones. These, again, are tones which appear more or less faintly as additions to tones actually sounded, yet they are entirely different from overtones. Overtones appear together with individual tones and above the fundamental tone. Combination tones are produced by any two simultaneous tones and their pitch is always less than that of the higher tone; it may, of course, be less than the lower, which is the case with all intervals smaller than an octave. They represent the pitch difference of such sounds; thus two tones with 120 and 180 vibrations per second, respectively, will produce a combination tone with 60 vibrations per second. The appearance of combination tones does not depend on any action of the singers and players. Such tones most likely are not physical facts, but are produced in our ear. They can be regarded as burdens an interval has to carry, and the general rule would be that the less an interval is burdened with combination tones, the more important it is harmonically. Thus the fifth, which carries a light load, is of the greatest harmonic value, while a minor second, carrying a heavy load of combination tones, is of little harmonic importance.

It seems clear that on these suppositions a series of harmonic degrees and of succession potentialities can be established. In the course of our investigation the importance of such a series will become more and more evident.

IV

Having traversed musical space and learned that both its smallest intervals and its widest chordal spans can and must be measured if the material for musical construction is to be selected from nature's unlimited supply of sound, we find that it is the musical element of harmony, and harmony alone, that causes the listener to have a feeling of musical space. But spatial units, be they intervals or chordal accumulations of intervals, are like cars kept without gas in the garage: they have no practical value unless we keep them running. We must combine spatial units with units of musical time if we want musical life to come into being.

Musical time, as we have seen in the fourth chapter, has two essentially different forms of appearance. Our customary terminology is none too scrupulous with respect to musical time: everything in this realm is referred to indiscriminately as meter or rhythm. However, it is necessary to make a strict distinction between the two terms. By meter we mean any kind of temporal entities — beats, tones, motifs — which are of uniform shape and which recur frequently and incessantly, temporal regularity being the principal condition. By rhythm we mean a succession of temporal units that are of unequal value and cannot be understood metrically, although meter may be attached to them and, in fact, in most cases is. In our own musical culture it is admittedly not easy to find rhythmical forms unmixed with meter. Nevertheless, the Gregorian chorale contains, apart from the hymns, sequences, and other strongly metrified pieces, many compositions based on this principle. If those free-swinging melodies are sung with any kind of superimposed meter, the real life immediately vanishes. Other examples may be found in the phonographic records of music sung by savage tribes who have not been infected with the Western "disease" of organized harmony and its inevitable companion, meter.

The characteristics of musical meter have always been clearly comprehended, the reason being its similarity to well-known facts in other arts, such as poetry and architecture, and to everrecurring events in nature, such as years, seasons, days, hours, and many periodic functions in plant and animal life. The temporal material in music, if it is to be used rationally, must be subjected to measurement, as was the spatial element, harmony.

Here again we are endowed with a rather reliable faculty for metrical judgment, similar to the natural feeling for the sizes of intervals, already mentioned. When we listen carefully to metrical structures — for instance, the series of one hundred uniform beats which served as material for our investigation in the fourth chapter — and analyze our faculty of auditory perception, we feel that there are accents which divide the series into small sections of uniform length. These accents are not stresses obtained by increasing slightly the length or loudness of beat or tone; they are not objectively apparent in the series itself, but are attributed to it subjectively by our faculty for metrical judgment. We cannot avoid such psychological interpretation, although usually we are not aware of its inevitability, since almost all music composed leaves us no choice as to the placement of such accents but strives to facilitate their being felt. Accents of this kind, if traced back to the smallest sections of a series, can ultimately fall only on one of two beats or on one of three beats. No other configurations can be felt; the one-beat component, like the one-tone spatial component, lacks any musical meaning, and more than three beats are interpreted as compounds of the simple two-beat and three-beat units. Although the hearing of such compounds is somewhat complicated by the interpretation of secondary and even tertiary accents, the metrical part of the temporal element in music is not in danger of getting too complex, since the primary accents are always felt very strongly and, at the onset of fragmentation or in cases of potential ambiguity, tend to usurp the functions of the secondary and tertiary accents. Despite this tendency towards a clear organization, metrical structure can be carried to the extreme if successions change quickly, frequently, and very irregularly from two-beat to three-beat units; or, similarly, if the time value (duration) of the metrical beat is changed. In the first case the numerator of the fraction designating metrical distribution changes rapidly (2/8, 3/8, 5/8, et cetera); while in the second case, a bewildering change takes place in both numerator and denominator (2/2, 3/8, 5/16, 2/4, 7/32, et cetera). Here, especially in the second case, we lose all feeling for metrical order; in our interpretational judgment the metric successions reach a critical point beyond which no meter whatever can be felt, but the feeling of the unrestrained power of free rhythm enters. On the other hand, free rhythmic forms can just as suddenly become metrified by the introduction of the slightest degree of regular temporal recurrence.

If we try to find methods of measuring pure, meterless rhythm, we are — at least now, and perhaps for some time to come — doomed to failure. In this respect we are as ignorant as were musicians one thousand or two thousand years ago. No scientist's research, no musician's intuitive genius, no layman's common sense has ever been able to find ways of measuring rhythm, in an attempt to establish a rational basis for the construction of temporal musical forms. This does not mean the establishment of such methods is impossible. From the very beginning of music on earth, temporal musical forms have been built. Each constructor, moreover, knows instinctively, or by trial and error, or by traditional experience, when structural parts are in good proportion and when they are not. Therefore, some rational, discoverable, and understandable law of construction must exist which could be put into effective operation. With its application, rhythm could be dragged out of obscurity into the clear light of reason. Thus far musicians have not cared about solving this problem; in fact, they have perhaps not even known of its existence. If they had been aware of it, perhaps they would still have preferred not to have their complacent intuition disturbed by exact knowledge. This protective attitude, valuable as it may appear for the immediate kindling of a musician's creative spark, is, of course, not tenable once he admits his musical intellect as an equal partner with intuition in the field of musical creation. The graveness of the problem will be evident if we compare the possible measurement of rhythm, apparently so elusive, with the measurement of intervals, chords, and meter, already discussed. Their compliance with the methods of measurement imposed on them proves that harmonic and metric material can be comprehended rationally; and this comprehension is facilitated by the technique of measuring their smallest units.

Measurement of rhythm would have to resort to the same method: the smallest rhythmic unit would have to serve as a standard gauge for all larger rhythmic organisms. But what the basic unit of rhythm might be is still an unanswered question. It cannot be what is called a motif, since even the shortest motif (whatever the precise definition of this term may be) is a compound of a higher order. Nor can it be a group of tones assembled around an accent, since this would be the characteristic mark of meter — and we can prove experimentally, as mentioned before, that meter and rhythm are independent powers with nothing in common but their temporal occurrence. Measurement with a stop watch is out of the question because of the nonidentity of ordinary clock time and musical time. We shall probably have to direct our search away from the mere physical facts of sound and into the field of musical psychology. Until an answer is forthcoming from that quarter, we must trust our empirical knowledge and our talent, as did all musicians before us. The many masterworks written by great composers of the past on none other than those very grounds seem to suggest that we would better follow in their footsteps and forego all artistic and scientific inquisition. Of course, it is admirable how musical genius has at all times and apparently blindfolded found the way of artistic truth and adequacy, and if we have geniuses among us, they doubtless will follow their predecessors' method of composing without ever listening to our sober admonitions. But this does not warrant a rejection of wisdom. He who believes he has a right to such rejection may not be a genius; and real genius may, after decades, be discovered in a modest man who, although he never thought of anything more than simply doing his daily chores, unconsciously invested in his creations more wisdom than did either the would-be genius or the omniscient toiler. Therefore it seems wiser to gather knowledge, in case our never-failing intuition should prove nonexistent.

v

If harmony was the element which entirely coincides with the mental concept of musical space, it is the element of rhythm, with its companion, meter, that represents musical time. We have found that for the attainment of musical effects both elements must be combined. This combination if applied in a restricted form — that is, so that rhythm exerts its power on the smallest harmonic unit, the interval — creates melody. The harmonic interval with its two tones in a vertical position must be tilted into a horizontal position in order to provide a surface for the attacks of rhythm. Then its two tones change their spatial relationship into one of time, and rhythm regulates their temporal relation: the harmonic interval has turned into a melodic interval. The harmonic strength of the original interval has, in this transmutation, been preserved; a fifth remains an interval possessing power and stability; a major or minor second, one with scant harmonic meaning. But since now, in the newly established form of interval, the melodic succession of tones, the movement, the temporal relationship are the main characteristics, it seems clear that any quality of an interval that emphasizes its former harmonic strength is unfavorable to the new melodic function. Consequently we see a complete reverse in the evaluation of intervals according to their spatial-temporal context: the harmonically strong fifth is of minor quality melodically, the harmonically poor seconds become the preferred intervals in melodies. In the middle ground between these two extremes we find the intervals that are not strong enough in either respect; they yield as readily to the attacks of the spatial powers as to those of rhythm. These principal factors of spatial and temporal construction, together with many secondary facts which cannot be discussed here, must, of course, be taken into consideration in the composer's practical work.

All this exhibits melody, genetically, as the offspring of harmony and rhythm. Yet it has qualities and potentialities of its own which are not explainable by, nor deducible from, rhythmic or harmonic facts. Thus musical space and musical time have produced a new spatial-temporal element which exists autonomously with them. The historical development, however, did not follow the genetic order. Primitive man, in singing and playing his primordial music, applies rhythms and melodic intervals, but has no feeling for harmony (the exclusively spatial component of musical structure), although the harmonic values of the intervals are also present in their melodic form, as we have seen. It took thousands of years before harmony as a consciously perceived part of musical construction could be introduced, and even nowadays we find many peoples who cannot or will not take the step towards a clear recognition of spatial effects in music. The reason for this contradiction between genetic and historic development is obvious. There are but two basic metrical units: those of two beats and those of three beats; and rhythm, once explained rationally, will probably also turn out to be an endless variation of very few and very simple basic units. The same is true with melody. Its temporal qualities are governed by these same metric and rhythmic basic units, partly known and partly yet to be discovered; and its spatial qualities, borrowed from harmony, are again vested in a few intervals: those with high harmonic value on the one side (fifth, fourth, et cetera) and those with high melodic value on the other (seconds), with some unstable ones in the middle ground. Such material, simple, unobscure, and lacking in great variety, presents little difficulty even to an artless musician.

With harmony it is different. The organized treatment of the simplest two-tone harmonies (fifths, fourths, thirds, sixths) demands a kind of purposeful musical thinking rarely found in an undeveloped state of musical knowledge, since not only the course of two different melodic lines must be calculated but also the harmonic effect resulting from it. Consequently, the more advanced harmonic material (the single, unmoving, chordal union

of several intervals) will prove to be a more conspicuous hurdle.
Of the simplest chords of three or more tones, indispensable for
tonal construction, there are more than twenty different forms
(triads, sixth-chords, seventh-chords, et cetera) and, counting all
possible combinations, the complete harmonic arsenal comprises
several hundreds — numbers that must have a dissuasive effect on
unsophisticated minds. But the chief difficulty arises when we
treat these chordal unions of intervals as we did the single
harmonic intervals: when we subject them to the influence of
rhythm and array them in chordal series. Since each chord of
such a series consists of several intervals, the possibilities of going
from any one tone of one chord to any one tone of the next are
numerous; and further complications spring up if these single progressions are not coördinated by a uniform melodic motion, the
driving power of rhythm acting with different degrees of energy
in the different strata of the structure. Such an infinite variety of
spatial-temporal possibilities (even if only a few are selected) cannot be incorporated into rational musical work until the simpler
combination of interval plus rhythm (equals melody) is clearly
understood and verified through countless practical experiences.
No wonder, then, that harmony as a consciously applied part of
the musical material of construction appears so relatively late in
the course of the art's evolution.

The rhythmically organized sequence of intervals, called melody, if it is to impress us as music, cannot be just a motley assembly of successive intervals: it must follow certain laws. It is obedi-
ence to such laws that guarantees us the possibility of mentally
coconstructing a perceived musical form and the probability that
emotional images can be conjured up. These laws, then, must be
of general validity. Later in this chapter some information concerning them will be given, although an exhaustive study of their
application is not within the scope of this book.

If the succession of mere melodic intervals is subject to laws,
the succession of chords cannot remain unregulated, since such
successions are structures analogous to melodies, containing mul-
tiple melodic progressions. They may be regarded as melody
spreading out in planes of different levels instead of advancing on

one level only. This kind of supermelody is called tonality. The laws ruling tonality must be of the same general validity as those applied to melody.

VI

Before the laws of melodic and tonal progressions can be established, we must be assured that the harmonic and melodic intervals to be used in music fulfill certain basic demands. One of these seems to be almost axiomatic: that in the arrangement of melodies or tonalities a given tone which recurs after other tones have intervened shall have the same pitch as before. If this were not the case, a reasonable stability of melody, harmony, and tonality could hardly be achieved. To find out how this demand and our basic material, the intervals, interact, we must undertake some easy numerical calculations.

Let us assume that the interval of the octave (1:2) is divided into 1200 equal intervals. This is not a simple division by 1200, but is done by the mathematical formula $2^{1/1200}$, that is, the twelve-hundredth root of 2, the number 2 being the symbol of the octave (1:2). The fractions thus obtained do not designate numbers of vibrations per second but are ratios of vibration numbers. This useful method of splitting the octave into 1200 "cents" was introduced by A. J. Ellis (1814–1890). We have no musical instruments which could produce such minute divisions, and no human voice can express them with sufficient distinction. But for theoretical purposes this division of the octave has the great advantage of showing the sizes of the intervals more accurately than does the twelve-interval division, thus being in musical space of the same service as a micrometer in real space. Furthermore it indicates in a more perspicuous form what is meant by the never very intelligible ratios.

In this octave system of extremely small intervals the fifth (2:3) contains 702 cents; the fourth (3:4), 498; the major third (4:5), 386; the minor third (5:6), 316; the major second (8:9), 204; the minor second (15:16), 112. If we now assume that we could sing these intervals with perfect purity — which is physically impossible, although, as stated before, we have a rather reliable feeling for this purity — we may try to sing the following little melody, in which the starting tone $c'$ (middle $c$) shall be represented by the number 0 (zero):

Expressed in cents the succession would read: $0 + 204 + 702 - 498 + 112 - 498$. The final tone is not, as we expected, $c' = 0$ cents, but $c' = +22$ cents, which, though only slightly sharper (one-fifth of the minor second, 112) is perceptibly out of tune. In one-voiced, unharmonized melody this fact may not be too disturbing, but if it occurs repeatedly in a melodic line, the final tone may come out a half tone or more removed from its intended pitch. In a tonal context in which not only the melodic effect but also harmonies as single units and in succession have to be taken into account, the slight deviation of 22 cents, afflicting a main tone of the structure, is so disturbing that it cannot be tolerated. From this we must not conclude that our intervals, the fifths, fourths, thirds, and so forth, are false — the fact that they are singable in a sufficiently correct form is proof enough of their high consonance — rather, we encounter the strange experience that in harmony and tonality the application of the purest material inevitably leads to impurity.

Further investigation acquaints us with the following facts:

(1) In successions consisting of any one kind of pure interval a critical point will be reached, after which impurity sets in. Example: The total of three successive fifths ($c$-$g$, $g$-$d'$, $d'$-$a'$) equals 2106 cents, or one octave + 906 cents. The same tone $a'$ (a major sixth above $c'$) may be obtained by deducting the known size of a minor third (316 cents) from the octave; but this $a'$ is only 884 cents above $c'$.

(2) There are intervals more susceptible to impurity than others. Example: The sum of two major seconds ($204 + 204$ cents) $= 408$ cents, which is a larger major third than the "natural" major third, 386 cents. We obtain the same result with four successive

fifths: *c-g*, *g-d'*, *d'-a'*, *a'-e''*, or 4 × 702 cents = 2808 cents, which is two octaves + 408 cents. This operation shows the greater purity of the fifth, as the distorted third of 408 cents was produced by the sum of only two major seconds, while four fifths were needed for the same effect.

In all the cases mentioned, the deviation from the correct, the more normal, or at least the reasonably expected, interval was always 22 cents. This small deviating interval is the syntonic comma 80:81, mentioned earlier in this chapter, but it is by no means the only deviation possible. Theoretically, any size of comma between one cent and a minor second may occur, although some commas appear more frequently than others in the computation of intervals. These comma-sized intervals not only may show up as the differences between the sum of pure intervals and simple octaves, fifths, thirds, et cetera, as demonstrated, but may also be deviations from these simple intervals that our ear will tolerate. The octave, however, we shall always demand in the purest form possible; the smallest deviation from its ratio 1:2 is felt to be disturbing. With fifths and fourths an impurity of two cents is tolerated, unless, of course, such tarnished intervals are compared directly with the corresponding pure interval. Thirds and sixths can endure deviations up to 22 cents (syntonic comma) or even 24 cents (Pythagorean comma) without seeming too much out of tune. With seconds and sevenths the tolerance may reach 40 cents, and the interval lying between the fourth and the fifth (augmented fourth or diminished fifth) has no fixed size at all: it varies between approximately 563 cents (13:18) and approximately 663 cents (15:22), any interval between these limits (which differ by a minor second) sounding tolerably pure.

## VII

All this considered, it may now be understandable that the demand which caused our digression into numerical calculation — namely, that a given tone recurring after intervening tones shall have the same pitch — needs an amendment to its simple form, since the tolerances conceded to the intervals may well modify an interval which contains the recurring tone, and may sharpen or flatten this very tone. Therefore the rule must include all possible cases, the equalities of recurring tones as well as the tolerances. We shall have to say: Each tone in a tonal system must be able to assume the place of any other tone; the system's content of intervals must be totally interchangeable. Practically, this means that a recurring tone which is off pitch by a comma-sized interval must be compensated by the tolerances of the following intervals, so that the original pitch context will be regained.

If we want to accommodate our material so that total interchangeability and the greatest possible purity are guaranteed, our common sense, the source of so much of our valuable information, will tell us that there are the following possibilities:

(1) We may build our melodic, harmonic, and tonal structures with intervals that permit the smallest tolerances only. (2) We may use all kinds of tolerable intervals, but stop short before impurity sets in. (3) We may use the main intervals (fifths, thirds) in the purest form and intersperse them with the less sensitive intervals, plus or minus tolerance. (4) We may divide the octave into equal parts which are so close to the "natural" intervals that these approximations fall within the limitations of tolerance for each. Let us examine these possibilities more closely.

(1) The use of this kind of melodic and harmonic interval would permit a very limited range of combinations. The great advantage of utter purity is offset by a lack of melodic and tonal variety. Melodies would consist of nothing but leaps in the sizes of fifths, fourths, and thirds, only occasionally interspersed with nondisturbing steps. Of the harmonies, the minor triad would be the most complicated chord. No change of the tonal center (tonic) — that is, no modulation — could take place. Our structures of sound would be like pigs or geese, kept in narrow pens to be fattened. Their hams or livers may taste better than those of their free-moving fellow pigs or geese, but only at the expense of the creature's own well-being. Throughout the evolution of mankind, no period has been satisfied with such limited tonal material.

(2) In arraying intervals according to our second method, we have somewhat greater freedom. The material serves equally well in both a melodic and a tonal context, but the moment of incipient impurity is always perilously near. Such a system, with its

limitations, can be only a transitional stage in a larger development. In the history of our own Western music we see it in effect
during the period of early harmonic exploration, before a conscious understanding of tonality, especially in its chromaticized
form, demanded a more efficient material. I believe that in the
organa of Perotinus (shortly before 1200) this material attained
the highest and final stage of its development.

(3) The more efficient material just mentioned, intriguing
practical musicians and theorists alike as early as the thirteenth
century, became fully explored by the end of the fifteenth century, and ever since has been the ideal arrangement of intervals
for singing voices and for all instruments not using keyboards.
What our singers and our players of wind and string instruments
do is exactly what we stated: they sing and play fifths, fourths,
and thirds in the purest form possible — or at least in close
approximation to the pure intervals they feel — and the commatic
adjustments needed to reëstablish melodic or tonal purity lost in
the succession of pure intervals can always be made by expanding
or contracting the remaining intervals, which for the most part
is done unconsciously. Even so, theoretically the danger of losing
tonal coherence is never absent; but practically the fixed points in
the tuning of instruments — such as open strings, or the immuta-
ble intervals between fundamental and overblown tones in wind
instruments — act like an Alpine climber's rope to prevent a sud-
den fall into an abyss. Doubtless this most nearly perfect method
does justice to our feeling for purity, in that whenever possible,
it uses the intervals of easiest intellectual and practical approach,
thus establishing a dependable basis for melody, harmony, and
tonality. On the other hand, it leaves us great freedom to broaden
tonality, without expelling us into the jungle of tonal disorder.
Even in the most daring, the most involved situations there will
always be a fifth, a fourth, or a third, perhaps supported by open
strings or otherwise fixed tones, that can be reached by some interval which is slightly modified.

Since the technique of constantly modifying the lesser intervals, which is the peculiarity in the application of this system, is
usually employed unconsciously, musicians have never found it
difficult to handle; in fact, few of them have been or are aware of

the peculiarity at all. It was the keyboard in its well-known form, with twelve keys to the octave, as it developed after all the chromatic additions within an octave had become common knowledge to singers, players, composers, and theorists, that brought out the full force of the problem: how could a compromise be found between the immovable tuning of the instrument's twelve keys and the mixture of purity and tolerances in the intervals used by the other musicians? An organ or harpsichord tuner using pure intervals would inevitably land in a range of impure ones, as we know. The apparent answer to the question was: to use as many pure intervals as possible and then forget about purity. You can imagine the result. If you start your tuning with the key producing the tone *c* and progress by bringing fifths, fourths, and thirds into correct relation to the tones already tuned, after several steps you will be out of tune with the starting tone. Your tone *a flat* obtained by this method may not coincide with the correct minor sixth (5:8) of the starting tone: it may even deviate by more than the tolerable comma of 24 cents. This *a flat* compared with the *d flat* which likewise may be out of tune beyond commatic tolerance would not produce a usable fifth, and the same may be true with the fifth *a flat–e flat* or any other fifth or third. Such discrepancies may show up in any part of the tonal range, according to the method of tuning used.

Thus the problem is not how to tune a keyboard in correct intervals; but rather, in which corner of the tonal range does impurity have the least disturbing effect? This reminds one of the lazy housemaid's deliberation, under which edge of the big carpet to put the sweepings. The room looks clean (the tonality seems to be satisfactory) but don't lift the carpet (don't listen to the intervals derived last; here all the refuse of the entire structure is deposited)! The question may arise whether one could not tune in seconds, in a scalelike fashion. The answer is that it cannot be done satisfactorily. Since seconds, as we have seen, are still seconds within a tolerance of almost a quarter tone, only approximate relations can be obtained and the over-all tonal range must necessarily be more out of tune than with a tuning using pure intervals, which, despite their spiraling into impurity, guarantee at least a partially clean tonality.

Methods of tuning keyboard instruments as described here were already known before 1500, and from that date until about 1700 many different suggestions appeared in learned books about the problem of where to place a tonality's weakest sector. Imagine housemaids publishing tomes on the best method of hiding the sweepings under the carpet!

(4) The reasoning underlying our fourth proposition ought now to be clear. If, instead of dividing the octave into an ever-shifting small number of preferred pure intervals and an undetermined number of others variably sized, we could divide it into twelve equal parts ($2^{1/12}$), all fifths would then be one and the same size, and this would be true with any other interval, provided, of course, that the eleven dividing points did not fall so that the deviations from any "normal" interval were larger than the admissible tolerances. In fact they are not. In our 1200-tone octave the half tones of the twelve-tone division are placed on the even hundreds, and thus the deviations from the main intervals are: fifth, 2 cents (700 now, 702 in pure form); major third, 14 cents too large, 6 cents less than the tolerated maximum (400, 386); minor third, 16 cents too small (300, 316). Even the major second 8:9 deviates by not more than 4 cents (200, 204), and the minor second 15:16 by 12 cents (100, 112).

The advantages of this system are evident. It permits an all-round use of the tonal range without any commatic adjustments, thus widening the tonal horizon more than any other system of a similar degree of complexity could ever do. On the other hand, it suffers incurably from its basic and omnipresent impurity. Even that interval which we want to hear and to use in the purest form, the fifth, is strained to the limits of its tolerance. From the eighteenth century on, this system (the so-called equal temperament) became the exclusive method of tuning keyboard instruments, and its influence was so powerful that many people, among them famous scientists, believed in an accommodation of our singing and listening habits to equal temperament. In their opinion we have learned to sing tempered, but they have never been able to prove their hypothesis. If they saw no harmful trend in this supposed accommodation of the producing, reproducing, and receiving mind to changing conditions, to others the constant absence of pure intervals resulted in an inevitable and never-ceasing perversion of musical intellect. The fact is that our feeling for the purity of intervals can be as little altered by circumstances and custom as the eye's ability to recognize colors, and no externally enforced system of temperament can influence our understanding and production of intervals in their natural purity. Singing and playing in combination with tempered keyboard instruments, which was thought of as the main reason for the reconversion of our ears and voices, does not change this fact. Such association is scarcely more homogeneous than a plow pulled jointly by horse and tractor! Either we feel that in such cases our temporary adjustment to the shackles of equal temperament falls within the limits of intervallic tolerances or we are superficially satisfied, in the belief that the collaboration of these unequal partners is necessarily of limited duration.

It is hard to understand how people can believe in the possibility of our singing tempered intervals (a cappella, that is, not guided by a keyboard). In doing so, their point of departure usually is to deny the capacity to produce pure intervals correctly. They obviously do not see that with commas and tolerances both correctness and freedom are guaranteed. If we did not base our singing on pure intervals, how could we ever believe in the accurate production of the unnatural, distorted, tempered intervals? If commatic regulations and tolerances were admitted in the use of tempered intervals, they would no longer be tempered intervals, since the characteristic quality of temperament is the once-and-for-all fixed amount of deviation from natural measurements. If, according to those assumptions, natural intervals cannot be produced correctly (which, with the possible tolerances, is not necessary anyway), the fixed, "unnatural" sizes of tempered intervals can to an even less degree be produced correctly. The assumption of purity as a basis would be more plausible and in fact would remain, as it always has been, the only possibility. The explanation for the rise of such ideas can only be the theorists' lack of practical musical experience. If they had ever carefully observed their own actions in singing parts of a cappella music, in which, inevitably, the ceaseless shifting of commas and tolerances is essential for the maintenance of tonal coherence, they would have felt the weakness of their assertion. As it is, this assertion proves either that they never sang in a chorus or that their musical gift is absent to such a degree as to prevent them from observing the most obvious of all facts in ensemble singing. Neither can they have had any experience in string quartet playing, where there is, as every expert knows, no such thing as rigid adherence to pitch.

Although we cannot think of a world without the advantage of equal temperament, we know that the benefits we enjoy in using it are as artificial as those provided by a monetary system: you can buy everything with money, but money does not satisfy your hunger. Equal temperament opens the entire tonal range and permits interchangeability of tones, but it cannot satisfy your innate desire for harmonic purity. Mankind will always turn to the latter, even if in times of transition or degeneration it may seem as though equal temperament and its slave, the keyboard, were the omnipotent dictators in the field of tonal construction. After all, we enjoy a clean living-room, although dust will inevitably penetrate various little nooks; and therefore the maid's concealing tactics are just as unappreciated as a versatile scientist's method of distributing the total amount of dust all over the place so thinly that it cannot be seen very clearly, yet covers everything with a perceptible film.

VIII

Once one has taken the step into the realm of equal temperament, one is tempted to increase the advantages it has over all other intervallic systems: unhindered access to every region of a tonality and absence of any commatic regulation. Could not the stimuli afforded by this carefree calculation be heightened if we replaced our twelve-tone division of the octave by a different number of tones? Numbers smaller than twelve would not do, for two reasons. (1) The intervals of such divisions would deviate from most of the main intervals (fifth, fourth, major third, minor third) by more than the tolerated aberration (divide 1200 by any of these numbers and compare the cent numbers of the individual tones thus obtained with the cent numbers given for the natural intervals earlier in this chapter). (2) Because of the

reduced number of tones within the octave, melodic and harmonic-tonal construction would necessarily be poorer than that
of the twelve-tone temperament.

However, if we take a number exceeding twelve tones within
the octave, we find it promising, the more so because we may get
a chance to reduce the minor but ever-present toxic effect of impure intervals by diminishing the amounts of the tolerances. Apart
from a greater number of tones, the multiples of twelve would
yield nothing new, because the deviations from the main intervals would remain the same as in the twelve-tone temperament,
the fifth being in both cases 2 cents below standard, and the major
third 14 above. Closer approximations to the natural sizes of the
simple intervals can be expected from temperaments that use a
prime number as divisor of the octave, but while some of these
produce better thirds (temperaments with 31 and 37 tones), in
none of these temperaments are the fifths superior to those of the
twelve-tone temperament, except in the temperaments with 41
and 53 tones. Alluring as such mines of tonal variety may appear
to those hunting for novelty in sound, keyboard instruments with
41 or 53 keys in a single octave and 400 to 500 throughout the
range will certainly prove as unwieldy in future as they have in
the case of the few specimens built experimentally in the past —
not to mention woodwind instruments whose modified forms can
only be a nightmare to normal, ten-fingered players. And where
would we find a cappella singers and string players who could
cope chromatically and in free successions with those microinter-
vals? Think of the cent progressions, as they appear in the space
of one whole tone, say the major second between the subdomi-
nant and the dominant, where the temperament with 41 tones
progresses 498 — 527 — 556 — 585 — 615 — 644 — 673 — 702; and
in the 53-tone scale we find 498 — 521 — 543 — 566 — 589 — 611
— 634 — 657 — 679 — 702.

However, one could imagine a total segregation of vocal music. It would have to adhere to its old-fashioned and almost sub-
human stammering, based on — shudderingly be they mentioned
— natural intervals, while the instruments would carry the ban-
ners of progress, freedom, and endless variety.

This kind of progressionism has about the same prospect of

surviving as had the civilized idea, formerly so enticing, of nourishing man with pills that contain all foodstuffs needed for his existence. We have learned that to the mere act of taking nourishment the enjoyment of eating and many other alluring features must be added if favorable effects are to be expected, and if this is true of nutrition, a most prosaic and inescapable business, how much more so of music, whose pleasure-born and pleasure-giving nature will be eternally opposed to automatization and dehumanization.

The conclusion drawn from all these considerations is this: of all possible tonal systems which fulfill the two primary conditions in combining melodic and harmonic material — which demand, as we know, that it shall be easily singable and that it shall provide complete interchangeability of all tones — our natural twelve-tone system, with its tendency towards maximum purity and its flexible commatic regulations achieved with the aid of expanded or contracted intervals readily tolerated, is doubtless the best one we can find. In its tempered form it is still close enough to nature so that its deviations are not felt as new intervals and so that it can be used together with the untempered form without causing serious disturbances. It is this latter advantage, in particular, which makes our system so handy but which cannot be maintained in more complicated systems. In the aforementioned temperaments with high numbers (41 and 53) the possible tolerances of a third or a sixth are almost as large as the scale's constituent intervals, and those of the major second exceed them considerably. Therefore sounding the tones at their accurate pitch would necessitate precision tools instead of musical instruments, and again would eliminate singers and foster automatization.

If, despite all the obstacles discussed, one wants to extend the possibilities of our tonal system, neglecting equal temperament, he will always find at his disposal a most reliable and most honest touchstone: unaccompanied vocal polyphony. A tonal system that cannot be used for a cappella singing is bound to die sooner or later of anemia. In a melodic-harmonic culture such as ours, the indispensable demand for total interchangeability includes the possibility of using the tones of the system chromatically — that is, in regular, uninterrupted succession. To invent a system of more than twelve tones which satisfies this demand and yet is feasible for choral singers doubtless requires a genius of extraordinary resources.

Of the systems of more than twelve tones (tempered or using natural intervals), the one closest to the twelve-tone one and yet entirely independent is a system with nineteen tones within the octave. It has the distinction of having been calculated and proposed — since its first appearance shortly after 1600 — more often than any other unusual system, but in spite of this it has remained theory — and theory in its vaguest form at that. It is one thing to propose tonal systems; another, to prove their practicability. Has anyone ever reported on his successful experiences with a nineteen-tone system, actually sung (and sung many times) by an a cappella chorus? No. Tonal systems grow and live like languages. They may develop from primitive forms into extremely involved idioms; worn-out systems may disappear. But they cannot be manufactured and put into use like motors and crackers, nor can they be enforced like laws.

### IX

A composer who has followed our path of discovery now beholds our musical material with all its potentialities, spread out in the vast expanses of musical space and musical time: harmonic intervals and the harmonic units of a higher order, chords; intervals and chords in succession, resulting in tonalities; temporal intervals generating both metric and rhythmic arches; and melody, the third element of musical creation, as an amalgamation of spatial and temporal powers. Such a composer, knowing the governing precepts and being so firmly rooted in this knowledge that for any technical necessity and for any stylistic demand he can draw from it adequate rhythmic, melodic, and harmonic means of expression, may ask how, before the disclosure of such principles, the historic development of our art endowed musicians with the knowledge of their constructive material.

Musicians have at all times tried to determine those governing precepts. Their ambition was to formulate them so that they would withstand the ever-changing conditions of performance, the never-stable correlations of music and society, the unending variability of tone combinations. Laws for the application of rhythm are known, as we have seen, for metrical structures alone; and this has always been so. Meter's characteristic feature being the incessant recurrence of two-beat and three-beat units, no formative problems had to be considered, beyond a mere assembling of such units. But rising metrical complications have a tendency to shift meter into the arms of rhythm, and here — to reverse our former statement — our ancestors were as ignorant as we are. Tradition, empiricism, sensitiveness to the material's potentialities, a gift for proportions, and a sharpshooter's unerring aim — without these they would have been living in lawless territory. Yet they felt the reins of the invisible law, and we may also assume that in the past clairvoyant musicians dreamed of a future time of enlightenment, when rational organization of rhythmical forms should have turned $x$ into a known quantity.

Similarly the application of melodic material was left to chance. Throughout the course of music history very few attempts at finding melodic laws have been made. If with rhythm it was the apparent incommensurability that frustrated all efforts at a rational understanding, with melody the negligence must have had other reasons, for we know the basic melodic material, the intervals, as the tilted form of the basic harmonic material, which, from the moment of its introduction, readily yielded to rational exploration and treatment — as we shall see. Melody was probably considered taboo, since in its sensuous flexibility it seemed to correspond so perfectly with our soul's innermost feelings. And who wanted his sanctuaries opened for public inspection! We nowadays, being freed from inhibitions, may think that we have found the laws of melodic construction. The resumé to come later in this chapter will acquaint us with the modern situation.

Harmony and tonality, their material being more extensive and varied than in the case of rhythm and melody, could not be left to the musicians' intuition. Here was a material that sprang up rather impetuously and demanded immediate investigation. If a composer wanted to use it at all, no reference to the experiences of predecessors would guide him; he was forced to study its qualities and potentialities. Thus we find, from the time of the first practical experiences with more-part sounds (that is, from the tenth century on), theories and directions for the application of harmonic and tonal material. They are founded on our well-known theorem which, although never enunciated as such, can be deduced from the theorists' writings: the two-tone interval is the basic unit of all harmony; chords are built up by combinations of two or more intervals. Although in its psychological effect a chord is more than the sum total of its tones (see our former statements), technically it is nothing but an assembling of intervals, and we can but admire the ingenuity which in those early times led the search for a rational application of the material in the obviously right direction. The concept of chordal inversion which in modern technique appears with the pretensions of an eternal law, could have no place in this old theory. A chord was seen as a thoroughly vivid structure, in which all the latent streams of energy, ready to spring up into tonal activity, were constantly observed. Here no unilateral and exaggerated relation of chord tones to all-determining roots and bass tones paralyzed a chord's inner life; no dull leveling of the faculties of hearing and interpretation turned chords into those degenerated tone clusters which in the styles of the nineteenth and early twentieth centuries made musical organisms appear like constructions built with the wooden blocks of a child's toy box. A healthy theory, combined with the unchallenged sovereignty of the human voice, prevented sliding from eloquent efficacy into mere sound; no keyboard could yet exert its devastating influence on the art of voice leading. No wonder, then, that the rules for this art of voice leading and for all other technical procedures were kept close to nature's own vocal prototypes, even if they were produced on instruments.

The rules for tonal organization regrettably did not find so persuasive a formulation. Progression from harmony to harmony in the individual voices of a setting followed the course prescribed by the church modes, a set of diatonic scales built on principles similar to those governing our major and various minor scales. Anything more than a confirmation of a mode's general mood could not be achieved, although modulation from one mode to another and the simultaneous application of several modes provided a greater variety than did the melodic one-line mode. However, church modes were originally and essentially intended for melodic purposes. In fact, they are merely precomposed, normalized, and generalized melodies; therefore they cannot be good tonal organizers. Theorist after theorist tries to reform this system of tonal organization, and the names of Odington, Prosdocimus, Ramis, Glarean, Vicentino, Zarlino — to mention only a few — are as many stations on the way of sorrows and errors along which music theory had to plod and toil.

In the eighteenth century, the older music theory, facing new technical and stylistic accomplishments, was unable to further provide a sound basis for the practical work of a composer. New ideas arose. Harmony became the mother of melody, not in the wide genetic concept shown in these pages, but in a very narrow sense; all melodic facts had to be understood as horizontal projections of vertical tone combinations. These, in turn, were not compounds of intervals, as before, but were considered independent and indivisible chordal units, the more complicated of which were derivations and modifications of the most primitive and fundamental harmonic structures, the major and minor triads. These two basic units were taken directly from nature, a fact that made a theory of this kind so attractive. The overtone series and the series of combination tones, both discovered shortly before that time, replaced the purely mathematical formula which in the older theory had served as the extramusical basis for melody and harmony. Thus the most important theorists of the new style, the French composer Rameau and the Italian violinist Tartini, provided a theory of harmony and melody that was to be a guide for a long time to come.

Rameau went even further. His theory of tonality was perhaps the most daring of all, and its consequences led directly to our most modern theories. According to Rameau, tonal progressions are directed by the so-called *basse fondamentale*, which is a bass line that does not exist in actual sound but only in the composer's and listener's imagination, thus providing a mental basis for musical activity in place of a solely technical one. It is indeed a far cry from the tonality-regulating church modes with their precomposed melodic shapes to this bass line which is in principle entirely removed from any scale succession. Strangely enough, this progressive idea was forgotten by Rameau's contemporaries as soon as it was introduced. They clung to the more obvious parts of his innovations and neglected the real original spark of genius which has only in our own time been resurrected as a leading idea in musical thought. Moreover, they leniently ignored the system's grave shortcomings and out of this indulgence and the neglect of advantageous formulations grew a strangely distorted system of theory. This system prevailed throughout the nineteenth century and is, with minor emendations, essentially the one used in our schools in teaching composition and all the related courses (harmony, counterpoint, fugue, and so on) that are the headaches of theory departments.

x

What are the leading ideas in our contemporary method of applying musical material?

For the application of harmonic and tonal material workable directions were evolved long ago. However, the formulations of the eighteenth century theorists concerning harmonies, so familiar to us from our theory lessons, have lost a good deal of their persuasive power. In none of their theorems, long believed to be of unshakable truth, can we any longer have confidence. Most of them we can disprove; others have proved themselves impractical. The inversion of chords — meaning that the harmonic purport and tonal potentiality of a fundamental arrangement of the chord's tones is retained in any other arrangement — one of the pet ideas in the evolution of the composer's technique during more than two hundred years, has turned out to be of very limited value. Beyond a certain degree of complexity, chords cannot be inverted; neither can they be reconverted into simpler forms of origin. Similarly, the "law," once so convincing, which required all chords to be built up by superposed thirds has, ever since the inclusion of more dissonant chords, lost right and title; so has Rameau's "borrowing" and "replacement" of chord tones, as has the subsequent chromatic alteration of scale tones, in which a tone could assume the functions of an entirely different tone, merely with our custom of applying matching names to nonmatching tones ($d - d\ sharp - d\ flat$) as an excuse. The worst setback was the waning belief in the unity and indivisibility of the natural triad in both its major and minor form, a belief that had forced the composer to handle each two-tone harmony as an incomplete chord. This theorem totally contradicted daily musical practice.

All this shows how reasonable the medieval musicians' ideas of harmony had been and how comparatively weak and far from reality the newer theorists were. Practically, our modern technique of writing has returned to the older method and it is merely music theory's backwardness which makes it cling to the cherished ideas of the eighteenth century. The older theory's principle of tonal organization, however, cannot be revived; church modes and any other precomposed scale lines as organizing agents of tonal progressions are forever abandoned. This includes major and minor scales as well (theory teachers making such statements had better look for another job!), since the tendency of the *basse fondamentale* to avoid scale regulation — a tendency reinstated nowadays, as mentioned above, but not generally accepted — is a genuinely comprehensive and reliable means of organization.

Melodies can, in our time, be constructed rationally. We do not need to believe in benign fairies, bestowing angelic tunes upon their favorites, nor is it necessary to be guided by the crude concept of melodically dissolved harmony. We can understand melodies as a sequence of intervals, linked together in a chain, with recurring tones, and welded into higher melodic entities by variably distanced steps of major and minor seconds. Application of the melodic material according to these considerations will do justice to both the technical demand for continuous sequence of smallest melodic units and the aesthetic goal of indivisible higher entities.

To summarize: In spite of our modern advanced technique of composing, the harmonic and tonal principles underlying this technique are those that were developed partly in the early stages of polyphonic music and partly by the theorists and practicians of the eighteenth century. Although their formulation is in many respects outmoded and obscure, these principles have at least been recognized, and attempts to use them as a foundation for a rationalized modern technique are bound to come. With respect to meter and rhythm we have not progressed at all but have tried to use the principles of musical time as a foundation for a rationalized technique according to the time-hallowed but by no means clever prescriptions that served our forefathers.

The situation is by no means satisfactory. The odd discrepancy between the refined technique of handling rich musical material and the obsolescence of this very technique in respect to its regulating laws has driven our musical culture in a deplorable state of uncertainty with such dangerous signs of decline as barbaric diversity of styles, total absence of some canon of beauty, senseless devotion to sound, emphasis on virtuosity and entertainment, and finally, esoteric escape, on the part of many musicians, from any responsibility towards society.

How our principles of application got us into this situation is not too enigmatic, if we recognize that there is one basic misconception in all the ideas of theorists and practical musicians: music which is entirely dependent, for its effects, on the movement of sound, was always dealt with in static terms. Music was not understood as a flowing medium, but as an assemblage of numerous individual sounds. To be sure, the understanding of single harmonies (intervals or chords) is founded on their isolated, noncollaborative harmonic qualities, but single harmonies do not cause musical effects; they must progress and thus produce the typical musical impression of streaming, of traversing spatial and temporal distances. In our old-fashioned precepts of applying the material, the evaluation of these inactive units, the single harmonies, was made (and still is) the criterion for the ever-moving structures of melody and tonality. This of necessity led to the definition of melodies as dissolved harmonies, and of tonalities as successive harmonized degrees of scales. Even the original concept of the *basse fondamentale* was not free of this static interpretation. With motion thus reduced to a mere train of numerous stationary points, the kinetics of music became those of Achilles and the turtle in the old fable. It is as if we were to understand a horse's gait as merely a summation of the individual movements of each foot!

Obviously, better rules for the application of musical material must be sought. If it is measurement that informs us of its qual-

ities, and if it is only with this information that we can find the
best rules of application, we must entirely abandon the principle
of measuring static points alone, no matter how many individually measured items we may collect, and evaluate the actual
stream of music. The discipline of music theory, endeavoring to
achieve such improved evaluation, will for the first time in its long
development face the same problem the younger science of elec-
trophysics had to tackle when it was forced to size up the properties of its material — electricity — in order to harness its power
and coerce it into useful service.

Basically, the problem of measuring musical current is not so
different from that of measuring the current of electricity, and it
can also be compared to the measurement applied to other currents, such as those of air and of water. Perhaps a comparison with
the current of water is closest for us, since no far-fetched technical terms will be necessary. However, we must be aware of the
limitations of such comparison. The known factors of the one
field of knowledge will lead us to the understanding of correspondences in the other field, but beyond this stimulus the qualities characteristic of the power to be investigated will have to
be apprehended in their own right. More than mere hints at
such apprehension cannot be given here.

Our parallelism begins with the chemical composition of water.
Here the combination of hydrogen and oxygen, in music the
unification of melody and harmony, is the indispensable condition for the creation of the end product. Once we have water, it
is subject to attraction and gravitation to a higher degree than is
true of its components. So is the musical compound of harmony
and melody: it is subject to rhythm in its two forms, metric and
rhythmic irregularity. The methods of determining the qualities
of this material would follow approximately the procedure outlined in the preceding pages of the present chapter.

Once the water begins to flow in rivulets, growing into brooks
and rivers, the following factors become measurable: (1) The
general tempo of the current, which corresponds with the tempo
of a musical piece as expressed in metrical beats; (2) the over-all
extraneous form of the water current, corresponding with the
over-all structure of a musical piece, with the infinite variety of

its irregular, nonmetrical constituents; (3) the water's rate of flow, or what in electricity is measured by amperes — the amount of melodic and rhythmic activity and the thickness of harmonic layers in any given moment of a composition's current; (4) the power or pressure the water exerts, or, as it is called in electricity, the voltage; in music, the harmonic and melodic intensity (as well as the density of melodic, tonal, and rhythmic successions); (5) the declivity of the stream's bed; in music, the differences in chordal complexity, the tensional gamut from the harmonious sound of a pure fifth to the most gruesome multitone dissonance.

And then would follow the correspondence of the water current to musical tonality: the direction of the stream as determined by the four cardinal points — by tonal centers. There would be changes in direction — changes of tonal center, modulations. During these changes the water in different sections of the current would flow with different velocities — the degrees of speed in the course of a tonality, and the amplitude (the degree of chordal tension needed) of this tonality.

Furthermore, there are the musical equivalents of waves, ripples, and eddies — figures, lines, and ornaments, the temporal course of which proceeds without commensurable relation to the general tempo, to harmonic density, to melodic and tonal speed. There are the undercurrents contradicting the main current — in music the changes of temporary tonics within a general tonality.

And finally there is the question of the usable amount of water in a current; which part can be used for drinking, which for industrial, which for chemical purposes. The analogy in music would be: the relationship of a composition's material and the physical space in which it is performed; its relationship to the mental and technical capacities of performers and listeners, to all other musical and extramusical conditions; in short, all those factors not of a strictly technical nature, as we discussed them in our early chapters.

XI

To laymen and, I am afraid, more so to musicians irretrievably engrossed in conservatism, not only will methods of composition following our ideas appear fantastic and unartistic; it will even be denied that they are workable. Why, the multitude of measurements and rules derived therefrom can only serve to prevent the growth of musical imagination; it will inevitably kill even the most profuse outpouring of an impulsive creative mind! Of course, such people forget how many knacks, rules, and procedures have to be learned before an ever-ready dexterity in traditional composing is likewise acquired. If they realized the magnitude of this barrier before undertaking their studies, they probably would be discouraged by an apparently insurmountable obstacle. In the course of time, the melodic, harmonic, and rhythmic material has become more voluminous and more complex. How can we expect to master it with the smaller set of regulations that were sufficient under simpler conditions? Would we not be in the position of an electrician who tries to control and direct electric currents with water tubes, pumps, faucets, and sewers? Although it is somewhat ridiculous to compare an art's technique with the skill displayed in sciences and crafts, sometimes a look at other laborers' work and their struggle with their material will prudently remind us that musical aptitude is not solely a gift from heaven, but has to be assiduously cultivated. Those musicians who do not agree with a more comprehensive, more rational, and altogether more realistic treatment of the musical material would nevertheless do well to face facts: neither sympathy nor antipathy will prevent the coming of an inevitable reform of our musical concepts.

To those among us who are willing to prepare and welcome the advent of this reform, the appendancy of musical thought from greater spheres of an intellectual evolution cannot remain concealed. Superficial coincidences, similarities, and analogies with other materials and techniques, as used here for the illustration of our opinions are of no significance; but quite apart from these, we may discover in music serious cross references to many fields of exact knowledge. Talking with physicists, biologists, and other scientists who are unaware of a crisis in musical thought, one is always profoundly surprised to how great an extent they operate with concepts analogous to those in musical creation. We have already seen how time and space have their musical equivalents, and there apparently exist similar equivalents to basic laws in the physical sciences. This could lead us to the belief that there is some sound foundation in the ancient idea of a universe regulated by musical laws — or, to be more modest, a universe whose laws of construction and operation are complemented by a spiritual reflection in musical organisms.

The time may perhaps return, when musical rules will be, as they were in olden times, an essential part of the code of the physical sciences. It is an alluring idea to think of a reorganization of scientific concepts on a musical basis. Instead of a plan for the world's destruction by superbombs, a blueprint of music theory would be drawn up to serve as a plan for a tremendous reformation of the universe. Harmonic, melodic, and rhythmic laws, as worked out in a most beautiful and exalted composition, would transform the world's woes and falsehood into the ideal habitat for human beings, who by the same process of musical ennoblement would have grown into creatures worthy of such a paradise.

# 6·

## TECHNIQUE AND STYLE

THE musical material described in our fifth chapter would remain mute and shapeless if the imaginative power of a composer did not force it into forms of sound having spatial and temporal significance. The necessary technique for doing this most adequately is a major factor in his considerations. In fact, it is believed to so dominate all other determinants of musical creation, that a composer's education, as known and applied in our culture, is almost exclusively concerned with problems of a technical nature. A broader view of the essential problems of composition, the problems dealt with in this book, is hardly ever opened up to the student. Both teachers and students usually plod along like those buffaloes or mules in primitive irrigation projects: their activities keep the region alive, but they themselves, blindfolded, follow one single narrow furrow, without sense of direction and purpose, never seeing the open world and the sun. And like those indispensable beasts they are not aware of their lack of direction and vision; they are satisfied with their mere technical function.

Among all the participants in the creation, distribution, and reception of music the individual with the keenest sense for the technique vested in a piece of music is always the performer. The impeccable technique of a masterpiece he transmits will be the most valuable stimulus for his own technique of re-creation; his performance will be carried along by the composition's perfection; his craving for the listener's satisfaction will most readily be crowned with success. Since, on the other hand, technical imperfections of a piece either prevent the performer from soliciting the listener's satisfaction or force him to cover by his own re-creative power the weaknesses the composer's inability has exposed, he is the one who suffers first and has to pay most dearly for others' faults. No wonder, then, that ordinarily he develops a judgment for technical quality which may at times appear biased, short-sighted, and directed by his own selfish purposes, but which in its uninhibited relation to practical demands is more realistic than the judgment of either the composer or the listener. The composer, busy computing the structural material, frequently loses direct contact with the effects his piece will release; and the listener is not interested in the technical arrangement of the dishes served as long as he derives any aesthetic satisfaction from consuming them.

As we stated before, there is a widespread opinion that questions of technique are irrelevant: that the creator of music, in particular, need not bother with the worldly problem of how to assemble tones, since he, the gods' favorite, cannot help simply and involuntarily fulfilling his superhuman mission. This opinion promptly leads to the often-heard statement that in music the question is merely one of quality: that there is only good or bad music. This is a statement you hear equally from the initiated, namely the composer, and from the layman, be he a plain music-lover or a well-trained philosopher. What the composer's attitude towards this statement ought to be we shall see later on. Here and now, in our quest to clarify the role of technique in the process of musical production and reproduction, we must resort to the experience of the performer, the man who, as we have found, is by his very actions necessarily closest to such decisions.

If all music ever written could only be classified as "good" or "bad" with some pieces perhaps occasionally falling short of either extreme, what would a singer or player do with a composition of the highest quality, viewed objectively, but not serving his personal purposes? Take one of the more florid Gregorian melodies, such as those sung at Easter time or on Whitsunday, which will doubtless be considered by every musician of some taste the most perfect, the most convincing one-line compositions ever conceived. Of course, in order to fully understand their overwhelming linear power, you cannot restrict yourself to just reading or hearing them. You must participate in singing these melodic miracles if you want to feel how they weld the singing group into a spiritual unit, independent of the individualistic prompting of a conductor, and guided only by the lofty spirit and the technical excellence of the structure. Now imagine that you are forced to sing them by yourself — solo, that is — transplanting those immaculate creations into another environment. Don't you feel as if you were expelled from a community of worthy friends? Has the music not lost its savor and assumed a taste of bitterness instead? And then play these same melodies, which were the precious vessels of highest linear revelations, on a wind instrument, then on a fiddle, and finally on the piano. The quality of the melodic line seems to disappear gradually, greatness turns into inexpressive melismatism, then becomes insipid passage-work, and finally ends in ridicule. If, as our aforementioned light-hearted philosophers believed, perfection remained perfection under all circumstances, how could such a disintegration of values take place merely by altering the means of performance?

Let us once more illustrate our point, this time with an example in which the change of the means of expression is not quite as drastic as in the gradual metamorphosis of a chorus into a piano, but which, due to its closeness to our everyday musical experience, is perhaps even more convincing. We all agree that in a fugue the linear arrangement of the musical material must be strongly emphasized, and this is often carried to the highest degree of contrapuntal rigidity. Consequently, any group of instruments that allows this contrapuntal fabric to appear in transparent lucidity should in principle be preferable to all others. Since linear writing for pianos or other keyboard instruments can only be an artificial projection of several independent melodic planes into one single plane, a keyboard fugue played on nonkeyed melodic instruments should reveal its linear spirit in a more appropriate and therefore more convincing manner than the original form could ever do. Now play some of the undisputed masterpieces of this species, namely fugues from Bach's *Wohltemperiertes Klavier*, as string trio or string quartet pieces. You will have a queer and rather disagreeable sensation: compositions which you knew as being great, heavy, and as emanating an impressive spiritual strength, have turned into pleasant miniatures. With the increase in contrapuntal clarity we have had to accept a deplorable loss of majesty and gravity. Although the supremacy of the piece has remained the same, the pieces have shrunk, despite the improved reproduction, and their structural and spiritual relation to the original keyboard form has become that of a miniature mummified Incan head to its previous animate form. In our fugues we have reduced to almost nothing the heavy technical resistance that a player of polyphonic keyboard music has to overcome, since the string players have produced their isolated lines without noticeable effort.

This example shows clearly that with the artless classification of good and bad, nothing is said about the real technical quality of a composition so long as no further criteria are introduced. One of these criteria is, as our experiments in the transformation of Gregorian and Bach pieces have demonstrated, the degree of resistance that the particular technical form of a composition offers to the players' or singers' technique of performance, a factor which the performer has to cope with before either the listener or the producer need be aware of it.

II

A composer may remain totally ignorant of the wider world of musical thought, musical creation, and musical reception shown in these pages; he may never outgrow his oxlike devotion to the moment's technical demands; but may we not hope that after he is told of the performer's keenness in respect to a composition's technique he, for his part, will comprehend that his own technique of assembling musical material should likewise be applied with utmost discrimination — a discrimination not arising out of his own preoccupation with the peculiarities of sounds and their application, but determined by factors more important than his individualistic speculations?

What are these factors?

There is, first of all, the prosaic decision concerning the space in which a piece is to be performed. In a very small hall, in a living room, we can readily discern the most involved melodic lines, the most complex harmonies, and the most intricate rhythmical patterns, because we are in closest spatial connection with the source of the sound. And besides, the instruments and singers can make use of the most refined subtleties of technique, because nothing will get lost, and the performers themselves can transmit their production as directly as in intimate talk. The composer, writing for such conditions, enjoys the greatest possible freedom to develop his technique into the most esoteric realms. Almost everything he writes will have a chance to be lucidly presented and clearly understood. No wonder, therefore, that chamber music has always, so far as application of the musical elements is concerned, been the preferred medium for technical audacity.

A composer writing for a larger hall loses a good deal of the freedom afforded by the smaller one. Melodies, in order to be understood, must be written so that the physical and mental distance between the performers and listeners cannot distort them. In rhythm, metrical structures will push themselves into the foreground, due to their greater intelligibility. Thus rhythmic patterns which, in order to be grasped intelligently, require a keen analytic mind on the part of the listener, ought to be avoided. Rapidly moving harmonies or harmonies of too great a complexity are not advisable, for the same reason. It is striking to see how sensitive our classical masters were in this respect. The technique of their symphonic works is essentially different from that of their chamber music, although all the basic material is identical. Nowadays we find many writers who neglect these necessities. Oftentimes we hear orchestra pieces written in a technique of complete linear independence, of great harmonic and tonal detail, and of rhythmic obscurity, all of which lose about fifty per cent of their substance before they reach the listener's ears. On the other hand, some chamber music pieces are presented in the rudest orchestral technique, which in small places of performance gives merely an impression of boorish awkwardness. What would an expert in steel production say, if a simple-minded waitress suggested the use of paper drinking cups as the most suitable molds for white-hot steel? Or what sense would there be in serving a milk shake in a Bessemer converter? In music we find many works the musical contents of which are no less incongruous with their containers — the places of performances — than milk shakes and steel in our metaphor. The larger such places are, the more the complexity of technique has to be reduced. So far no music has been written that would fit our gigantic stadiums and bowls.

We are using them for the performance of classical music, music that depends on the closest physical and mental proximity of not more than a few hundred listeners, and now this music is blown up to fill spaces in which the listener in the last row of the third balcony hears the fiddles' tones about a second after he has seen the players' bows executing them (a second equaling one half measure in 4/4 time at ordinary walking tempo!). Here again we could learn from the past — from Perotin, for instance, who about 1200 wrote his Organa for the then overwhelmingly new spatial conception of the Gothic cathedrals. These pieces, by no means primitive, provided in their technical planning even for the echo within those columned and vaulted halls, so that retarded echoing harmonies, intermingling with the straight progress of the normal harmonies could not disturb the over-all impression.

Once I heard a performance of Beethoven's Ninth Symphony in one of those tremendous stadiums which seat thirty thousand or more people. The piece was performed by a chorus of about one thousand singers with a five-hundred piece orchestra. The group of performers, although of a high quality, and the dimensions of the place were so utterly disproportionate to the shape and character of the piece, that it sounded ghastly. One could not make head or tail of it. After this symphony a dance was performed by thousands of school children to the accompaniment of some specially manufactured music of no significance. It was written for a couple of recorders, two or three lower-ranged instruments, and some soft percussion. This music, transmitted by loud-speakers, made a masterpiece appear like an amateurish attempt at composition by some nincompoop. Had Beethoven, while writing the symphony in its familiar technique, conceived it for the spatial conditions just mentioned, we would have to accuse him of the grossest technical miscalculation. Fortunately, he had the finest feeling for the proportional relationship between space and compositional technique and he cannot be blamed for the sins of his interpreters. Our performers may, for their own ephemeral glory, adhere to such barbarisms as playing a Brandenburg concerto, written for not more than fifteen players and an audience of fifty to one hundred, with eighty or more players before an assembled audience of forty thousand, but the living composer should at least try to prevent his own pieces from being performed under adverse conditions. Alas, he usually is only too elated if his compositions are played at all, no matter what the conditions of performance are.

There are other factors besides places of performance that influence — or, let us say, ought to influence — the composer's technical considerations. There is the intellectual capacity of his listeners. If he writes for an audience well acquainted with symphonic music and its performance, he can apply a technique more involved than the one he would use for unaccustomed listeners. For instance, an orchestral piece that is good for New York or Boston is not necessarily good for Musselshell, Mo.; and chamber music, enjoyed in a salon by a sophisticated, overcritical bunch of highbrow intellectuals, may be boring to people with plain musical intelligence or those with a desire for uninhibited directness in musical communications. Of course, there is always the haughty point of view of the composer who does not want to step down to the populace. "My music is as it is. I am not influenced by all these considerations. If people want to understand my music, they will have to grow up to my standards." It is one thing to write down to the bad instincts of the unrefined listener, and another to satisfy by technical means the just demands of a cultured customer. The attitude of the arrogant composer is similar to that of the millionaire who cannot understand that other people are in want of money. Even the loftiest musical spirit grew from a state of simple-mindedness to its superior position; thus, it is acting the parvenu to look with contempt upon those left far behind on the road to success. Moreover, there are many people who never will be and never want to be millionaires, financially or musically. Are we to lose them and their propensity towards music merely because we are unable or unwilling to write music that satisfies their demands?

Another important factor in technical decisions is the performer's degree of skill in playing and singing. For the Boston Symphony you can write anything from open strings to complicated arrangements approximating those that only Harvard's "mechanical brain" could be expected to handle with a formidable consumption of electric current; they will play it. But what about orchestras in small towns, amateur groups, and school orchestras? What about amateurs who have perhaps one hundred times the good will of the professional musician but only one hundredth of his technical skill? If the nature of our pieces is such that they can master them only after fifty rehearsals and even then never to their own satisfaction, they will gladly consign their fiddles and voices to cold storage and become one hundred per cent listeners, driven away from practical music by the very musician who usually complains bitterly of the public's ever-growing aversion to practical participation in music.

Finally, do we want to drive away all those who have all the culture and education that make them perfect listeners; and those excellent players or singers, professionals or amateurs, who simply are not always in the mood to solve intricate musical problems? Shall we leave them to tin-pan alley and the juke boxes? There is a great choice of technical possibilities that can take care of their needs.

III

Once, in the Rocky Mountains, I had a strange musical experience. In a gorge famous for its waterfalls and filled with aerial railways, summer guests, cars, and ice-cream vendors, a well-coördinated loud-speaker system screamed Isolde's *Liebestod* all over the place, as part of the gorge's daily routine. I am sure the managers of the establishment wanted to please their customers, true to the rule which seems to be one of the leading theses of the American way of life: enjoyment plus enjoyment gives you more enjoyment.

We cannot blame them for the idea that the accumulation of single enjoyments results in an accumulated sensation: that *Liebestod* plus waterfalls plus ice cream give us more pleasure than *Liebestod* or waterfalls or ice-cream solo. After all, it was the composer of the *Liebestod* himself who concocted the idea of the *Gesamtkunstwerk*, in which singing voices, orchestra, stage, light effects, horses, rivers, cardboard mountains, artificial beards, et cetera, et cetera, were part of the over-all enjoyment. The catch in this conception is that our over-all enjoyment cannot be more than one hundred per cent. Hence, three factors of enjoyment, which each by itself would provide one hundred per cent enjoyment, do not add up to three hundred per cent; they are, rather, compressed into the one hundred per cent, so that each of them, if participation is equal, has but thirty-three and a third per cent of its original effect. I personally even believe that too much of an accumulation of artistic or presumedly artistic enjoyments not only reduces the percentage of the single constituent enjoyment, but also reduces the over-all effect from its one hundred per cent to a much lower degree. Thus the effect of the aforementioned *Gesamtkunstwerk* in the mountains will most likely be that you will take your car, cursing waterfalls, *Liebestods*, and ice cream in equal percentage and drive to a place where there is nothing but a hundred per cent view.

This time the disproportion between the composition and its performance was not, as it was in the case of the Ninth Symphony, of a musical-technical nature. Although the operatic piece was originally not written for gorges and waterfalls, the many loud-speakers provided an even distribution of sound, so that acoustically the conditions of a big opera house were reproduced not too inaptly, and thus the technical shape of the piece was not in disturbing disagreement with the space in which it was performed.

The disturbing effects in this case originated in a discrepancy between styles. The piece with all its technical, intellectual, historical, and aesthetical implications belonged to one certain sphere of style, from which the style of the pleasure-voracious crowd with their dull, indeterminate, and resistless surrender to anything sensuous is far removed — if ever such brutishness can be honored with the name style — a term that usually indicates at least a faint tendency toward a cultured life!

It is obvious that the gorge's managerial benefactors of the vacationing crowd thought "If *Liebestod* is good in the Metropolitan, it will be equally good in our gorge." They forgot that the composition deals with the most refined feelings of two sublime lovers, expressed in exalted music for those who come especially prepared for its reception, and that it should not be projected into an environment which, although gigantic, has become nothing but a tremendous prop for the proverbial having-a-good-time of thousands of daily vacationists. The discrepancy between the vacationists' good time and Isolde's unfortunate experience is more than disgusting.

If we make the distinction between good and bad taste, between things that are in style and others that are not, there must be some agreement about taste and style. This ought to be easy in respect to the performance of players and singers, and somewhat more difficult in respect to composers. Even the layman readily recognizes differences in the playing of various pianists; he recognizes each player's individual manner of performing as being unlike another's, although he may not be able to put his observation into words. There are many attempts in science to do this for him. Players' and singers' performances have been recorded, and with special methods of research their mode of performing has been analyzed. One finds as constituent elements in such analyses: tempo, registered with all its countless deviations from the player's main speed applied to a given piece, such as accelerandi, ritardandi, rubati, the slightest retards emphasizing expression, et cetera; dynamics, with a range from utter pianissimo to the loudest outbursts of fortissimo, and all the infinite shades of accents, crescendi, diminuendi; tone color, including the refinements of a pianist's touch and a violinist's application of the bow; pitch, with all its modifications, such as portamenti, glissandi, vibrato, and so on. From the end of the past century on, a good deal of time, money, and intelligence has been invested in these analyses of the interrelationship of performing technique and acoustical effect, or, as the title of a more recent publication puts it, "in search of beauty in music." The attitude towards music, covered by this title, appears to be the last pinnacle of a building erected in the time of purest materialism — a philosophy which tried to know and explain everything in the arts by taking it apart, analyzing it; and which, in counting every component part, believed that it had found the secret of artistic creation and re-creation. But we have seen many times how in musical composition the whole is by no means the sum of its constituent parts, but is a new, indivisible, and unchangeable unit. The same is true with reproduced musical forms.

If we followed the reasoning of those seekers of beauty in music, all we would have to do would be to take Paganini's or Liszt's playing — provided we had records of it — take it apart, copy it in every detail, and a new Paganini, a new Liszt could be manufactured. If human beings reacted to treatment as does metal, wood, leather, and other working material, it would be easy to reproduce the Paganinis as we produce automobiles, wholesale and at a reasonable price. Science, however, has long ago abandoned the idea of creating artificially a living being of higher organization, and only in the artistic field do people still adhere to the homunculus idea. Let us tell them that in music we still have to rely — and probably always will — on the most time-honored methods of production; that no artificial creation can be introduced, and that all those very accurate methods of research will bring us not one step nearer the inner secrets of produced and reproduced music. They cannot reveal any rationality in the factors which determine musical effects: the spontaneity of the human imagination; music's ability to arouse intellectual participation and release memories of feelings; and finally, the musical producers' and reproducers' ability to utilize their technique to this end. In the face of all these incalculable factors, this particular search for beauty assumes the same role as that of the telephone directory in respect to the minds and souls of the human beings listed in it: you see their names, know their lodgings (and in certain cases their professions), and by implication you may guess certain facts about their social position; but beyond all this the telephone book is a very poor source of information.

We must, of course, not deny that there is and always will be a search for beauty in music; but if it is to consist of more than a mere registration and analysis of musical sound or a vague description of impressions, it will have to revolve within the intellectual and emotional realms outlined in our preceding chapters.

IV

In addition to the performer's style of playing or singing which he adds as his personal contribution to the technically established form of a composition, this composition itself has an individual style which differs in varying degrees from the style of other pieces of the same kind, from the creations of other composers, and even from the other works of its own creator. We talk about an operatic style, the style of oratorios, of chamber music, of church music, and so on. In listening to a piece we can determine with sufficient accuracy the century of its creation. We can attribute it to a certain composer; we may even sense in which period of his life it was written. According to the statements made at the beginning of the present chapter, it ought to be clear that all these distinctions are, strictly speaking, not concerned with the style of a composition. It is, as we have seen, a question of the writer's technique, how the musical ingredients of a piece are mixed, this technique being determined by the locality of performance, the intellectual readiness of the consumers, and the dexterity of the performers.

Style is not wholly identical with technique. It is the peculiar manner in which a composer adds further component parts — parts, however, that are not essential to the structure's functional mechanism; parts that are added after the main decisions of construction have been made, after the technical part of the composition is virtually completed. To be sure, these structurally unessential additions are also part of the producer's technique, but since they do not influence the purpose of the composition, its place of performance, or its relation to the consumers and performers, they are left entirely to the composer's fancy. Due to their basic structural unimportance we are justified in separating them from technique as such. On technique itself the entire vitality of a composition depends. It is responsible for touching or failing to touch our intellectual and emotional capacities; while fanciful stylistic additions give a composition its particular flavor. We must not underrate the role of their seasoning or soothing or stimulating effect. Listeners and performers alike are addicted to these effects, oftentimes to such a degree that they become spellbound and lose a clear concept of all other elements in a composition.

The composer's stylistic amenities, despite their conspicuousness, really constitute a minor consideration in his craft. We even may assume that the majority of those writing music never bother to analyze their stylistic efforts. Nevertheless, we must ask what are the guiding thoughts in the selection, application, and distribution of the stylistic means of expression.

There are, at least from a layman's viewpoint, several answers to this question. One is that the composer follows his inspiration. Some undefinable power determines his actions. We, the other people who do not write music or are not artists at all, do not feel within ourselves the command and guidance of this power, and this fact alone seems to many of us proof enough that stylistic manifestations can only be of supernatural origin.

Another answer is that each period in musical history develops its own style without dependence on the efforts of individual writers. The ingredients of compositions would, according to this theory, be formed by the actions and counteractions of the total musical movement of a period; and the extent, the internal pressures, and the dynamic force of the movement would mold these ingredients into a certain technical and stylistic shape, a process similar to the shaping of the earth's surface in times of geologic upheaval. The productive mind, being in this case hardly more than an executive of some kind of formative *Zeitgeist*, is, by virtue of his technical and stylistic decisions an inseparable part of those shaping forces. There is believed to be a general tendency in the technique of composition throughout the course of music history to become increasingly and gradually complicated. Composition is thought to have first begun with simple harmonies, simple melodies, and simple rhythms. Our modern music, compared with the music of earlier times, has reached a very high level of complexity. An individual composer, aware of this fact, usually wants to contribute his share to this presumed progress of music, and thereupon he adds complications of his own — complications of technique which will eventually fracture the framework set up by the physical and mental conditions of musical performances, and complications of style which in their ultimate esoteric loneliness are bound to reach the borderline of unintelligible enigmas. There are numerous instances in which a creative artist made extraordinary efforts, consciously and deliberately, to accelerate this process, and they are not to be found solely in our most modern literature. Inevitably we find mentioned Beethoven's Grand Fugue, the piece he wrote originally as the finale for the string quartet opus 130. But, strangely enough, music written before 1750 is seldom cited as proof of the constantly growing complexity of style in composition. There is a very simple reason for this: The evolutionist theory of music's unceasing development towards higher goals is untenable. To be sure, an unbroken development towards technical and stylistic complexity can be observed from the middle of the eighteenth century on; but the following statements will show that in periods prior to that time there is evident no such straightforward urge towards the technical virtues and stylistic miracles — assertedly so desirable — of our own time.

I have mentioned the fact that in some cases of primitive music, music sung by savages without any conscious knowledge or culture of musical styles, musical forms are produced whose rhythmical structure is of a complexity not present in any music of so-called higher cultures. The same is true with the highly ornate melodic lines found in the music of a purely melodic, nonharmonious culture, as in some of the more elaborate Gregorian melodies and their close relatives, melodies in Arabian and in some classes of Asiatic music. When harmony was introduced to our Western music, this wealth of melody and rhythm shrank to forms of comparatively little significance. After several centuries of musical development, in which harmony had become a regular part of the musician's working material but in its own realm was still on a low level of growth, the style of composition, as established in the form of the isorhythmic motet (thirteenth and fourteenth centuries) reached such a degree of intellectual involution with its interplay of rhythmic and metric patterns, that no later period could boast of such artistry. And what about other techniques and styles between 1400 and 1750, which likewise achieved formulations never surpassed? Consider the contrapuntal technique from Dufay to Josquin; the miracles of vocal treatment in the choral works of those composers; the unbelievable concentration of harmonic and melodic material with its assimilation of a whole nation's treasury of folk song in the German *Liederbücher* of the sixteenth century; the superhuman balance of forces and the perfect adequacy of every technical means of expression in

Palestrina; the exuberance of Protestant church music in the eighteenth century. Consider, too, the developments in style: Obrecht's and Josquin's highly polished sweetness; the Tintoretto pomp of the Gabrielis; Gesualdo's nervous tensions; Schütz's probity; the ultraexpressiveness of Monteverdi — climax after climax, each emphasizing another aspect of technical and stylistic formulation, and each followed by a decline. What we see is certainly not an ever-ascending line; we are reminded, rather, of a landscape with many hills and mountain summits, no one of which can be said to be the most prominent, the most important, the most dominating. Perhaps the one nearest to us may impress us somewhat more than the others, for we can see its structure in greater detail; but we know about perspective and have to admit that despite the more detailed view the other summits are by no means less impressive. In music, however, it almost seems that either we never had this sense of perspective, projected from spatial into temporal views, or that, fascinated by our own achievements, we have lost it. We do not know what our musical future will be, but we can be quite sure that the wave that has carried us technically and stylistically through the past two centuries has risen to its crest and in due time will be replaced by one of a different character.

Our era may have brought the technique of instrumental composition with its accompanying stylistic curlicues to a climax never before attained. In other fields, however, we have achieved little. Do we have any vocal creations of significance? Have we found a singable but nevertheless original and aesthetically satisfactory choral technique of general validity? Do we know how to provide music with the characteristics of our time for the amateur?

The necessarily negative answer to these and similar questions may lead us to the conclusion that our contemporary techniques are in some respects notable, perhaps even remarkable, while in others they are far inferior to the standards set in former times. Stylistically it seems that our era has not found the strength, obviously so effective in earlier periods, to direct the composer's individual and voluntary stylistic extension of a purposeful tech-

nique towards some kind of unification — unless one considers
our centrifugal tendencies and our apparent inability to create
a widespread contemporary style a kind of style in itself!

Once we permit doubts to enter our judgments, we may refuse
to take Beethoven's Grand Fugue and other recommended masterpieces as models of technical and stylistic endeavors, and consider
as the ideal contemporary composer not the man who forces himself into technical exaggerations and his material into an over-
strained style, but the man who strives among other things for
balance, evenness, and conscious proportionality — ideals which
for the past one hundred and fifty years or more have scarcely
ever been postulated.

v

This brings up the question of how far an ambitious craftsman
can go in developing his style. After all, he wants to be modern;
he does not like to stand in the second rank of pioneers. His music
is to excite his listeners by its novelty; his combinations of harmony, melody, and rhythm with all the additional ingredients of
dynamics and color must be of a never-heard-of intensity.

In the light of our formulations concerning technique and style,
some remarks made in the second chapter will now be more
clearly understood. There we pronounced our disbelief in a continuous advancement of music, but conceded that a certain kind
of short-range progress was possible. It ought to be clear now that
this progress is nothing but the ever-changing stylistic organization of the surface in works of art. The principles of technical
construction, however, do not permit any further advancement
once they are thoroughly investigated.

The desire to be modern, new, and exciting is nothing that our
age of excitement has introduced into music. In fact, it is as old
as any competition between singers or players — in other words,
as old as music itself. In certain periods the urge towards novelty
is particularly keen. There was the famous Ars Nova in France
and Italy after 1300; there was the strange attempt in the sixteenth century to revive ancient Greek music, which led to
another ars nova; then we see in the eighteenth century the rise
of a new style which put the great Bach in the odious position of

a reactionary; and finally, after Beethoven's death, music again went through an ars nova period, with Wagner as its leader. All these artes novae, in addition to uncovering new aspects of music and providing both producers and performers with challenging tasks, added new experiences to the common store of practical and theoretical knowledge. Apparently new musical forms were introduced, new ways of curving melodic lines were discovered. But, for the most part, it was harmony which was constantly amplified and extended.

It was always harmony that fascinated musicians more than the two other elements, melody and rhythm. From about 900 through more than one thousand years we see an uninterrupted flow of harmonic discoveries and ever changing applications of the harmonic material. And even nowadays, when we might think that an all-round knowledge of musical material would teach us a well-balanced attention to every branch of technical and stylistic application, it is again harmony which is the musician's main concern. Hardly ever do we hear of attempts to invent new musical forms; the most radical inventors adhere to the traditional forms of the sonata and the symphony, and even such period pieces as menuets, sarabandes, et cetera, have had to be taken out of the moth closet. Melody, although it is for the layman perhaps the most obvious and, in its effects, the most direct of the three musical elements, has played a less important role in the expert's considerations. But harmony seems to everyone to be of such importance, that many writers have almost nothing in their minds but the search for never-heard harmonies and harmonic progressions. You may read articles about modern music; periodicals may report about the fights between creative artists and their followers; music appreciation may instruct students about the progress of music in our time — the theme is mainly, and sometimes exclusively, harmony.

Yet, if anything seems to be of little reward, it is the search for originality in harmony. After a thousand years of research, experiment, and application, harmony has become thoroughly known; no undiscovered chord can be found. If we have to depend on novelty in harmony, we might as well write our last funeral march for the death of our own music. Fortunately enough, the question of novelty in harmony is of no importance except to those whose stylistic creations have no other foundation. With the relatively late discovery of harmony, music came to the full development of its possibilities after all the other arts had become old and wise. Music has now entered the phase of its life that corresponds with the natural permanent state of poetry. Unless a poet invented his own words and constructed his own language, no new material could ever be introduced into poetry. Everybody who understands the national language of a writer knows his poetic material of construction thoroughly. Yet poetry has not come to an end, and never will, so long as there are spoken and intelligible languages. Why, then, should music have reached the final epochs of its existence, after all the material of harmonic construction is equally well known?

We may ask, however, whether we could not assemble chords novel in their succession (even if not in their individual arrangement of tones) to produce less traditional patterns of sound. Would not such novelty in succession be proof of a further extensibility of the harmonic material, thus showing that the steadily ascending line of harmonic development had not reached its end? This idea, like so many others concerning musical styles and aesthetics, is extravagant, born of fancy, and defies reasonable investigation. If we are justified in calling any structure of ideas naïve romanticism, this theory concerning harmony deserves that name: it is unsurpassably naïve and romantic. Mere observation and the knowledge of simple empiric facts prove beyond any doubt that there is only a limited number of harmonic and tonal combinations, and no matter how big this number is, it will be exhausted after centuries of continuous use. A few thousand or so combinations left over may postpone but cannot eliminate the final exhaustion. But why argue with the proponents of such ideas, who, after all, defend nothing but stylistic gadgets? No one any longer argues the stylistic problems of the past, that once were so awfully exciting. It is only several generations ago that composers fought and became martyrs for such stylistic credos as program music, leitmotifs, or even orchestration, all of which have lost a good deal of their importance — so much so, that the mere thought of people putting up fights for or against them makes us chuckle. We are sure to see our contemporary stylistic trifles, for which people are fighting, notwithstanding the discouraging experiences of former battles, become the laughing-stock of the future. As long as stylistic arrangements do not serve a higher moral purpose, they are bound to become ridiculous, once the first charm of novelty has worn off. And current stylistic inventions in harmony certainly have not proved to have any moral aim, in the sense so often expounded in this book.

## VI

Let us investigate briefly some of those allegedly "modern" achievements. The best known and most frequently mentioned is the so-called twelve-tone technique, or composition in preëstablished tone series. The idea is to take the twelve tones of our chromatic scale, select one of its some four hundred million permutations, and use it as the basis for the harmonic (and possibly melodic) structure of a piece. This rule of construction is established arbitrarily and without any reference to basic musical facts. It ignores the validity of harmonic and melodic values derived from mathematical, physical, or psychological experience; it does not take into account the differences in intervallic tensions, the physical relationship of tones, the degree of ease in vocal production, and many other facts of either natural permanence or proven usefulness. Its main "law" is supplemented by other rules of equal arbitrariness, such as: tones must not be repeated; your selected tone series may skip from one stratum of the texture to any other one; you have to use the inversion and other distortions of this series; and so on — all of which can be reduced to the general advice: avoid so far as possible anything that has been written before.

The only segment of our conventional body of theoretical musical knowledge which the dodecaphonists have deigned to admit and which, in fact, alone makes their speculations possible, is the twelve-tone tempered scale. We have already been told of this scale's weakness: because of its basic impurity it can be used only as a supplementary regulative to a tone system containing natural intervals — at least, so long as we want to save our music from total instrumental mechanization and have human voices participate in its execution. True, some kind of a restricted technique of composition can be developed on a foundation of compromise scales and arbitrary working rules, but doubtless the general result will always be one similar to the kind of poetry that is created by pouring written words out of a tumbler without calling in grammar and syntax. A higher tonal organization is not attempted and cannot be achieved, especially if one permits the technical working rules to slip off into the aforementioned set of supplementary statutes which are nothing but stylistic whims and, as such, not subject to any controlling power of general validity. Of course, there are those superrefined prophets who proudly claim that they can, by the rules of this stylistic method, write pieces in C major, which seems to be a procedure as direct as leaving one's house in New England through the front door and entering the back door by a little detour via Chicago.

Twelve-tone operations are not the only nightmares that haunt the composing zealot who wants to be up to date. Are there not city sky lines whose ragged contours demand to be reproduced in melodic lines? Some other composers invent, with the aid of addition, subtraction, and other numerical operations, ways of combining tones mechanically; and finally, there are always colors as organizing agents. It is easy to recognize the underlying principle in all these and similar methods: it is a simple equation between a given number of tones and anything else that consists of an equal number of constituent parts. We could go on counting such methods of tonal equations, but only to enter a sphere in which there is almost nothing that could not be brought into direct equational relationship with harmony and melody: fever curves, cooking recipes, railroad timetables (the music resulting from them may be rather monotonous, though), catalogues of country fairs, the depth of the ocean between Halifax and Ireland, and so on.

If the inventors of such systems had looked into music history, they would have found that their methods are by no means as modern as they think. Moreover, their predecessors' lack of lasting success should have made them suspicious. The earliest attempts at composing by a method of this kind can be found in several treatises of the eleventh and twelfth centuries, in which an equation of the five vowels of the Latin language and five successive tones of a church mode is used. The melodies thus constructed must, even to the inventor of this system, have sounded trivial enough, because we see an additional, transposed equation recommended to heighten the poor melodic effect somewhat. (I was never quite sure that this invention was not contrived with tongue in cheek.) Obviously this method did not appeal to contemporary composers, since in spite of the medieval theorists' fondness for plagiarizing each other, it did not reappear in later treatises.

Other equations were devised with the spots of dice, a pastime very popular in Mozart's time — in fact, some of the methods of composing with this recipe are published under Mozart's or Haydn's name, one even in Boston, Massachusetts.

The method which in my opinion showed the greatest subtlety is one suggested in a little book published in 1751 by the English musician William Hayes. Its title is *The Art of Composing Music by a Method Entirely New, Suited to the Meanest Capacity*. It is a satire on the wave of Italian music, with its composers of frequently inferior quality, which at that time swept over London. His advice is, to take a brush with stiff bristles (like a toothbrush), dip it into an inkwell, and, by scraping the bristles with the finger, spatter with one sweep a whole composition onto the staff paper. You have only to add stems, bar lines, slurs, et cetera, to make the opus ready for immediate performance. Whole and half notes are entirely absent, but who cares for sustained tones anyway! (What a striking forecast of one of the ugliest modern musical diseases!)

Despite the intentional humor of these directions, the similarity with our twelve-tone technique cannot be overlooked. The characteristic difference seems to be that Hayes's method gives the composer, or whatever you want to call the fellow who uses the brush — the "spruzzarino," as he calls it — a greater freedom in artistic enterprises than does the rather rigorous twelve-tone technique. Moreover, it prevents the once accepted technique from degenerating into stylistic irrelevancies.

Movements of this kind spring up like epidemics of measles, and they disappear just as enigmatically. We have already once seen a twelve-tone movement die, due to lack of interest on the part of musicians who liked music more than operations on music. That was shortly after World War I. At that time the germ was introduced to this country and caused minor disturbances, which by now have all but disappeared, with a few scars remaining. After World War II, Europe was again infected, but already the patients are feeling better and there is hope that after some minor relapses only a few diehards will survive to be the prophets who, in quiet solitude, will prepare the next big outburst. This, if we can trust past experience, will probably occur after World War III, provided any people are left over to be interested in tone combinations. One little sign of reconvalescence may perhaps be seen in the following fact, which could not remain hidden even to the most stalwart dodecaphonists (or is it dodecacophonists, as many people have it?): with this method no pieces can be produced which could fill big spaces with broad symphonic colors, or which could satisfy many people's demands for simplicity, directness, and personal sympathy.

A strange feature of all these movements is their sectarian character. It is almost as in the Nazi state or in a Red dictatorship: the supreme condition for your participation is that you have no disbelief whatsoever in the perfection of the system. You will have to fight against the adherents of other "systems," against the writers of program music, and against those who use sky lines and numerical equivalents other than the permutations of the numbers one to twelve, although your "meanest capacity" would tell you, that their activities are of the same kind as those you adore. The parallelism to religious sects goes so far, that an idol is felt to be necessary, to whom everything of importance ever created or uttered in music is ascribed, although for his glory some real instigators and inventors may have to be obscured and rendered innocuous. It is all so reminiscent of some kind of voodoo cult, and the idolizers of the superstition seem to bear a painful similarity to the haruspices in ancient Greece and Rome. The entrails of sacrificial animals by means of which the haruspex predicted the future have just as little to do with world events as have numerical permutations with musical creation.

I would not have dwelt so long on these strange peripheral endeavors, were it not for the fact that such a discussion shows how far one can be led astray by the emphasis upon a musical factor of secondary importance — namely, style. The ethical power of music is entirely neglected; the composer's obligations towards his fellow men are degraded to a game of double-crostics, which certainly gives enough stimulus to one's self-content but leaves the other fellow like the doleful child outside the house in which the Christmas tree is shining. If music written on this basis has any message for others, it is the crassest order "you have to obey, you have to believe in my constructions," in a time when we all are so terribly in need of some shiny little reflection of that other message, the one that Schiller and Beethoven gave to mankind: *Seid umschlungen, Millionen* — be embraced, ye millions.

## VII

It would be a major miracle, if the composers' technique and style could be spared the horrors of detrition, disintegration, and degeneration. Our artistic life, tending to address ever increasing masses of consumers and losing more and more of its original loftiness, is not favorable to technical and stylistic refinement. The composer, being the victim of everyday prosaic demands, frequently will not find the moral strength to maintain in his works standards of technique and style which would distinguish him from hordes of other providers of public entertainment. Why, then, should he keep a tool keen and most efficient, if a technique, having grown dull by its daily use for base purposes, satisfies his artless customers just as well? Why should he care for the development of a personal, cultured style, if they reject it because it forces them to apply some mental effort when all they want is simply to be doped by music? Technique then loses all the characteristics of a wonderful tool; it sinks down, drawn by its own weight, into the quagmire of drab routine. Style, the crown and flower of technique, if bereft of invigorating imagination disintegrates into fashion. Routine and fashion — these are the worst snarls that can entangle the creative mind.

Routine does not attempt, as does genuine technique, to find the best solution for any problem arising; it is satisfied with the one most handy, most commonplace, and most easily accessible.

It is not the right answers that are sought; one is satisfied with mere assurances, no matter how vague. Decisions on matters of fashion, in turn, are made on the principle of least resistance. No effort is made to find an individual form of expression; for everything models will be found, prepared by others, which can be drawn upon whenever needed. Routine and fashion turn a musician's life into the perfect incarnation of the subman's intellectual desire: the high-geared mechanics are working infallibly, spirit and personality are entirely abolished.

Of all the abject forms that music, regulated by routine and fashion, can assume, two have struck me as particularly significant and symptomatic for our era.

One shows how denaturized an art can become once it is made a part of an industrial production system totally inhuman and dictatorial. In Hollywood they keep composers and arrangers in little booths provided with staff paper and piano, and here on the assembly-line music is produced in which all the normal virtues that are part and parcel of the composer's profession — imagination, enthusiasm, original talent — are just so many factors hindering industrial production. Versatile mediocrity is the password for admission to these temples of streamlined utility, abnegation of any individuality the condition for success. The musician who submits to this life of a musical slave can hardly be blamed. The fact that he is able to sell his abilities to exclusively industrial purposes shows his low artistic value anyway, and usually he enters the gilded porticos of his job fully conscious of the warning *lasciate ogni speranza, voi ch'entrate*, in this case abandoning the hope of ever returning to a more reasonable kind of music. The few exceptional individuals who try to reconcile their job with former ideals by writing long-haired music in their spare time, confirm by their notorious ineffectiveness the old adage that no man can serve two masters.

The other most despicable form of technical and stylistic degradation in music is practiced in totalitarian countries. If, with the capitalistic misuse of music aforementioned, our art was deprived of its artistic dignity, at least it was still treated as music. With our omnipotent and omniscient dictators this superfluous consideration has been abandoned and music has become nothing but a lubricant for their political machinery. The effects of this abuse of musical creation, the stunting of all imagination, can in superior cases produce scarcely more than pieces in the Tchaikovsky style already too long perpetuated. Experiences during Hitler's thirteen-year millennium proved this true; and more recent information has not added any evidence to the contrary. Wretched creators, who have to suffer artistic emasculation without daring to escape or even to shriek out in pain! Some of those whose music is admitted to the governmentally directed lubricating process have stated, and probably will state again, that they cannot think of any higher goal than being thus admitted, and that their music, before it was turned into refined political greasing fluid, was the regrettable error of an absurdly misbehaved mind. Knowing musicians, we may be convinced that they will confess anything else demanded by a brutal power that now points a gun at them and then again benevolently permits them to continue with their ephemeral writing. Even technique and style of a musical creation, although they are but the external hull of the work of art and not its essence, can grow only in unfettered minds. Those who pretend that under the knout of industry, dictatorial governments, and other nonartistic agencies they can produce more than routine and fashion can never have known how an unfettered mind works. If they ever knew, they may have forgotten voluntarily or may have been forced to forget.

After our lengthy preoccupation with technique and style, let us draw a rather anticlimactic but, with reference to our former chapters, none the less logical conclusion. Technical skill and stylistic versatility have only one purpose: to bring into existence what we called the vision of the genuine composer, or what comes closest to it in the imagination of his minor colleagues. Technique and style are obedient servants so long as they are kept under control. Once out of control they either totally dominate the process of constructing a piece, or they degenerate into routine and fashion. They are indispensable aids to our work; without their help we cannot produce any musical form. Yet, like many versatile but stupid attendants, they must be held in subservience if they are to give their best service; they must be treated with contempt. Thus we have the grotesque situation that the man who writes music has to go through many stages of learning, experimenting, and constructing in order to achieve technical and stylistic adequacy, only to despise all these achievements, because they must remain the humble slaves of superior ideas.

# 7.

## PERFORMERS

"TEMPORIBUS nostris super omnes homines fatui sunt cantores" — in our time the silliest of all men are the singers. This sounds like the statement of a modern composer who time and again finds that singers have great difficulty in singing what he has written. Or the director of an opera company, mindful of his singers' antics, may resignedly sigh in this key; or a poor theory teacher, after many fruitless attempts at acquainting singers with an elementary knowledge of harmony and counterpoint, may in his desperation burst into tears with those words.

Surely the man who wrote this depressing statement ought to have known what he was saying. He was one of the most famous musicians of all times. It is the opening sentence of a little treatise (*Epistola de ignoto cantu*) addressed to his friend, the monk Michael, in which he describes an invention of his — an invention the benefits of which we enjoy every minute of our musical life. The invention — or at least what he thought was his invention, similar experiments having actually been made before — was our notation, and the writer is Guido of Arezzo, who lived around the year 1000. Even at that early time the discrepancy between the composer's demands and the singers' inefficiency was not a recent discovery. But if despair over the singers' incompetence led Guido to his invention, as he tells us, it was the first time in music history that dullness was the cause of something very useful and intelligent, and we might as well be grateful for the fact that among the singers of the tenth and eleventh centuries there were a number of stupid ones.

An elaboration of Guido's statement we find in the treatise of a later writer, Arnulf of San Gilleno, who wrote in the early fourteenth century (*De differentiis et generibus cantorum*): "There are singers who have neither talent nor knowledge, but only vanity. This makes them audacious. They do not even know plain chant, but nevertheless tackle the most complicated music, singing more loudly and more brutally than the jackass, producing the most terrible cacophonies, and with their false phrasing they turn music into barbarism." Then he goes on to tell us how they criticize and correct real singers in public, how they can never be silenced, how they tap time while singing, and then he concludes: "Those singers, not worthy of the name of musicians or singers at all, ought to be excommunicated from the society of decent singers."

Arnulf's statement sounds like a confirmation of Boethius' classification of musicians, in which the performer, the player, the singer, occupied the lowest place, since he was, owing to his emphatic devotion to the means of performance, unable to participate in any profound knowledge of music.

These two quotations from early writers are meant to show that the performer's eternal dilemma, his dualistic soul with both halves fighting each other, was well known centuries ago. The permanent and obviously inescapable contradiction of the singer's or player's specialized technical achievements and the artist's comprehensive understanding, these factors of artistic work confined in one single mind like two grim animals in a too narrow cage — doubtless this problem had already arisen in primitive form when the stone age man, the bone-flute player of whom we talked earlier, tried to reproduce on his flute a tune that another flutist had played before.

If we take Guido's sentence not as a mere temperamental outburst of a grouchy teacher but see in it a true description of the conditions of performance at that time, we find that those lowest-class musicians, the performers, were in no enviable position. Due to the lack of a practicable notation before Guido's time, their job consisted of a parrotlike imitation of other performers' accomplishments, and such secondhand activity was neither fit to strengthen the mental powers of the performer nor did it place him on a high rung in the ladder of society's esteem.

By the time Arnulf wrote his treatise the situation had changed. Notation had become sufficiently reliable to free the performers

from the fetters of dull imitation, and with the development of
more-part music they were obliged to lift their musical accomplishments to a higher level of general intelligence. With the
knowledge of notation and harmony the composer's craft also
developed more and more into a highly specialized art instead
of a rather esoteric branch of science. This more efficient and
more elaborate method of composing led to an ever increasing
strain exerted on the musical material, which forced the performers to adapt themselves to demands hitherto unknown. Once
used to these new conditions, they started inventing new technical devices and virtuoso tricks of their own which in turn
again influenced the composers' technique. The immediate effect
of all this was a revaluation of the performer and his work. From
now on, the composer was dependent on the performer, and only
when a composer's own performance of his work was of equal
value with that of the virtuoso, was the old Boethian classification
again restored. Therefore Arnulf's derogatory remarks are not,
like Guido's, of general validity, and, in fact, in the following
sentences of his description he turns into an ardent admirer of
the good performer, thus giving us a just estimation of the singers'
and players' abilities.

If we like to hear the performer extolled without reservation,
we have to turn to the *Compendium musices* (1552) of Adrian
Petit Coclico, a French musician and pupil of Josquin. He tells
us about an extraordinary class of musicians, in which we find
those singers who without any doubt surpass all others: the Belgians, Picards, and Frenchmen in the papal, imperial, and many
royal chapels. "They know the rules of art, which they learned
from the composers. We may even count them among the composers, in that they improvise free counterpoints over given chorale melodies. The knowledge of all musical means of expression
and possibilities of effects enables them to delight and enrapture
men with their well-sounding, sweet, and solemn execution."

We see in our quotations two extreme opinions of the performer's position in the musical world. For some critics he is nothing
but the low-grade medium of transmitting music, a contrivance
to produce tones; a fellow full of vanity, jealousy, and misconduct, and totally unable to apprehend either music or his role in

reproducing it. For others he is the almost superhuman being who, with the wings of his divine talent, carries us into heavenly regions, who ranks as high as the man who creates music, and sometimes even higher, since he "improvises over given chorale melodies," while the ordinary professional composer has to follow the slow and cumbersome procedure of figuring out his music on paper.

In our own times performers outnumber composers to a degree never known before, and their abilities, attitudes, and tastes are perhaps the strongest power in determining the development of our musical life. Even the style of emotional expression in our compositions (as well as their outward technical form of appearance) is largely determined by the performer's talents and demands, so that in many cases the composer has become but a purveyor of sound effects for pianists, string players, orchestras, and so forth.

II

This high evaluation of the intermediate transformer station between the generator of a composition and the consumer — as we called the performer — is dangerous. It not only deprives the composer of his liberty of thought and imagination: it diverts the listener's attention from the more momentous properties of a composition. It seduces the listener to slide down irresistibly until the lowest point of perception is reached, when nothing else counts but the performer's virtuosity, the pleasant-sounding emptiness, the uninhibited superficiality. In the early stages of a musical culture this danger is of no consequence. A composition improvised and sung simultaneously by the individual who is both composer and performer flashes across to the receiving listener without any transmitting medium. Here it is entirely the composer's fault if the perceptions of his audience degenerate to a low level. With the progressing development the insertion of the performing mediator becomes inevitable, and from now on the fate of a composition depends on a factor that in rare cases may boost a bad piece to success (a procedure of very doubtful moral value), in many other cases cannot match in quality of perform-

ance the qualities of the composition, and ideally can but dup-
licate the preëstablished values of the composer's creation. The
listener is a rather helpless prey in the performer's net, once the
technique of performing music follows its inherent tendency to
enter esoteric regions, into which the listener is unable to follow,
so that he has to take the singer's or player's production as a *fait
accompli* without further questioning. However, confronted with
a too highly specialized performing technique the listener does
have the power of simple refusal — which the performer is careful to challenge! — or the listener may mobilize his own moral
strength against a performer's tendency towards shallowness, thus
offsetting the influence of a bad reproduction. That music for its
realization has to count on the performing mediator is an inherent
weakness, although it cannot be denied that the multiplied tensions between composer and listener, added in the course of a
composition's performance, are a source of further intellectual and
emotional sensations which may heighten our enjoyment.

Once we accept the performer as an inevitable necessity in spite
of his basic dubiousness, we may as well try to determine what
properties make him estimable.

There is in the first place the mere sentimental appreciation of
his productions, which, however, is not of a strictly musical nature. We submit to some qualities of his (or her) personality,
either actually perceptible in personal appearance, or suggested
to our emotions by the performance. This is particularly true
with singers, with whom no intervening instrument complicates
the emanation and transference of the personal influence. Doubtless this bewitchment through personality is a barrier put up
between the music and our desire to own it, and we must be
watchful not to let it grow beyond the size of a minor hurdle
the surmounting of which remains enjoyable without being det-
rimental to genuine musical appreciation.

This genuine musical appreciation of the performer's accomplishments depends considerably on his technical dexterity. The
singer or player with the more nearly perfect technique of reproducing and delivering a composition is more likely to uncover
its qualities than is his colleague who is hampered by his own

inefficiency — provided of course that technical perfection does not assume a dictatorial attitude that overshadows all other factors of musical reproduction.

III

There is no doubt that our modern performers have developed their technical skill far beyond any goal imagined in earlier times. Two hundred years ago violinists hardly knew how to reach tones higher than those in the so-called third position. In Bach's works exceptionally advanced passages make use of higher hand positions, but the discovery of handling tones up to the twelfth tone and even to the double octave of the open string was reserved to the Italian violinists of the late eighteenth century and, in their wake, Mozart. Today unexplored regions of the stringed instruments' fingerboard are nonexistent; even the arctic zones of the eternal rosin (near the bridge) have become a habitable abode for fearless climbers. The technique of handling the bow has also undergone important changes. Up to Bach's time the simple up and down movement (with the bow's hairs always in touch with the strings) was the exclusive manner of bowing. Nowadays extensive use is made of bowings that utilize the bow's saltatorial elasticity. The players of the other string instruments have by no means been idle. The 'cellists' technique of fingering and bowing is wholly equal to the violinists' and the double bass has been transformed from its proverbial function of a dog house into a musical instrument with a variety of expression and technique almost equal to that of the others. Even the violists, who in former times retired to this instrument because they were either half-wits or half-deads, converted their tool into something useful and indispensable.

The other instrumentalists went through a similar development in playing technique. In each single case we can observe that in our times this technique has reached its climax. Singers, however, arrived at their state of perfection long before instrumentalists did, and from that time on they merely maintained their status. Their apparent progress in successive generations consisted of generally accepted changes in the style and expression of singing, that is, in making their already perfect technique serve ever-changing purposes.

Besides the sentimental and the genuinely musical appreciation of the performer's work there is another important criterion that guides us in our judgment: the social classification of the instrument he is playing. Some musical instruments are regarded as low-class utensils, others enjoy a high social position. Some are low-class in one period, while in others they are climbing the ladder of social esteem. Our double-reed instruments, the oboes and bassoons, had to travel a long way from their lowly ancestors till they became the noble members of our instrumentarium they are nowadays. Bagpipes, reed organs, and most of the plucked string instruments, formerly an aristocratic assembly, have all but lost their reputation, and their players are proceeding on sidetracks of musical advancement, some of them being regarded as members of sects devoted to queer or even hopeless pastimes.

The changes in social evaluation that the guild of brass players went through is an apt illustration for our statement. In the centuries of early more-part music the trombone players, at least, must have been musicians of a higher quality and authority, while the trumpeters occupied positions of great prestige socially, but hardly musically. In Bach's time the art of trumpet playing reached an extraordinary peak, with the trumpeters being so clan-conscious in their civil importance that they could force a lower-class instrument, the cornetto or zink, on those players who were not admitted to their ranks. Then, during the nineteenth century, it was the horn players who gained in technique and musical reputation, leaving the trumpeters and trombonists almost in a state of musical illiteracy. Today brass players have again pushed forward and in both technique and social position are now equal to the players of stringed and wind instruments.

The players of keyboard instruments always occupied a very high place in the social order, but the veneration once accorded the organists has now changed into a fashionable admiration of the piano players.

The singer, with his instrument never subject to any change, throughout history maintained his social position. If he was of excellent quality, the glory, the amenities, and the riches this world has to offer were always bestowed upon him without restriction; and as an insignificant croaker he always had to creep along in choruses and mediocre teaching jobs together with the low-class instrumentalists.

IV

There is one group of performers which in earlier periods of musical communication represented nothing but the simplest means of keeping several musicians, performing simultaneously, in line, but which has gained so much in importance that nowadays to most people its representatives alone are the figures that direct music, literally, socially, and spiritually. I am speaking of conductors. The earliest description of a conductor's duties, as we know them, can be found in the *Tractatus de musica* of Elias Salomon, a clerical writer on music in the late thirteenth century. Although his description is not of great significance, it shows how the conducting of groups of musicians started, and therefore is worth reading. Elias' conductor had no orchestra to deal with, he was merely the director of a vocal quartet that sang the church services in the provincial town of Perigueux in France. It was the time when more-part music in the form of free organum had come to a certain perfection at the musical centers, that is, in northern France, Paris, and Limoges; and places like Perigueux with low-class performers and a conservative taste had just arrived at a style that in the centers was already outmoded: the old, improvised simple organum. It is the performance of this old-fashioned form of more-part singing which Elias describes. One of the group sings from the big chorale book in front of them, the three others singing in parallel octaves and fifths (or fourths) with him, occasionally modifying the strict parallelism with oblique or contrary motion of the voices, according to certain standard rules. This kind of shackled voice leading could be applied to slow-moving and simple-structured Gregorian pieces only, but even so, frequent opportunities were afforded for making mistakes, the singers being of minor quality and the rules of voice leading not unambiguous. Here the conductor's duties begin. He is one of the singers, and according to Elias "has to know everything about the music to be sung. He beats time with his hand on the book and gives the cues and rests to the singers. If one of them sings incorrectly, he whispers into his ear 'you are too loud, too soft, your tones are wrong,' as the case may be, but so that the others don't hear it. Sometimes he must support them with his own voice, if he sees that they are lost."

Elias' conductor has essentially the same obligations our conductors have, the difference being that nowadays the practicing, correcting, and prompting is done at the rehearsals, while at St. Astère in Perigueux it was part of the performance. Unfamiliar to us is the complete lack of emphasis on the leader's work, the tendency to keep him the *primus inter pares*. Times have changed; no modern conductor would like to be hidden among his collaborators.

Of course, we all know that a group of musicians, especially one as large as our modern orchestras, could not play together without being directed — unless they spent sufficient time and money to satisfy their individualistic desire to live without a conductor. We further know how beautiful music can be if performed under inspiring leadership, and how a poor conductor turns even the best music into dullness. There was a time when leading an orchestra was the exclusive task of men with a universal musical wisdom, when outstanding musicianship and great musical and human idealism were the foremost requirements. Granted that today we have many conductors with these old-time qualities, we nevertheless cannot overlook the fact that with the many times greater number of orchestras and hence the multi-production and consumption of conductors, their musical wisdom is frequently anything but universal, their musicianship doubtful, and their idealism replaced by an insatiable vanity and a deadly fight against any other being who happens also to wield a baton. That a great conductor, one of the first-mentioned class, has all the success he deserves according to his talents and efforts is understandable and praiseworthy, but that in general the caste of conductors plays a role in our musical setup that seems out of proportion when compared with that of other musicians, must have reasons that are not purely musical. Yet sentimental admiration, as accorded to players and singers, is hardly the source of this, since that admiration is an affection devoted to the immediate producer of the musical impression. We cannot recognize the conductor as such, since scores of musicians are needed to make the sounds he planned come true.

Certainly it is not the technical difficulty of the conductor's work that leaves people breathless. Even the most refined technique of beating time requires scarcely more skill than a good percussion player needs for his job, and considerably less than the ever-ready promptness of any first desk player. Frequently enough we see greatest conductorial success and a bad technique appearing together; likewise the combination of excellent beating dexterity and poorest musicianship is not infrequently found.

Musical proficiency as a general trait cannot be the reason for the estimation in which the conductor is held, since there are many solo players equal or superior to him, who with all their efforts will never impress the public as profoundly as he does. And it cannot be his overwhelming wisdom or human greatness, since everyone knows that just as among all other people we find among conductors every shade between dullards and wizards, quacks and cracks.

The extramusical reason for this somewhat disproportionate regard seems to be based on the following fact: In an era that leaves little opportunity in the individual's life for the application and the display of overt despotism, the demonstration of some refined and stylized form of oppression seems to be imperative. The listener in the audience who in his normal behavior has to suppress, thousands of times, his most natural human desire of governing, ordering, dictating to, and even torturing his fellow men, projects himself into the conductor's personality. Here he sees a man who with the consent of human society exercises a power which we would look upon as cruelty if we saw it applied to dogs or horses. Identifying himself with these activities the listener enjoys the perfect abreaction of his own suppressed feelings: he now swings the teacher's cane, the dignitary's mace, the general's sword, the king's scepter, the sorcerer's wand, and the slave driver's whip over his subjects, and quite contrary to the effects such dictatorial manners have in real life, the result seems to be pleasant to all concerned.

This is the reason why the conductor has to do his work in full visibility. Should he be hidden, it would be too much of a strain on the listener's imagination to identify himself with an authority whose directions can be felt but not seen. It is the reason why conductors who perform their work with musical perfection but neglect the showy part of inciting, soothing, spurring, urging, and whiplashing will lack the real conductor's success. It is the reason why we pay so much money for an almost tribal despotism which in this democratic world seems to be rather anachronistic.

And it is the reason why we have never heard of great conductors coming from countries in which political dictatorship is the form of government. One dictator can never permit another dictator to be his rival. Although the political dictator is the more powerful of the two, it is always dangerous for him if the people can choose their form of slavery, especially if one form is so much more agreeable. Under such conditions a great conductor would have to submit both politically and musically to his superior superconductor — but a submissive conductor is an absurdity (except to the lady members of his orchestra's board of trustees). However, since the musical conductor is merely a symbol of dictatorship and not the real thing, we must be glad that he exercises so salutary an influence. Who knows whether the world would not see more delinquency and unhappiness if the beneficial habit of going to see a conductor at work did not cause so many people to get rid of their repressions. They enter the concert hall as unidentifiable members of the human crowd, filled with evil instincts and bad intentions against everyone and everything, and they leave as purified individuals, suave and with an appreciative understanding for the world's weaknesses.

Needless to say, these statements are not intended to minimize a conductor's work. On the contrary, they try to shed some light on acts which obviously cannot be explained on a purely musical basis, thus providing ground for a more profound understanding. I know that intelligent conductors are aware of their essentially nonmusical function. For them such knowledge is not disturbing but helps them in exerting their full power. A conductor who thinks that his successes are nothing but a just remuneration for

his musical efforts short-sightedly underestimates his higher signification as a humane institution.

v

Our conductors have conquered the most powerful position
that a musician could ever hope to occupy. Our players have
reached the state of utmost technical perfection. Even our student
instrumentalists are of a caliber far surpassing that of the average
player a few generations ago. But if you are acquainted with performers and know their thoughts and feelings, you will soon discover that the conductor in spite of his power, the players and
singers in spite of their technical perfection, and all of them in
spite of their successes give the impression of people walking on
uncertain ground. It seems to be the curse of public success and
of technical perfection, that they leave one's soul unsatisfied. The
time comes in every serious performer's life, when he feels that
it cannot be the final purpose of his existence to be some elevated
form of public jester, that there must be some higher aim than a
lifelong concentration on the question how to hit the right tone
at the right time with the proper strength. So you see them almost
without exception striving at some additional musical goal that
sets their minds at peace and gives their existence a somewhat
profounder justification. Rude people are inclined to call the
satisfaction of such desires hobbies, but it is more than that. Hobbies cannot be taken seriously beyond a certain point without
losing their function as hobbies. Furthermore a hobby must never
be used to bother other people. In our case something faintly
tragic seems to enter the picture.

A very popular activity that satisfies such longings is producing
arrangements of other people's creations. How do you do this?
You take some older music written for harpsichord, organ, or any
other relatively unattractive instrument or group of instruments,
and dress it up with all sorts of more fashionable trimmings. For
the connoisseur this is an artistic procedure of about the same
value as providing a nice painted skirt and jacket for the Venus
of Milo, or dolling up the saints of Reims and Chartres with tux-
edos, mustaches, and horn-rimmed spectacles. Yet, if accused of
ordinary falsification, you only need to point out that without

your efforts those wonderful compositions would remain unknown to the great public or that some sparsely covered branches
of instrumental literature need some afforesting. It is of course
understandable that musicians who for want of creative talent
cannot experience the power of the vivifying fire directly, try at
least to catch a little reflected spark of it.

In the case of orchestral arrangements it is most frequently the
apparently inexhaustible source of the works of defenseless J. S.
Bach, whose name, followed by a hyphen and some necessarily
anticlimactic name, covers all kinds of Tchaikovskynized or Grie-
goid versions of his works on programs which with his legiti-
mate works for orchestra he hardly would have "made." Since
Bach himself was a great arranger of other composers' pieces, our
arrangers love to cite his name as a vindication of their own work.
They forget that an arrangement is artistically justified only when
the arranger's artistic effort is greater than the original composer's.

There is, however, one work which is the *pièce de résistance*
of the more art-conscious set of arrangers: the *Art of Fugue*.
They may say: We agree that objections to a rehashing of other
composers' works are generally justified, but here we have an
opus the arrangement of which no musical moralizer could in-
terdict, since the composer himself invited us to do so, if not verbally then at least implicitly. As you perhaps know, Bach wrote
this piece without giving any indication of the instruments to be
used. Not only that. He died before he could finish the last fugue
of the work. Is this not a more than enticing challenge to supply
the orchestration and possibly finish the piece — unless you prefer
to perform the unfinished version, which gives the listener the
impression that it is your genius demonstrating how death takes
the pen from the composer's hand. But if we are opposed to the
arrangers' tampering with a masterwork, what are we to do with
this incomplete piece? The ideal behavior is to enjoy it in the
same spirit of nonsounding abstraction as the composer did when
he wrote it, thus executing consciously and in the highest degree
the emotional and intellectual actions and reactions demanded
in our introductory chapters. If we are not experienced enough to
have emotional images and intellectual coconstructions conjured

up by the mere act of reading music, we may resort to an audible reproduction of the piece; but there is only one form of performance that is in the spirit of the work: to play it with the soloistic instruments at hand, essentially as an act of edification for the participants, and with not more than a handful of understanding listeners present, if any at all — never in large halls and never for an emotion-seeking audience. Don't say that this mode of performance would deprive many listeners of the enjoyment of hearing this composition. Why should everyone have everything? Even with the most liberal and most democratic distribution of goods there will be many things that the average citizen will hardly ever have in sufficient quantities, such as diamonds, caviar, and Stradivarius violins. Should we not be glad to have certain pieces of music similarly kept away from the ordinary musical goings-on, if for no other reason than to give the ambitious seeker of higher musical truths an opportunity to grow? Since Bach did not grant us any access to his piece, we can merely try to understand it our own way, always knowing that we are only guessing and assuming: but we should not permit any arranger, even one with the best technique and the most honest intentions, to make any decisions for us. Consequence: the arranger is always wrong, and particularly so in respect to the *Art of Fugue*.

All this shows that one of the most primitive laws in the realm of food production — namely, that for the protection of the health of a population food has to be kept pure, under penalty of severe punishment of the adulterator — is not valid in the nobler field of artistic production. You are not permitted to sell unsanitary macaroni or mustard, but nobody objects to your undermining the public's mental health by feeding it musical forgeries.

The irrepressible desire to arrange, to participate in the creative process, at least by nibbling, seems to belong in the same class — although on a higher level — with the cannibal's eating of his captured enemy in order to add the enemy's strength to his own. But among nibblers also there are qualitative distinctions. Having discussed the highest class, the arranger, let us now have a glance at the lowest category, thus marking the extreme limits of a long series of paracreative activities.

Those performers who, craving a modest share of the creator's glory, feel unable to compete with the glorious deeds of the arranger, find their satisfaction in adding fingerings, slurs, dynamics, and other symbols to other people's compositions. This means that they leave the mere notes of a piece as they are, but otherwise feel free to forge, interpolate, and adulterate as they please. It would be hard to understand what satisfaction people draw from the sinister enterprise of besmirching existing compositions and publishing them with their own name added to the composer's — in parentheses, to be sure, not with a hyphen — were it not done for the benefit of vocal and instrumental teachers, who thus need not bother with these questions in their lessons. If this is necessary, if our teaching system is ragged and degenerate to a degree that teachers cannot show their students how to read and play the composers' own notation of the pieces they study, it really deserves to fall into the hands of our editorial blowflies. To what extent this despicable disease has penetrated our musical body may be seen in the fact that of at least ninety-five per cent of all nonmodern music taught and studied in our schools and private classes, no printed edition of the composer's original is available. Some of these editions have, with the careless ignorance of our teachers as the sole reason, gained fame and belong to the standard teaching material. No wonder that by some ambitious secondhand editor they were published in a new, revised edition, which in turn did not satisfy the fingering and slur convictions of a thirdhand editor and consequently were again reëdited — which means that the composer's work reaches the student like a piece of furniture covered with three thick coats of oil paint instead of its natural color.

VI

As the instigation to the aforementioned activities and similar ones of our arranging pseudo-creators we mentioned the feeling of insecurity, of dissatisfaction in the performer's soul. One may wonder why a successful artist should be dissatisfied. What more can he want in his life than success, based on a perfect mastery of his craft? Would he not be the ideal performer who never doubts the importance and justness of his profession? If he had doubts, could he ever do his playing or singing or conducting with an outright and all-out conviction of his mission? Would not the listener inevitably be aware of this defection, would he not feel cheated of his due, which he had a right to expect after having paid for a ticket and mustered his good will and patience? We must admit that immovable and unshakable self-confidence may well be found in the soul of the low-grade performer, who never outgrew the primitive struggle with the petty necessities of performances and who works merely for the immediate effect of his endeavors — like a radio comedian's script writer to whom language is nothing but a medium to produce a salvo of laughter after each sentence. The higher up the path of perfection a performer climbs, the more he is usually tortured by doubts, distrust, and desperation. Most of his successes he will achieve as victories over those dark powers, and an experienced listener will be aware, mostly subconsciously, that this artist did more for him and his artistic satisfaction than the other performer who storms from conquest to conquest with lighthearted brutality and almost without knowing what he does. An unproblematic performer of this kind may be admired like some beautiful plant or other natural growth, but in art it certainly is not admiration of strange facts we are seeking; it is, as we know, participation. An attentive listener identifies himself with the performer — we mentioned this fact when we spoke about conductors — and the effect of the performance on the listener is the greater, the more he has the feeling: "This is the very way I would like to act, although I know I never will have the ability." The artist exerts on a lower and temporary basis the same attraction that moral or philosophical ideals exert on a higher and more permanent one: the model example guides you; you seek to attain it, yet it will forever remain unrealized.

We hear our listener's reply: "Looking at the problem without sentimentality, we need not bother with the artist's insecurity and dissatisfaction. If he makes me envy his perfection, he has done good work which ought to satisfy him. Moreover, if he evoked in my mind inspiring images of emotions and if he leads me with his performance to the intellectual coconstruction of it, he has fulfilled his artistic duty and has also satisfied me, no matter what his own mental condition may be. Beyond this objective he has no obligation and therefore has no right to feel insecure."

The listener is right. His cruel statement shows the reason for the performer's feelings. The singer's and player's task is to do as the listener stated: to prompt him to the highest auditorial activity. But when the artist succeeds in bringing the listener to his moral goal, he himself suddenly loses all importance. The listener's satisfaction is exclusively his own; he was given what could be given to him and he received it emotionally and intellectually with an open mind. The artist, in turn, had to be the giver, and the other's moment of highest satisfaction was the moment of his greatest loss. His duty was merely to reproduce a composition without any disturbing individualistic admixture, so as to prepare for the listener the perfect ground for his mental collaboration. This fact, namely to spend a life's work and, again and again, your heart's devotion and your mind's ambition in performances, with conviction that you did your best only when you and your work disappeared behind the piece performed; gone and forgotten the moment you climbed to the highest summit of perfection and self-denial — this seems to me the essential tragedy in the performer's existence.

Giving away one's precious properties certainly brings unselfish satisfaction, but to do it incessantly one has to be a saint. A more profane being now and then needs the stimulus of receiving some recompense. With a performer, the feeling that for his altruistic donations he never will receive any compensation of the same moral significance must lead to melancholy. Melancholy in turn leads to artistic sterility. The faked fertility that manifests itself in the production of arrangements, fingered and bowed editions, and other secondhand trifles, cannot hide the dwindling of the vigor once so impulsively productive in the artist's endeavors. The top soil of a garden, robbed of its contents of nitrogen by generations of plants that needed it for their growth, cannot provide further nutrition for such plants. It must be replenished with new nitrogen in its natural, most readily assimilated form. This most common of all gardening rules has not yet become a part of the musician's considerations. Once he enters the concertizing or teaching profession, he unceasingly pours out the supply of music he had stored up during the receptive years of learning and collecting. He is unaware of the approaching exhaustion of this supply, he does nothing to preserve or renew it. Even the cognition of ultimate exhaustion cannot penetrate his consciousness as he works his treadmill. Routine replaces enthusiasm, feelings lose their genuineness, endless repetitions of the same restricted number of facts create an atmosphere of fictitious truth.

Not with diversions, amusements, hobbies, and pursuits of various natures can the lack be supplied. The missing nitrogen had to be replenished with new nitrogen. Here music is missing, music that got lost in the dreariness of musical business. The vacuum must be filled up with music, music in its natural state: that is, music without any professional flavor, without intentions of demonstrating, instructing, or entertaining, without performing or listening purposes, without admission of other than purely musical sentiments — in short, music as it is made by children or incorrigible dilettantes. Musicians who try to regain this state of rejuvenating musical innocence will be shocked by the difficulty of shedding all their pride, professional inhibitions, and crampy habits, but after the first steps on this road they already will feel the invigorating briskness of a new atmosphere. The most reliable way to the fountain of youth is coöperative singing in small groups of like-minded seekers; the least recommendable, the use of keyboard instruments with their tendency to force the player into musical and mental isolation. Of all the hundreds of professional musicians I have met, there are few who found their way back to the source of musical life, and there is hardly more than a handful who retained their wonderful freshness from the time of their musical infancy.

A world-famous instrumentalist, talking with a colleague who played chamber music as a means of musical recreation, expressed envy. Asked why he could not do the same, he said, "I cannot afford it." Either he would have lost money while devoting his time to nonprofitable music, or his hopelessly professionalized mind could not be distracted without his losing his direction. It is the most depressing statement a musician ever made: it expresses the horrible emptiness of fame; it is the perfect illustration of the utter senselessness of a musical specialism that has lost all ground and reason.

Let us hear a comforting report of another musical attitude. After a Chinese musician, a great virtuoso on his native instruments and a celebrity in his home country, had given an enthralling performance of Chinese music, a discussion of musical customs in China sprang up. Would he make his living by playing his instruments; would he be a traveling virtuoso; would he try to educate, elevate, and entertain audiences? Almost offended, he answered in the negative, displaying a Boethian contempt of musical professionalism. How, then, would the perfect musician exercise his art? "He would take his horse and ride to a mountain far away from houses and men. There he would play his instrument and sing for his own enlightenment."

Instead of escaping one's own self by participating in another summer school, another refresher course, another series of informing lectures and concerts, would it not be advisable to do as this musician did: to go away from the pell-mell of public music and regenerate one's musical soul by communicating with the true spirit of music, with nature, with the universe?

# 8.

## SOME THOUGHTS ON INSTRUMENTS

THERE are many people to whom an orchestra is a strange institution. They cannot see or do not want to see any plausible reason for its existence; to them the men who spend their physical and mental capacities in the production of queer noises belong to some class of irresponsible creatures; discomfort is the least of the feelings they have if their presence at an orchestra's long-haired stampede cannot be avoided.

There are others who professionally spend a good deal of their lives working within, for, and in front of the orchestra. They are familiar with its secrets in all their soberness. Sometimes a certain weariness from too much occupational ado will make them overcritical, somewhat cynical, and keenly aware of ridiculous factors.

These two attitudes towards an orchestra's productions can in their extremeness hardly be surpassed. Fortunately the uneasy novice's bewilderment is as far removed from the accustomed concertgoers' assent as is the detachment of the overfed professional. If it is discouraging to be wholly ignorant of an orchestra's purpose and function, it sometimes is not too pleasant to see the veil of illusion drawn away from one's complacent consent.

It was in this mood that I listened to one of those important-sounding, empty-pompous, symphonic pieces in which the crowded players on the stage, their stern bustling, and their inciter's antics put you in the situation of a helpless onlooker in a rolling mill. Six players in the percussion section beat, rang, whizzed, banged, and rattled on a multitude of contrivances, producing rhythmical patterns of a devilish intricacy — for the player, but without any meaning for the listener — which in the program book were explained as the most sophisticated synthesis of Parsee, Hellenistic, and Greenwich Village *Weltanschau-*

*ung*. We all know what happens when too many visible and audible distractions and too much of a strain on our credulity disrupt the connection between a performance and our attention: one either giggles or in plain boredom regards most of the events before him as absurdities.

I concentrated on the triangle player. Here he was, a grown-up man, wife and three children waiting for him at home; a man perhaps owning one of the greatest stamp collections in the country and being Exalted Potentate of his Shrine; in short, a man of highest social repute. Now he meekly counted his rests and once in a while elicited some tinkles from his triangular bread basket, an activity which in this case absorbed about as much mental exertion as the unlacing of a shoe, but was backed by five years of conservatory instruction, a bachelor's degree, auditions and victories over competitors. Of course, we know the difference between good and bad triangulists and nobody wants the triangle's violent trill of the last *tutti* to appear in the following *pianissimo subito*. But one refuses to see in a sporadic triangle tinkling the ultimate purpose of a human being's earthly existence.

It is not so much the incongruity of effort and effect that here arouses our indignation, but rather the fact that something which under normal circumstances had at least a slight significance as a part of a higher entity has been deprived of even this scant *raison d'être* by being thrown together with a host of badly calculated, insufficiently organized, and altogether unessential stuff. Intrinsic low value — such as the triangle's sound — emphasized by its placement in an environment made worthless by disorganization, that is what has offended our sense of proportion. The greatest sin in art is not boredom, as frequently stated, but the lack of proportion, and he certainly is a bad composer who has no feeling for the balance of all his means of expression. If he had, how could he boost a childish dalliance into artistic pseudo-importance? How full of vanity his mind must be that for this he claims the right to engage a serious man's intelligence and honest musical efforts! His is the oppressive attitude of an Egyptian Pharaoh to whom human lives were nothing but utensils for hewing and carrying stones at the building site of his pyramid, the difference being that the Pharaoh by birth, education, and governmental power had at least some token justification for his tyranny, while to the bad composer, all the power — although on a lower and less dangerous level — is conceded without any merit of his own. True, magnificent deeds need the combined efforts of a multitude of nameless and faceless toilers. Our armies of workers, soldiers, and intellectuals are similar tools in the hands of governing powers for the achievement of superindividual goals, and the more the word "people" is mentioned, in reference to their actions, the more we can be sure of a considerable amount of disproportion: it seems to be inevitable that some Pharaonic fathead will always stuff himself with the glory derived from his slaves' drudgeries.

If this cannot be avoided in our ordinary political and economic life, we could at least keep music free from painful exaggerations. Music had the distinguished task of charming us into an atmosphere of space and time symbols, it touched our emotions, inspired our better self. Why, then, must music be misused for the megalomaniac exhibitionism of some composers and performers? Why must a group of about one hundred orchestra players submit to the individualistic caprices of disproportionate tone arrangements? And why must whole audiences be the guinea pigs for any immature experiment in sound?

The provider of all those inadequacies, the trivial tone compiler enjoys all the advantages of a situation circumscribed by the works of the genius and meant to be saturated with masterworks. Thus being in his own status already out of proportion with his surroundings, it is not too surprising to see disproportion perpetrated and cropping up in all his musical creations.

II

Among the many and varied reasons for the aforementioned facts is the sheer weight of the apparatus involved. It is undeniably impressive to see scores of people work for one's entertainment or enlightenment, and a piece of music, be it of the worst kind, can hardly be thought of as being devoid of any value, since it was deigned to be accepted for a representation in so glorious a frame. The mastermind who with his harmonized fancies keeps this mechanism humming doubtless knows his reasons for all these strange goings-on. Besides, we do not want to hurt our self-respect by admitting that with our dignified presence we are assisting something base and worthless. How could it be worthless, if so many artists and instruments are employed? See what they have marshaled! Rows of fiddles, an impressive phalanx of basses, shiny brass tubing galore, an entire family of kettle drums, several pianos and other menacing keyboard instruments, not to mention the six busy men in the percussion section.

Poor Bach and poor Haydn, you did not know how to capture an audience, and your scanty-looking orchestra pieces are just good enough as mere preparations for more demonstrative exhibits. Poor oratorio singers, you may appear in hordes, dressed in alluring gowns and singing like cherubs, but you cannot compete with the illustrious diligence of the full orchestra. And poor adagio movements, in which everyone plays unattractive long notes without much motion of fingers, bows, valves, sticks, and keys, and with many players waiting idly for cues anyway. Ah, torrential cascades from the gargoyles of the orchestra! Ah, ocean full of roaming prodigies! Ah, Manhattanesque assembly of pipes and strings and reeds and membranes!

The instruments, the immediate providers of all this bliss, can to the nonprofessional listener and onlooker have any meaning between the extremes of a fetishistic charm and a mere decorative piece of musical household equipment. The musician who sounds them is devoted to them, as is every craftsman to his more or less reliable tools. In a composer's work they may talk with the same directness a man uses in his most heartfelt and affectionate speech, or in the hands of nontalent they may degenerate into insipid noise makers.

What is our own position? We look at them with the enthusiastic allegiance that is our attitude towards all things musical; on the other hand we do not ignore their imperfections. They are close to our heart, so close that we understand them almost as living beings, in all their radiant beauty and their pitiable evanescence.

III

When we think of string instruments, the violin with its close relatives, the viola and the violoncello, come to our mind as a princely family. Are they not instruments of a perfection not to be surpassed? The creations of Cremonese masters and their successors are by general consent the *ne plus ultra* of an instrument maker's craft.

Can we believe in fateful coincidences? If the clear recognition of necessities, a common artistic feeling, noble trends in a period's attitude, a flawless handicraft, and the readiness of a genius all worked towards one single objective, then the period four hundred years ago was in fact the ideal era and northern Italy the right place for the birth of so versatile a musical tool as the violin. As long as those conditions prevailed, the instrument's kingly rank and dignity remained stable.

The early forerunners of the violins, the rubeba (rebec) and vielle, had died out in the fourteenth century. They had lived under conditions less favorable. Almost exclusively coupled to singing voices, theirs was not an unbridled existence. They had to recede when a more presumptuous instrumental conscience demanded more expressive and more efficient tools. The viol family took their place, its members being wonderfully balanced in sound, size, and manipulation throughout the compass of that period's tone system. These soft-voiced instruments had to yield to the violins, answering the individualistic call of the Cinquecento and the Baroque period for more soloistic, personal, sensuous means of expression. The only viol which survived amidst the newcomers was the tenor gamba, submitting to the new trend with a sophisticated solo literature in the early eighteenth century, but then with its own disappearance sealing the final downfall of the viol family. The violins' domination now was undisputed. Gone was the complacent, charming frugality of the predecessors, but gone also their clanlike homogeneity. Vigorous individualities, the violin and the 'cello permitted the evolution of a slender and speedy technique of playing which by leaps and bounds reached the climax of its expressive possibilities about eighty years ago. The other two members of the family, viola and double bass, of a rather disproportionate construction in comparison with their luckier relatives, could not make up for their physical drawback and probably never will, although — as mentioned in the seventh chapter — modern players have done their best to overcome all structural obstacles.

If the violins and 'cellos were built mainly for soloistic purposes, their collective use in our modern ensembles — up to forty fiddles in an orchestra — contradicts the creators' original conception. What is worse is their placement within an entirely different scene of action. The same little wooden boxes the sound of which was intended merely to fill the living rooms or halls of some nobleman's private palace, are pressed into service in our enormous concert halls with the number of listeners multiplied a hundredfold and more. The instruments had to be reinforced if they were to satisfy the new acoustical requirements. As the boards of the instrument's body could not be strengthened and the form altered without entirely changing the character of its sound, the only part of the sounding body that could be adapted to the new conditions was the strings. Replacing the smooth-sounding, soft-speaking gut strings with sturdier materials, more and more metal was used in stringing the instruments of the violin family, and on the violin proper, as it is used today, uncovered gut strings are practically never used. Now, since solid metal strings or strings wound with metal wire increase the pressure on the instrument, this tiny wooden body of the violin, built originally for the low pressure of gut strings, and thinner gut strings, at that, at present has to endure a considerable amount of overpressure. To be sure, the actual difference in pressure may not amount to much. Physicists may even tell us that metal strings of an appropriate thinness will exert less pressure than a gut string four or five times thicker sounding the same tone. But the conditions in the physicist's laboratory with its weight-loaded strings are not the same as in actual use. A corresponding thinness of metal strings would make them less resistant to breaks than gut strings of the same pitch; consequently, heavier metal strings exerting more pressure must be used. Furthermore, the assortment of feeble wooden shreds called a violin is without doubt sensitive to changes of pressure amounting to fractions of an ounce, especially when applied continuously, and the virtuoso who sorrowfully tunes down his instrument after each use knows perfectly well what he is doing.

Another source of overpressure is our manner of handling the bow. The soft strokes of earlier times have given way to our notorious production of the "big tone," and our technique of jumping and hacking upon the strings subjects the instrument to a terrific beating. Although we can but admire the constructive genius and foresight of the early builders, whose constructions are useful under the most adverse conditions, we may as well state that the surest way for a violinist to ruin his Stradivarius, the price of which may have been anywhere between ten thousand and forty thousand dollars, is to use it our modern way with high-pressure metal strings and reckless manners of playing. I am sure that no instrument can stand this kind of treatment longer than a few decades. We are so unreasonable as to expect from those dwarfs superperformances which are against their very nature. Why the happy owners of those treasures subject them to such ruinous treatment is not clear to me. Many experiments have shown that in our large concert halls it makes no difference whether one uses an overpressured Baroque violin or an equally overpressured one of modern decent make; only in smaller spaces where subtlety of sound rates higher than brilliant loudness can the difference be felt.

The accommodation to new concert halls, greater numbers of listeners, and changed social conditions is not alone responsible for the changed treatment of our bowed instruments; the replacement of the soulful gut strings with blaring metal does not spring solely from the desire for a louder, more penetrating sound. It is a new ideal of sound, a longing for colors and expressive qualities unknown in the past that either produces new instruments or tries to modify the sound of the older ones until the new desire is satisfied. Strange as it may appear, the new ideal of sound has grown up as the result of the technical improvement of a device that was not conceived as a producer of musical tones. It is the radio amplifier, the loud-speaker, which has become the standard sounding instrument, towards which the sounds of most of our musical instruments are aimed. In an ever increasing degree they try to sound similar to the loud-speaker's tone. Not until the loud-speaker's general acceptance as a transmitter of music (that is, about twenty-five years ago) did we experience the rather radical conversion of our instruments' sounding qualities. A transmitter device, in respect to music originally nothing but a reproducer with a well-meaning tendency towards undistorted rendition of the sounds it received, has turned into an independent ruler with a voice that directs taste and fashion. Our fiddles with their high-tensed metal strings ape this newfangled usurper's tone only too well, and even the players' methods of attacking these strings with fingers and bow strive for a close reproduction of the reproducer's intermediary moans. As a further confirmation of our opinion we hardly need mention certain more than obvious mannerisms in singing and in the playing of wind instruments, which without the loud-speaker's tutelage would be entirely senseless.

Those among us who still believe in backgrounds of culture and musical discrimination which determine the exterior appearance of music may deplore the sad fact of the submission of musical sounds to an eternally secondhand acoustical gadget. We are probably in a situation similar to that of a musician in the eighteenth century who sheltered his genteel gamba against the reckless onslaught of the violins. An intruder felt to be a proletarian takes over; his regime will grow until it in turn will be outmoded and conquered by the next lower proletarian, who will go through the same circle of evolution — and thus ad infinitum.

Seen from this angle, the chances of our violin family having a much longer life seem to be slim. To be sure, people will continue to build violins, violas, 'cellos, and basses; our devotion and that of future generations to music of the past will keep them alive for a while, but theirs will be an artificial existence. The vigorous idealism which created them and carried them through four centuries has vanished; they have lost the power of regeneration and their assimilative agility. After a few more decades, those fiddles that have not been killed by our unreasonable treatment will survive merely as exhibits in a museum of sound, as part of the antiquated tool chest used for historic performances of those legendary composers of the nineteenth and twentieth centuries. Our successors, finding them just as we had used them, without their original charm and mellowness, will probably ask how peo-

ple ever could use such inappropriate tools: tools too small for the
required tone volume and too inadequate for the constant over-
strain demanded of them.

IV

The prototypes of wind instruments can be found in every
nook and cranny of the world of organic growth. Hollow bones,
bamboo sticks, or any other kind of tubelike part of an animal's
or plant's body, blown upon at a certain angle; stalks of grasses
and grain plants, compressed at one end by the lips blowing upon
them; dry reeds and sedges, a half-splintered piece of their surface
vibrating in the respiratory air of the mouth; an animal's horn,
the air forced through it with tight lips — these are the basic
types of all wind instruments, of flutes, double-reed tubes, one-
reed tubes, and those with cup-shaped mouthpieces. Their tone
color, range, and loudness is determined and modified by the
tube's building material — which comprises any imaginable solid
substance from glass to leather — and by the form of its interior
bore, which may have any shape from a cylinder to a wide cone.
Whole families of any one type have been built, each reaching
through the entire compass from lowest to highest tones: flutes
of all sizes, double-reed instruments of every imaginable shape,
bore, and range, mouthpiece instruments of a similar variety of
forms. But the general evolution of the wind instruments has
been somewhat different from that of the stringed instruments.

We saw how the viols as a complete family succeeded the old
rubebas and vielles, and how they in turn were replaced by the
violins. It is always one family at a time that reigns in the field of
the stringed and bowed instruments. With the wind instruments
several families of an analogous type may exist simultaneously,
while others are at that time nonexistent and still others imper-
fectly represented. Thus in the sixteenth and seventeenth centuries we find an abundance of double-reed instruments. Dulcians
and bassoons cover the whole range of the tone system; so do the
softer shawms and bombards, the schryari and bassanelli, the
sordunes and doppioni. Krummhorns (cromorni) with their cap-
suled mouthpieces and restricted range come in at least five
different sizes; bagpipes, of all dimensions, and bladderpipes add

more color to the already multicolored palette, with rankets completing the set. Flute families of two different species were in use: the one with wedge-formed mouthpieces — the recorders; the other the well-known traverse flutes. Trumpets and trombones with narrow tubes and flat-bowled mouthpieces extend through most of the compass; the cornetti, preserving the form of their model (animal's horn) to a greater degree than did other instruments, appear in three sizes; and finally there are the horns proper, which, however, as lowly hunting horns were not admitted to the artists' set of instruments. Single-reed instruments were entirely unknown in the sixteenth and early seventeenth centuries.

With the beginning of the eighteenth century a deadly disease seems to attack the life of the double-reed instruments. Soon the krummhorns are extinct; bombards, dulcians, schryari, et cetera are forgotten; the bagpipe in all sizes is banished from the society of so-called decent instruments; the cornetti vanish, too. Today all that is left from the former plenitude is the oboe with its larger brother, the English horn, and the bassoon in two sizes. Most of the flutes also became victims of the deadly germ; all the recorders withered away, and two traverse flutes is all we inherited. The trumpets and trombones maintained their position, but a powerful low-class contestant gained strength who in the nineteenth century all but pushed aside the venerable elders: the French horn. It is only in the last few decades that the three standard brass instruments have been welded into a group of equally able and equally well-equipped associates.

### V

The strangest fact in this cycle of life, atrophy, death, and rebirth is the rise of the clarinet. This instrument towards the end of the seventeenth century begins to push itself into the ranks of the tone producers, first as an ordinary intruder. Soon it is recognized as a useful addition with great potentialities, and its shape and fingering mechanism is subject to a continuous improvement, so that already towards the end of the eighteenth century Mozart can write his clarinet concerto and the clarinet quintet and the trio with clarinet, pieces which use the new instrument in the most perfect and exhaustive way. The newcomer is strong enough to develop a complete family, and nowadays the clarinet is the only woodwind instrument that has a representative in each section of the musical tone range, from the bass clarinet to the E-flat soprano, or even (with the inclusion of two extreme outsiders) from the contrabass clarinet to the small A-flat piccolo.

Although the modern flutes, oboes, and bassoons still have basically the same form as their predecessors had several centuries ago, it has been the flute in particular which, due to the general tendency to reinforce instruments and thus increase their volume of sound, has gained in strength and lost in sweetness — followed closely by the clarinets. The modern oboes are still very similar to their earlier relatives in color and volume; and the bassoons, especially in their French form (which seems to be on its way to extinction) have changed less than all the others and therefore are the least fitted to serve modern purposes. Keys had to be added to all of these instruments' finger holes, first merely as a means of bringing the holes at the lower end of the tube into reach of the hand, later as a more dependable and more flexible way of governing the entire scale. The players, in collaboration with instrument builders, scientists, and composers, tried to transform their tools into precision mechanisms, and it seems that the flutes have now reached the peak of this development; the efficiency of their structure, the technical possibilities for the player, and the resulting sound effect being in a state of perfect balance. Clarinets and oboes are still up to some improvements, mostly in the arrangement of their keys, and for the bassoon, with its clattering long levers and other obsolete features left in a somewhat fossil condition, there probably will be a thorough reconstruction.

Brass players have also seen a good deal of change in their instruments. In some periods narrow-built conical tubes approaching the cylinder were used; in others wide forms or tubes of a pronounced cone shape were preferred. Sometimes the mouthpieces were shallow and sharp-edged, then again kettlelike and with soft edges. Later on, valves were added to trumpets and horns, so that the players could use the uninterrupted chromatic scale. Here also these factors had a considerable influence on the tone quality and the technique of playing. Nevertheless, the families of these instruments have shrunk: only one type of trumpet remains; of an entire set of trombones two sizes are still in existence; and horns are in the same situation.

With the brass instruments the struggle to attain a greater efficiency was not quite so successful as with the woodwinds, since with the addition of each valve a certain amount of impurity is added to an instrument's pitch. Devices designed to avoid this, such as the Sax valves, have not met with general favor because of their unwieldiness. Future improvements are still possible, although they are limited if the traditional fancy shape of horns, trumpets, and trombones is to be preserved.

The fatal blight that bereft the musicians of the eighteenth century of a colorful set of instruments, had left a vacuum which, even with the clarinet's intrusion and eight or ten individual remainders of the old splendor, could not be filled to the players' satisfaction. During a few decades in which the attention of the musicians was absorbed by the new technique of composition displayed in the progressive works of the young Mannheim school, the demands on the players' technique remained modest. Not before the end of the century did the Viennese masters in their symphonic works and the orchestra's rapid progress in French, Italian, and German opera require an instrumental expressiveness and agility which the old-fashioned wind instruments failed to provide. Now we see all the aforementioned improvements in the instruments' structure appear, and once the spark of technical inventiveness flares up, attempts at restoring the old variety of instruments become more and more numerous. Again an abundance of forms, sounds, and mechanisms comes into existence: the golden age of the wind instrument seems to have dawned. But only one of the many newcomers proves sturdy and important enough to survive. It is the saxophone, which becomes a regular member of our list of instruments. Similar to the clarinet it appears in a complete set covering the entire tonal range, but unlike the clarinet family's well-balanced members the saxophones are of uneven quality, some of them being ugly-sounding and unbalanced. However, one of them makes up for the deficiencies of all the others: the alto E-flat saxophone shows a balance of unhindered technique, expressive range, and directness of speech that has its equal only in the modern flute.

All the other wind instruments introduced during the past one hundred and fifty years are definitely nothing but hybrids, combining in manifold ways the basic features of tube-forms and mouthpiece arrangements. There is, of course, nothing to be said against hybrids, either in corn or hogs or musical instruments, and sometimes they will produce an offspring of superior quality. The saxophone, being a crossbreed of a wide horn tube, the clarinet's one-reed mouthpiece, and the oboe's fingering, certainly has proved their vitality. The conditions for hybridizing instrumental qualities are not quite as promising as those for hogs or corn; for since we have many robust strains of hybrid plants, our hybrid instruments (save the saxophone) have remained a shadowy crowd, and probably nobody will ever inflate with the breath of persistent musical life all those varied bugles, cornets, mellophones, sarrusophones, sousaphones, Wagner tubas, baritone oboes, and valved trombones.

It seems that the exaggerated hybridization of musical instruments indicates the terminal phase of a period's structural and technical imagination. The inventiveness of the constructors and users is directed by a sense of utility and adaptability rather than by the free imagination and adventurous spirit of the earlier explorers who created all those fanciful contrivances out of sheer pleasure, or with a religious urge, or as an enrichment of a period's treasury of artistic values, but never with the prosaic curiosity to combine the advantages of several existing things for the sole purpose of constructing something different.

Compared with the hybridization of wind instruments (which, after all, served the significant purpose of filling the gap left open by the disappearance of the older set of wind instruments), crossbred string instruments, although numerous, never gained any importance. There has been Bach's five-stringed 'cello and his viola pomposa, the bowed guitar arpeggione for which Schubert wrote a sonata, the many attempts at finding some better balance between the playable size and the pitch of the viola, the tenor fiddle in the lower octave of the violin — but how could they ever hope to live, with nothing but their constructors' speculations as the vitalizing power that brought them into existence?

## VI

The man who for the first time in history made a fluting tube speak with the aid of compressed air instead of his own breath necessarily had to invent another technical device: a lever opening and shutting the tube's flue. A series of such levers, arranged in a handy form, could eventually be nothing but a keyboard which, after some minor adjustments, would end up as something similar to the arrangement of either the piano or the typewriter. The decision had to be in favor of the piano type keyboard, as this obviously clumsier structure could be built to a certain perfection by people who had not yet acquired enough skill for the construction of subtler types. For the conduction of air into a set of pipes — an organ, that is — the keyboard in its simple lever form was a necessity and, before the introduction of electrical transmission for the organ, doubtless the only dependable means of releasing the valves of the tubes. But why the keyboard's lever work had to be built into other instruments, especially those with strings as tone-producing bodies, is one of the unanswered questions in our musical evolution.

A keyboard inserted between the player and the sounding strings, or whatever nonorganlike tone producer is used, eliminates the direct touch without adding any essential improvement to the player's action. Remove the keyboard from a piano and what remains is basically a harp. The simpleton who took the harp for a nude piano did not know how in his innocence he touched one of the mysteries of musical genetics! Nevertheless, the harp in its natural form, unhampered by a keyboard, has, in spite of its closeness to the player's touch, enough weaknesses to prevent it from assuming a place in the very first rank of important musical implements. A defender of keyboards may point out their superiority in respect to velocity. However, their ability of producing successions of tones more rapidly than other instruments could not have been the force that in the period of early keyboard experiments determined the shape of this sound-releasing mechanism, since in that golden age it was more the weight and meaning of tones that counted instead of their number and tempo of succession. Also the possibility of playing full chords cannot have caused the insertion of a mechanical impediment; for the harp and other plucked instruments like the psaltery or even the ancient cithara would have more than satisfied the modest demand of the Middle Ages for harmony. Perhaps unconscious psychological considerations led the old constructors to heighten the aesthetic satisfaction of the sounding end product through the greater resistance of the inserted mechanical hurdles — a none too convincing assumption, since, save for the player directly involved, nobody could have shared this particular satisfaction after the subjugation of obstacles. Could it have been a normalization of sound, the elimination of the disturbing irregularities of the human touch that was to be achieved? Again this is not likely. A keyboard in those past centuries must have suffered from imperfections to a greater degree than its builders and players were willing to stand. A distinct playful urge towards variety in sound and means of sound production probably was the only reason for adaptation of a lever-shaped releaser that in organlike instruments had proved its usefulness — the same urge that had so fancifully conditioned the shape of many other instruments. This releaser, during a long period of evolution, has from its playful beginnings turned into a mechanism that nowadays quite distinctly separates itself from others, has caused the development of its own unique style of expression and composition, and has become more reliable than any other musical implement. Yet, keyboards have remained basically what they were, and as tone releasers they are in the same class with timpani sticks and far below the keys and valves of wind instruments.

Real enthusiasm for the keyboard will simply ignore such statements and will refuse to regard it as an interposed and intrinsically superfluous gadget; playfulness will never be acknowledged as the creative power that produced the apparently most sensitive and most perfect mediator between the player's emotions and the sounding string. Admittedly, the action of the piano key, compared with the mere switch function of the organ key, is highly sensitive, and strangely enough it had reached the highest degree of sensitivity in its most artless form, namely with the key of the clavichord. This instrument's strings are touched without any intervening medium by the rear arm of the key lever and are kept sounding as long as the finger presses down the key. Thus the duration, loudness, and color of a tone, its sustentation and, to a certain degree, even its pitch remain constantly under the control of the player; and although the inveterate weakness of all keyed instruments using strings, the sharply attacked and rapidly fading tone, is also characteristic of the clavichord, this keyboard instrument more than all other claviers can, in respect to expressive and sensuous playing, compete successfully with the more directly speaking, nonkeyed tone producers.

Nothing of this kind is desired with the harpsichord. Here the sharply attacked tone just mentioned is emphasized without compromise. Artificially the player is deprived of any direct expressive influence on the instrument's tone by the insertion of a secondary set of levers between the key's rear arm and the string: the jacks which on impulse from the keys pluck the string with a tiny quill plectrum. It is the principle of plucking lute or guitar strings that here is driven to the extreme. The desire for this kind of discontinuous tone production, which in spite of its peculiar charms undeniably suffers from an exaggerated artificiality, must have had its reason in the culture of ensemble playing in the late Renaissance and Baroque periods. The sound of bowed or blown instrumental groups, uncontoured and somewhat floating with all their sustained tones needed some contrasting element that would articulate the sounding forms with fresh color, with buoyant looseness, and with inescapable rhythmic abruption. Without the harpsichord that period's ensemble playing would have been in permanent danger of deteriorating into a more or less amorphous sounding mush.

The key mechanism of the modern piano restores the player's control of the production of sounds, although it was unable to reinstate the utmost sensitivity of the old clavichord keys, for the adaption from the harpsichord of inserted secondary and even tertiary levers could never, even in an arrangement of greatest technical perfection and precision, permit the almost undisturbed directness of the clavichordist's touch. After the abandonment of the clavichord's mellow tangential pressure that vibrated the strings, after the obsolescence of the harpsichord's rapping device, a hammer mechanism was finally achieved. A hammer will always and basically remain a tool that lengthens and modifies the hand's actions, and the fact that it is covered with tender felt cushions and is equipped with numerous additional refinements will never make it equal to the violin player's finger that touches the string without any intervening transmission of forces. Pianists do not appreciate such statements.

VII

The worst blow the admirers of the hammer keyboard ever received was the discovery of physicists that in the sound tracks of an oscillator no difference can be seen between tones produced by the adept touch of a great artist's hand and those stemming from manipulation with an umbrella. Piano antagonists liked to gloat over this humiliating experiment which, by the mere fact that it could be performed, seemed to prove the uncouthness of the mechanism in question.

The scientifically proven fact cannot be doubted, in spite of all disavowals by the pianists. There is no mysterious power acting in a key and no reason can be found why an arrangement of several levers should be more than a device for the transmission of physical energy. In my opinion both the clavier addicts and the umbrella conspirators are arguing facts that have no bearing on music and musical effects. It is of no importance whether a single tone is produced by Franz Liszt or by Mr. Smith's umbrella. A single tone, as we have stated repeatedly, has no musical significance, and the keyboard does not provide any exception to this rule. The tones released by the keyboard receive musical value only if brought into temporal and spatial relations with each other. Then the infinitely subtle gradation in the application of pressure, the never-ceasing interplay of minutest dynamic hues and temporal length proportions, all the bewitching attractions of good piano playing — only the artist can produce them convincingly; and it certainly is not his hand that reigns within the microcosm of musical diversity but his musical intellect as the master of his playing hand. Even the application of the world's most perfect umbrellas could never cope with this diversity, gradation, and interplay.

Whatever the pianist does, using intellect, hands, and lever arrangements in the process of enlivening musical forms, will always be derived from musical experiences with the human voice. The player may not be conscious of this fact, yet if he genuinely wants to move his listeners intellectually and emotionally, he would better stay close to the conditions of vocal expression. Even in prestissimo tone successions, so easily produced by faultlessly working keyboards, the reference to the basic musical material of the singing voice should always be recognizable. Probably one of the main reasons that the harpsichord could not survive the assault of the *Hammerklavier* is the relatively strong alienation of its sound and treatment from that of the human voice, which made it an easy prey to an instrument that was somewhat closer to the prototype.

The closeness of instrumental utterances to their vocal model finds its expression mainly in a judicious articulation of tone successions, which means that temporal relations must appear in well-proportioned balance. This balance is by no means identical with equality in length, or with time proportions expressed in lowest numbers, or with symmetry. On the contrary, such short-range balance would be totally alien to human song, whose freedom and variability is subordinate to a higher order of large-scale temporal proportions, the computation of which is the task of a performer only after a composer has done all the constructive calculations in advance. Thus the singing and playing of motifs, phrases, melodies, and other small components of musical forms cannot be done with evenness and petty symmetry. We may even go so far as to say that in vivid music two successive harmonic, melodic, and rhythmic units must never be of exactly equal duration, even if their written form suggests absolute temporal uniformity. The distasteful effects of short-range symmetry we experience frequently enough in fast-moving passages of many short-valued tones; with the increase of tempo and evenness such successions gradually approach the effect of a mere motoric noise, in which nothing but the ever-changing pitch level differentiates between a musical structure and the relentless motion of a machine. Many players apply this machinesque evenness also to structures which by no means suggest any traces of it, the reason for this fear of vocal proximity being either plain ignorance or their horror of distorting a composition. Their performance may sparkle with technical perfection, but it will remain musically dead, for it has not found the way to living articulation; even a slow-moving motor does not evoke any effects of a musical nature.

Instruments like the organ and the harpsichord which permit every temporal gradation but are entirely devoid of any micro-dynamic discrimination, incite most easily to inarticulate playing. Without great musical intelligence and taste, the restriction to the application of rhythmic proportions cannot make us forget the absence of dynamic expressiveness. Not many of the modern players of these rigid instruments display the required intelligence and taste! Much of the organ playing we are exposed to nowadays suffers from the stupid uniformity of a hurdy-gurdy, and between the performances of so many harpsichordists and the performance of a punching machine not much of a difference can be discerned.

With the ingenious player or singer the problem of style in performance is practically nonexistent. They play and sing, following the infallible guidance of their natural musical talent. They cannot avoid re-creating the intrinsic proportions of a musical form; they make the listener feel how a performance is for a composition what a precious crystal goblet is for an exquisite wine: the wine's quality remains unchanged, but its color and bouquet unfold in all their splendor. The term "interpretation," once meant to designate the intelligent performance of a composer's artistic mediator, now is almost synonymous with all kinds of obscure doings in the rather uncontrollable middle field between a composition and its reception by the listener, and frequently is nothing but an excuse to gloss over the ungifted performer's imprudence. For him the styles of performances are subject to frequent changes. Only a short time ago he used to perform everything that came across with that unsavory super-expressiveness which made each piece of music appear like an exaggerated and unhealthy hothouse plant. The well-proportioned inequality, of which we talked before, was in his playing and singing distorted to an uncommensurable temporal and dynamic arbitrariness. In the meantime he discovered the more up-to-date soberness, and in comparison to his metronome-born productions we came to appreciate a rattling automaton as a sympathetically unstable and capricious contraption. One might, in fact, regret that science has not yet advanced so far as to replace his ten fingers by as many of our legendary umbrellas.

VIII

The adaptation of the keyboard from organlike instruments to those equipped with strings may have come about with no better reason than a playful desire for variety — as we have seen. No particular urgency can be discovered in that fateful step. Quite to the contrary, the accommodation to an ideal of novel sound which brought into being the host of Renaissance and Baroque instruments and later the clarinets and the saxophone, almost precluded any arbitrariness. It seems that the building material — tubes, strings, sounding boards, membranes — assumed forms and functions almost without the aid of a builder. The phantasm of a sound, hovering in the musician's minds, sought its manifestation in new instruments. These instruments, in turn, stimulate the composers' imagination; the composers invent tonal configurations which again lead the players and constructors of instruments to improvements of their crafts. It is a never-ceasing mutual provocation which inevitably leads to an exhaustion of the technical and expressive possibilities of the instruments and eventually insists on their replacement by other types.

Such mutual forming-and-being-formed of music and musical tools is a factor which lays us under certain obligations when performing the music of periods past: we must not destroy this coherence. All the traits that made music of the past lovable to its contemporary performers and listeners were inextricably associated with the kind of sound then known and appreciated. If we replace this sound by the sounds typical of our modern instruments and their treatment we are counterfeiting the musical message the original sound was supposed to transmit. Consequently, all music ought to be performed with the means of production that were in use when the composer gave it to his contemporaries.

Of course, we know the objections to this opinion. How can we restore the sounds of an earlier time without having the proper instruments? True, in many museums we find them exhibited in glass cases, but permission to practice and perform with them may either not be granted at all or else granted with extreme reluctance. If perchance we can get hold of some obsolete instruments, they will most likely be in a bad state of preservation and usually will not match in pitch. Reeds and strings of the proper type are not obtainable. Our modern accessories, being built for a heavy tone production, would, again, prevent the revival of ancient sound qualities. Assuming that all material hindrances could be overcome, no skilled players would be available.

None of these objections can be upheld. Some of the older instruments are not so entirely out of our reach, the harpsichord having been reinstated to its inherited position, and the recorders, by a long detour through kindergarten and school, slowly regaining their old importance. The use of the tenor gamba, the lute, and the clavichord is on the increase. Already it is a widely accepted conclusion that performing an eighteenth-century orchestral score with a modern piano as the continuo instrument is to be rejected as being unbearably out of style. Why should the other groups of instruments not be granted the same consideration? Enticing the benevolence of museum directors will become superfluous once we come to the decision to use replicas of old instruments unrestrictedly instead of trying to revive the mummified originals. Modern copies can be built without difficulty; they are in every respect more reliable than the models. Similarly, the strings and other accessories in their original shape can be provided by following the many directions given in old books. After all these achievements take place, some instrumentalists will doubtless specialize in the playing of the reconstructed tools. Three trumpet players, having been trained as virtuosi on the trumpets used in Bach's time and before — not their surrogates, the modern small D trumpets — thus reviving the old art of clarin playing, would inevitably be called to Bach performances over a whole continent, not to mention their prospects as teachers of a forgotten craft. Nowadays we find at some universities and other cultural institutions *collegia musica* where music of the past is performed in its original form, although hardly ever is more than the minimum number of required instruments available: a harpsichord, some recorders, and now and then a gamba or even a set of viols. Nevertheless, this is a beginning, and eventually all the historic instruments including the very early bagpipes, psalteries, trombe marine, vielles, and rubebas will again be used in performances of music written for them.

Those who have ever tried to get acquainted with the manipulation of a recorder will have discovered the difference between our modern instruments and their ancestors: the elementary technique on those revived contrivances is of an enchantingly treacherous simplicity. There is no one who, after a few harmless attempts, could not produce something that sounds pleasant; but the catch is that after the acquisition of an initial technique, which will be found sufficient for many unassuming pieces, a disproportionately steep ascent blocks the road to virtuosity. Therefore a virtuoso cornetto player will always remain a rarity, the more so as his comparatively undeveloped instrument makes his performance more hazardous and more subject to accidents than that of a clarinetist. Fortunately high virtuosity is usually not counted upon in old music. Bach's solo instrumental parts are exceptional in their demands; in general the texture of the orchestral parts is of a simple nature. A look at the orchestral pieces by Schütz or Monteverdi and a comparison with these composers' vocal technique gives us a good impression of the relatively low artistic ability of the average orchestra player in those times.

It is just this fact that presents further aggravations in our realization of old music, as it provokes the opinion that the sounds produced on the old instruments are, after the experiences with our modern ones, more than rude and undependable. Our instruments are superior, they produce perfection of sound instead of mere implications. Moreover, to our modern players with their brilliant technique the old orchestral parts provide but ridiculously small hurdles; thus the musicians' abilities would be quite out of proportion with their actual task. Surely, so one could think, the composers of the past would have preferred our perfect instruments to their own impractical tools, had they only known them. Bach must have envisioned the modern piano, since his mu-

sic sounds thin and noisy on the harpsichord. Beethoven's or even
Wagner's orchestra would have been more satisfactory to him
than the handful of musicians of moderate quality who were at
his disposal. Why, then, should we not let the dream of past musicians come true by liberating them from the shackles of their
shabby set of instruments?

If for this innocent belief in a perpetual progress of musical
achievements any support could be found in actual facts, we
would have to assume that a musician in the fifteenth century,
who in no case could foresee the conditions of our time, would at
least have dreamed of the sounds of the Bach period as the ideal
for which he wrote his pieces — sounds that in our own opinion
are just as obsolete as any other sounds of the musical past. And
what are the facts that could assure us of the perfection and finality
of the sounds used nowadays? Will not another ideal of sound
again change music's audible universe and turn our present inven-
tory of sound into one and the same state of obsolescence as
Bach's? With the more comprehensive intellectual view that dis-
tinguishes our reflections from those of our forefathers should it
not be possible to predict the kind and extent of future instrumental superperfections and then accommodate our own creations
to this vision? No; we are writing and enjoying music with
unshakable confidence in the reality of our present sounds. This
same attitude we must grant our musical ancestors. Bach wrote
with fullest conviction for the instruments of his musical environment; he was as little a seer of future musical experiences as
had been all other composers before him. To all musicians, our
contemporary ones as well as those of the past and the future,
their instruments, collectively, constitute a world of natural
growth, the appropriateness of which they must not question
so long as they retain their belief in any dignified mission of
musical art. How could a misanthropic mind that loses this belief
ever maintain a fruitful connection with music!

We saw that there exists no serious technical obstacle to the
authentic restoration of the sound of old music, yet in spite of all
our efforts the music of olden times can resurge only as a symbol
of its past reality. It is our yearning for musical revelation that
animates this symbol. Our spirit of life is not identical with that of

our ancestors, and therefore their music, even if restored with utter technical perfection, can never have for us precisely the same meaning it had to them. We cannot tear down the barricade that separates the present world from things and deeds past; the symbol and its prototype cannot be made to coincide absolutely. Even if this were possible, would it be a criterion for the value of our enterprise? Certainly not, for here, as in every other moral effort, it is not what we actually achieve that is accounted valuable, but the lofty endeavors which marked our progress towards the goal.

IX

The human voice is the instrument that has never undergone basic changes as have all the other instruments. Although it seems clear that our modern mode of singing — with the mouth and throat wide open — was not introduced before the time of the High Renaissance, it was at all times the uninhibited directness of vocal tone production, its human touch, its essential familiarity, that made singing the most easily understood and most highly appreciated form of musical reproduction. It is quite natural that with the universal familiarity of its instrument, the technique of singing reached its highest degree of perfection and virtuosity relatively early. The music of the fourteenth century demands singers of considerable technical skill, not to mention the intelligence required for reading the clumsy notation of that time and for fitting the singers' parts together with those of the accompanying players. Still other styles forced singing techniques into extreme forms of expressiveness.

Our modern vocal education has doubtless raised the average level of singers' technique and musical knowledge, and instead of producing superspecialists it aims at versatility. Yet it is not possible to produce all-round singers, who, like instrumentalists, can take over any part written for their range; for, due to the directness of vocal performance, the singer's human quality, his individual shade of tone color, and his personal expression are part of his musical reproduction to a much greater degree than in the case of the instrumentalist. Thus some form of specialization will always determine a singer's place on the concert or operatic stage, although extreme forms of such specialization are somewhat contrary to our taste; so much so, that nowadays it is rather difficult to find certain types of singers common in former times. Almost extinct is the typical Lieder singer, who, with his art of insistent and intelligent declamation, knew how to transform the small dramatic, epic, and lyric structures of his repertoire into overwhelming musical and human events. One can scarcely find singers who have the technique and stamina to perform convincingly roles like Tannhäuser or Norma, not to mention the heroes and heroines in the operas of Handel and other Baroque composers.

In one field of singing a complete deterioration has taken place. Ensemble singing — that is, singing in small groups — hardly exists except with enthusiastic fans who are determined to revive a formerly flourishing form of artistic creation. Amateurs and professionals alike brought this art of madrigalesque singing to a climax in the sixteenth and seventeenth centuries, and for such groups a literature was created that contains the most remarkable pieces ever written by musicians. The quality of a society's art of ensemble singing and the value of the compositions written to satisfy the demands of the group singers is quite likely the best gauge of a period's musical culture. This art cannot grow except in a fertile ground of general human culture, of mutual understanding and a desire to share the joy and sorrows of one's neighbor; it is dead in times of great political activity, of marked social progress, of conquest and glory, no matter how much such periods foster the more representative forms of music. Should not an art which neglects all external glamor and instead emphasizes inner musical values, thus forcing the participant into an inescapable mood of active devotion, be esteemed more highly than symphonic or operatic creations which, instead of soliciting the participant's devotion, beat him into submission? Our own time, with its overweening estimation of instrumental music, possibly in its most obtrusive orchestral form, will perhaps, in a later evaluation of music history, count as a period of lowest artistic culture, compared with those epochs in which the art of ensemble activity with the emphasis on vocal participation flourished most noticeably. I refer to the period of Machaut, Dufay, and Josquin; the time of Isaac, Senfl, Finck, Hofhaimer, and many other contributors to the art of the German *Liederbücher* in the sixteenth century; the madrigalesque style of Marenzio, Monteverdi, and other Italians; the English madrigalists; and finally, the cantatas of Bach.

As time went on, the subtle pleasure of ensemble singing gave way to the sturdier practice of choral singing, probably for the reason that in a more democratic world more people wanted to participate in the performance of music, and to them the ensemble style did not correspond with the feeling of grandiose collective effort which they put into their musical endeavors. The Venetian art of the Gabrielis and their followers introduced this style and with the Passions of Bach and Schütz it went on to its great and hitherto unsurpassed climax in Handel's oratorios. But this impressive art lost its significance in spite of the progressing democratization. It degenerated into a banal mixture of singing and social gatherings practiced in glee clubs, church choirs, and choral societies in which either the zeal of the conductor or the ambition of the choir occasionally produces something that goes beyond the limits designated by the Messiah or by the St. Matthew Passion. And yet, if there is any form of musical reproduction that is able to touch the collective feelings of large groups of people, it can only be choral singing. I am convinced that such singing, on a scale completely unknown thus far, will be one of the important forms of musical life in the future. Although it will make use of all possible achievements that an advanced knowledge of conditions of performance can provide (new instruments for accompaniment, effective means of amplifying and transmitting, adequate localities for performance), the heaviness of such tremendous musical apparatus will force the composer into stylistic considerations foreign to our present writers.

An art of this kind can never be a replacement for the cultured musical communication of ensemble singing. Nevertheless, subtlety may not entirely disappear from the musical world. Musical development may progress on lines parallel with general social advancement. After further wars, political and economic upheavals, after destruction, grief, and desolation, after the final detrition of generalissimos, führers, and dictators, a human society may emerge that in addition to its grand collective deeds strongly emphasizes the small-scale gregariousness of the individual. The reason for such gregariousness is the eternal longing for human warmth and sympathy, which can never be provided by a government-organized mass movement, and without which such mass movements would in the long run lose their driving power. If in some political theories the mass movement is proclaimed as the fulfillment of the human being's desire for mutual understanding, one should note that this is true only in times of low culture. The genuine satisfaction of such a desire is achieved in the voluntary union of individuals who may then project it onto the background of the general human community.

If the fear of earthly loneliness is the reason for all this, we may see in music the sublime way of dispelling it. Since there is no nobler way of making music than ensemble singing, we may nourish the conviction that with a clear recognition of man's collective desires a new epoch of madrigalesque musical art will spring up as an encouraging model for other collective enterprises.

# 9.

## EDUCATION

L ET us assume that a country has, at a given time, five thousand active music teachers in colleges and music schools
— a number not too high compared with the number in this country. The duty of these music teachers is, of course, to instruct
professional musicians and amateurs, and among the professionals
so instructed, new music teachers are produced. Now, if each
music teacher produces not more than two new music teachers
each year — which is not an exaggerated estimate — and if no interfering war, plague, or earthquake hinders this happy propa-
gation, the result can easily be foreseen: after the first year we
will have an additional ten thousand music teachers, in the fifteenth year every man, woman and child in the United States will
be a music teacher, and after about twenty years the entire population of our planet will consist of nothing but music teachers.

I admit that the example slightly exaggerates the results of our
teaching system, but it demonstrates clearly that we are suffering
from overproduction. There is in each country a certain capacity
for absorbing music teachers. Once the saturation point is reached,
they will either go idle or have to look for other jobs. In this
country nobody knows this fact better than the directors of music
schools and the deans of music departments. Each year the problem of finding teaching jobs for their graduates becomes more
and more desperate, because the saturation point is reached. For
musicians not looking for teaching jobs, especially for players of
string and wind instruments, the situation is not quite so gloomy.
Orchestras with their constant demand for players will be the
most natural goal for those musicians' proficiency, although here
also the danger of overproduction is imminent. The teacher, how-

ever (mainly the teacher of piano playing), has been pushed, both artistically and socially, into a hopeless position.

If such difficulties could come into existence, something must be wrong with our teaching system. What is it?

We are teaching each pianist or violinist as if he had a chance to become a Horowitz or a Heifetz, although we know that the entire concert life of the civilized world can hardly absorb more than ten or twelve great soloists in each field. Even if for regional demand in each larger country another ten are acknowledged, what in heaven happens to the remaining hundreds and thousands?

Some recognize right away that there is no chance for them on the concert stage and try to go into teaching. If they find a job, they will have to teach all their lives and mourn for a career they were prepared for without ever being rewarded for their pains and sacrifices. Others work up in their prospective career till their Town Hall recital, provided they can raise the money for its expenses. If the reviews they receive are bad, they have no other choice but to join the group that went into teaching in the first place. Good reviews mean, perhaps, a contract with a concert agent and a consequent state of slavery, compared with which the life of a bondman on a plantation is a pleasant little paradise. New expenses, hard work at establishing a repertoire, a brutal fight against competitors — and the result? For a few exceptional cases the dreamed-of concert career, for the rest again: teaching.

Among those taught by our endless phalanx of pedagogues the nonprofessional, the man who wants instruction for his own amateurish fondness of playing with musical forms, hardly counts at all. He who normally ought to be the music teacher's best customer has, as a numerical factor, dwindled to almost nothing, and as a musical factor he usually wilts away after several years of a training that, instead of flattering and fostering his layman instincts, has administered an indigestible virtuoso treatment. Thus the clan of music teachers is now living in a state of ever growing artistic isolation and infertile self-sufficiency. Their teaching of teachers who in turn teach teachers, a profession based on the resentments of the frustrated concert virtuoso and not aiming at any improvement of human society's civilization, by its very activity removed from the actual demands and duties of a real musical culture, must inevitably lead to the sad goal reached by every other kind of indiscriminate and large-scale inbreeding: after a short period of apparent refinement a gradual degeneration and slow extinction.

I have dwelt on the music teacher's (notably the piano teacher's) predicaments, because they show us in a relatively familiar field all the problems which in a more aggravated form beset the teacher of musical composition and theory. Not only is he bereft of a sound foundation for his job by the fact that, basically, artistic creativeness cannot be disseminated by teaching the multitudes, but he suffers in a higher degree from our teaching system's lack of responsibility towards human society. His teaching of the technical aspects of composition — nothing else can be taught in this discipline! — has become a highly specialized craft that in its growing isolation even from practical music drifts toward senselessness. And his teaching of theory has degenerated into merely providing embellishments to the other music teachers' course of study.

In earlier times composition was hardly taught at all. If a boy was found to be gifted for music, he was given as an apprentice into the care of a practical musician. With him he had to get acquainted with many branches of music. Singing was the foundation of all musical work. Thus singing, mostly in the form of group singing, was one of the most important fields of instruction. The practical knowledge of more or less all instruments was a *sine qua non*. Specialization was almost unknown. Frequently a musician may have been better on the keyboard than with the bow and with woodwinds or brass, but that would not have absolved him from playing as many other instruments as possible. And all this playing was done with one aim in mind: to prepare the musician for collective work; it was always the community that came first. Soloistic training was nothing but a preliminary and preparatory exercise for this purpose. Hand in hand with this daily all-round routine in instrumental training went a solid instruction in the theory of music — not only what we call theory in our modern curricula, namely harmony, counterpoint, and other branches of practical instruction, but true theory, or if you prefer another name, the scientific background of music.

This vast stock of general musical knowledge was the hotbed in which the germs of composing grew. If a musician had any talent for composition, he could always draw on this tremendous accumulation of practical experience, once he wanted to convert his ideas into audible structures. Composing was not a special branch of knowledge that had to be taught to those gifted or interested enough. It simply was the logical outgrowth of a healthy and stable system of education, the ideal of which was not an instrumental, vocal, or tone-arranging specialist, but a musician with a universal musical knowledge — a knowledge which, if necessary, could easily be used as a basis for a more specialized development of peculiar talents. This system, although it provided for the composer the best preparation possible, did not guarantee him any success. Only posterity decided whether he was to be counted among the few extraordinary creative musical figures each country had produced throughout the world, or among the many preparers and pioneers who had to blast the way for those great fulfillers, or finally among those who generalize, smooth out, and popularize the more original work of the genius.

II

Today the situation is quite different.

First of all, it is almost never the gift of composing that sends young people into this field of musical activity. Musical creative gift cannot, in my opinion, be recognized until after a rather well developed general knowledge of practical music has been acquired. If there is no such knowledge, the sole evidence of that gift can be afforded by written-down attempts at building musical structures. Usually such attempts are not at all a sign of creative talent. The minimum requirements for entering the creative field, such as a good ear for musical facts and perhaps even a feeling for absolute pitch, are too common among all people, musical or nonmusical, to be taken for the foundation upon which to build a composer's career. Their presence acknowledged, the further creative inclination of a youth inexperienced in practical music normally is the desire to express himself in some way or another. The ordinary urge to put something on paper is most readily attracted by notation symbols. Their being distinctly remote from the banalities of written language symbols, the widespread talismanic belief that by some power of their own they may turn from a vague conception into a work of art, and finally the pictorial satisfaction they give to people otherwise lacking the gift of drawing or painting — all these factors make the writing of notation symbols, following some self-imposed rules of combination, the ideal medium for minds who in their youthful innocence try to compensate for confusion and immaturity by means of exorcistic mysteriousness.

Another familiar starting point for presumptive composers is the ambition to imitate somebody whose name is known, to become a famous man, which in the opinion of most candidates can be accomplished in the field of musical creation with less effort and with a greater expectation of success than in other activities. In all these cases the driving factor is the inclination towards release of some tension — frequently but not necessarily of a general artistic nature — and not primarily a musical gift that decides in favor of composition.

True, all these factors must not be underrated. Once a workable knowledge of practical music is acquired, they can aid the assiduous mind considerably. Alone, however, unbacked by solid experience, they are of no greater value than an infant's determination to become a streetcar driver or a garbage man.

Although genuine musical knowledge is lacking, some experience with music is usually evident with those intending to enter musical composition. The main fact in their favor is that they listened most frequently and eagerly to music, predominantly in the form of records or radio transmissions, and that their actual musical activity consisted in turning the radio dial, or putting the records on the Victrola, which latter effort grew obsolete with the introduction of automatic record turners and long-playing disks and was reduced simply to an admiring and utterly unproductive attitude. The fellow who comes as a fiddler or a wind instrument player from a high-school orchestra or band and sees in the study of composition a complementary discipline of his general musical education that eventually may or may not lead him into specialization is already a rather rare bird. And the case in which people come from the place that ought to be the normal breeding ground of future composers — namely, the family that has made singing and playing a part of their daily cultural life — is almost nonexistent.

The situation we described shortly before as the ideal seems to be reversed. In former times one had to be a good musician before he could take up composing, and it was up to history to decide whether or not he was to be regarded a great creative genius. Nowadays we can be sure to find in most applicants' souls, openly shown or bashfully hidden, the conviction "I feel that I am a great creative genius, therefore people have to take me for an excellent musician"; and the equally meaningless and boastful addition "I am feeling an irrepressible urge to compose" can be taken for granted. Frequently ominous amendments follow these basic statements, such as: "I do not play any instrument, and I never had any regular instruction in theory and composition, since several attempts in this direction failed due to the fussiness of the teachers who wanted me to go through years of boring technicalities instead of promoting my creative gift; I have written many pieces, some of which have been performed and won awards; in a recent nationwide competition I won the first prize over a number of trained composers and theory teachers." We may count ourselves lucky if the courageous ignoramus does not end up with "My compositions are written in an atonal vein."

If you are a good-natured person and want to give this fellow a chance, you may ask him to submit his compositions for an examination, although you know from hundreds of preceding experiences that there is no hope of discovering a creative musician this way. Nature doubtless has her whims and sometimes permits him to appear, meteorlike, among hundreds of thousands of regular cases, unprepared, uninhibited and full of talent, energy, and fervor, and you want to assist this prodigy in coming to the fore. But despite all well-meaning midwifery, untrained natural talent has not the same chances in music that it has in poetry or painting.

In the latter arts the material is much more easily accessible, since language is everybody's property anyway, and there is nobody who does not, from his earliest childhood, have access to pencils, colors, and drawing paper and with them the possibility of acquiring some rudimentary artistic knowledge. In music, however, as in architecture and in sculpture, the materialistic obstacles that rise between the first mental conception of a creation, no matter how naïve, and its final form are stupendous and cannot be applied without a proper knowledge of the material. Ignorance in architectural or sculptural technique cannot remain cloaked. Thus our applicant turns to the gratifying mysterious symbolism of musical notation, gets doped by writing down his uncontrolled inventions, and uses notation's imperfection as the mask that deceives not only his amazed family, but first and permanently himself — and frequently the teacher and, later on, possible audiences.

Who would ever expect a young man without any experience concerning the carrying capacity of beams, pillars, and walls, or the rules of organizing living spaces three-dimensionally, to enter an architect's office with the words, "I never did anything in this field, but I am a great architectural genius"? In music, this is quite common. How common, is shown by the answer a student gave me when he was told about the years he had to spend in acquiring a decent technique, provided he showed some talent. He said, "But Mr. H., there must be some short cut." This typical remark did not properly assess the situation. Do we not know how long an extraordinary musician like Mozart had to struggle till he was able to bend, press, and mold the tonal material into the shape he wanted it? As a boy of five he wrote little compositions, at nine he was as qualified a composer as many others of that period, at twelve he had thoroughly mastered the technique of his time; yet it took him about twenty more years of his short life to write himself free from all restraints, so as to reach that superior technique — not to mention the uninhibited power to reveal his visions in musical forms — which for us is one of the intrinsic qualities of his works. No short cuts for the Mozarts! And none for other great masters. Even such an apparently

easygoing composer as Schubert — what a colossal arc of technical
and mental development he had to traverse from "Hagars Klage"
to the "Taubenpost."

### III

The most conspicuous misconception in our educational
method is that composers can be fabricated by training. If you
go through two years of Harmony, one of Counterpoint, fulfill
your requirements in Composition I and Composition II, have
some courses in Orchestration and Form, throw in some minor
courses for credits, and do some so-called "free" work in a post-
graduate course, you are inevitably a composer, because you
paid for your courses — or somebody else did — and you can expect to get something for your good money. We produce composers the democratic way, as we produce congressmen. The
citizen is by provision of the law entitled to the career of a con-
gressman, and with elbow power and persistence he merely has
to convince the majority of about three hundred thousand people
of his superiority in order to gain a seat in Washington. Why cannot the man who writes music have the same kind of a career? If
a method of production is good for one class of people, why
should it not be applied to others?

It cannot be done. Elbow power and persistence are in this field
no proof of your superiority, and seats in highest assemblies sig-
nify neither quality nor knowledge on the part of a composer.
We have never heard of a natural gift peculiar to and indispensable for congressmen, but music cannot be invented without a
specific creative talent. This talent cannot be implanted in people,
like good manners or smallpox bacilli, and composing cannot be
taught the democratic way. If there is anything remaining in
this world that is on the one side basically aristocratic and individualistic and on the other as brutal as the fights of wild animals, it
is artistic creation. It is aristocratic, because it is the privilege of a
very restricted number of people. If it could be democratized, it
would lose its quality as an art, become reduced to a craft, and
end as an industry. In many branches of our musical life we already have reached this lowest, industrial phase, as we let musical

democracy have its unbridled way. Artistic creation is individualistic, because it is as private as your dreams; nobody can interfere with your artistic phantasms, and although physical powers may prevent a work of art from coming into structural existence, the individualistic act of creation in the artist's mind can never be touched. And finally, artistic creation is excessively brutal, because works that have no strength are eliminated and forgotten like living beings that cannot survive the struggle of life, and no reasoning, no excuse can prolong their life or protect them against the crude power of the stronger work.

Although artistic creation cannot be governed and rationalized by democratic methods, although democratic methods of teaching cannot produce a creative talent, nothing is to be said against a spirit of true democracy in the admission to creative instruction, provided we develop an equally well-functioning weeding system that removes the weaklings, the unfoundedly presumptuous, and the untalented. Nowadays many are admitted to an artistic education who in former times had no chance, and with this broad accessibility we have at least reduced the possibility that a supreme artist could be overlooked or lost. But with the influx of the masses the percentage of geniuses in a population will not be increased. A fair estimate is that in our time and in countries adhering to our way of producing and consuming music, about fifty million inhabitants are needed to produce a composer of classical rank. Of course, we know that all these terms, "composer," "classic," "rank," have no accurate meaning; each of them would have to be explained and fixed in its significance before it could be used in a scientific way. But we are now talking about art, art in a very general sense at that, not art in its clearly definable technical aspects; and artistic statements in spite of their inevitable vagueness convey a rather clear meaning to those who agree to a common basis of understanding, namely to the sum total of our individual experiences with music and our knowledge of musical development at least during the last three hundred years with all its social, political, economic, in short, human implications. Fifty millions, producing one significant composer, can only mean, that after years, decades, and perhaps a century this one composer will finally be recognized as the musical apex of his epoch, but that tens of close runners, hundreds of camp followers and competitors, and thousands of miniature contributors had to do their share to make the great creator possible. However, the tragic destination of the individual will hardly ever permit him to understand his role in this gambling for future glory. In no case can he foresee the fate of his production. The creator of the surviving and significant works may not be recognized in his own time, he may feel himself to be the lowliest, the most insignificant musician; and simultaneously some minor writer may think of himself as the master mind of his time, may even see all the glory and admiration of the present bestowed on him, and yet may be forgotten before his last note is written.

If we believe in the truth of these statements, it will be hard to understand how support can be given to a system of musical education which hides this reality from the students' eyes, deceives them with each exercise they are given. It is extremely dishonest to give every student the education that is meant to turn out a Beethoven, while we know that he will never be more than a medium-sized commonplace composer. Would it not be better, more honest, and even more economical, to provide him with an all-round technique of general validity, on which his talents may thrive. In other words, don't feed people with caviar and champagne which in the long run they cannot digest, but bring them up with a solid fare and teach them to appreciate the extraordinary as a unique donation of heaven. Tell the student: "The gift of composing is nothing that exists by itself, nor can it be nursed and trained separately. It is the fruit of a plant, this plant being the entity of musical experience and talent of a musician. We cannot have healthy and sturdy fruits, if the plant is weak and underdeveloped. Consequently we must first of all raise a healthy plant. It will bear its fruits in time, and we may even have the chance to produce an extraordinary prize-winning fruit. If our labor is not to be blessed with the production of a fruit, we at least have the satisfaction of having done our utmost to raise a healthy plant."

And, for heaven's sake, have the courage to discourage his ambitions as a composer, if his productions are worthless as an artistic communication.

## IV

Once this conviction has become our pedagogic credo, we will have to change our education of composers entirely. In fact, we will have to reconvert it into the old, solid, and reasonable system of teaching described above — the system that was, by a wave of general megalomania, distorted into our production line, the result of which can only be battalions of composing mediocrity. This means that practical music would again be the backbone of instruction, composing would not be taught as an end in itself, no illusions would be implanted in the minds of students. Fewer composers would be produced, but the few who grew out of the fertile field of general musicianship would have better prospects of surviving and representing our time than hundreds of half-gifted or ungifted writers. One figure who is nowadays the most deplorable product of our system of education would disappear entirely: the composer who is unable either to sing or to play his own composition, who has to rely entirely on the ability and the good will of other performers. Our era is unique in having produced this pseudomusician, and for this sin alone our educational system deserves every punishment possible.

Trained in this old and renewed system — if the most natural musical activity can be called a system — composers would again be musicians, who could be used in many fields of music equally well; who are useful players, not of one instrument, but of several; who sing acceptably, who know how to handle classes, choirs, and orchestras; who have a decent knowledge of theory, and beyond all, who certainly know how to compose. For them the idea of extreme specialization is abhorrent. They must be good performers, but never at the expense of their comprehensive musicianship. If amidst this wealth the gift of composing shows up, it will be fostered by all possible means, but even then always with the understanding that composing is never a profession, that it can hardly be regarded as a job which nourishes its proprietor, and that the talent may one day cease to yield further fruits, or may disappear altogether, just as mysteriously as it appeared. There will be little similarity to those frequent products of our average instruction: the fellow full of vanity and empty of real erudition; and the other fellow, who caught, along with some wisdom, all the frustrations a never-fulfilled aspiration creates.

Teaching according to these maxims, I never found vanity or frustration as a result. How can you be conceited if the overwhelming number of musical facts you can learn makes you conscious of your smallness every moment of your musical existence? And how can you be frustrated, if you know composing is not necessary unless the creative talent shows up unexpectedly? Musicians brought up this way will by the very nature of this instruction see their initial enthusiasm preserved throughout their musical career; disappointment in their vocation will most likely remain unknown to them.

Once I had a discussion on this subject with a well-known composer. He said: "I think your system of teaching composers is all wrong. It discourages young people, to face an almost unsurmountable heap of knowledge and technique. When I studied with a famous teacher in Europe, every student in the class had the feeling that he was the elected genius of the future, that the piece he was writing right now was superb, and that it was merely a question of time and practice before his fate as a successful composer was confirmed." The response to this reproval is: If one cannot face the obstacles lying before a composer's career he should not be permitted to embark upon it at all. Why must an apprentice composer be wrapped in cotton, when instrumentalist students come in touch with those obstacles from the very first day in obvious and mostly discouraging forms? Certainly it is not necessary to emphasize obstacles, but an honest teacher can never hide them. And what else is the result of a constantly flattering instruction but a pampered egotist who to the end of his life will be the only one convinced of his greatness, when everyone else ceased to share this opinion shortly after the performance of his first composition? There is but one conclusion that can be drawn from these statements: Don't teach composition the way it is usually done. Teach musicians. If once in a long while one of your students shows creative talent, let nature have its course. A fellow educated in the way here described will use all his manifold experiences to the right purpose, and what you can teach him beyond all this is more valuable than the teacher's instructing a pupil: it is the united effort of two equals in the search of perfection, in which the one participant is mostly but not always leading, for his is the greater experience.

v

Knowing that in spite of our teaching methods creative talents find their way to the surface, one is inclined to believe in the old adage, "Good teachers are nonexistent; there are only good students." Since, as stated before, nothing but the technical part of a composer's work can be covered by organized instruction, a teacher may not be able to prevent the unfolding of a talent; on the other hand, he may unduly delay the student's development either by applying bad methods or by forcing him into technical and stylistic realms alien to his peculiar talent. Furthermore, he may, by arousing false hopes and pushing nontalents, ruin the mental capacity of many otherwise useful musicians. Provided we had a valuable and nevertheless generally accepted system of musical education and we knew accurately what had to be done in individual cases to make them blossom and ripen, the quality of the teacher would still remain as a factor of uncertainty. This is true, of course, in all branches of scientific and artistic instruction, yet in teaching musical composition this uncertainty perpetually threatens like an overshadowing cloud the relation between teacher and student. The technique that can be taught corresponds roughly with the subject matter of our fifth chapter, although the conclusions there drawn are (and will remain for some time) ideal requirements which for many teachers are of no practical value. If uncertainty prevails concerning the apparently so well-known basic truths of music and their technical application, we cannot expect any clear-sighted confidence in the other intellectual and emotional aspects as shown and discussed in the other chapters of this book. They are beyond all technique, lofty and evasive, and cannot be brought within the regulating fences of a normalized teaching system that will give an account of their presence; no marks and credits can honestly be given for their achievement. Here from the very beginning it is artistic talent and artistic achievement that count; the clumsy net of our scholastic evaluation cannot catch them.

This is the reason why many teachers who according to school standards are of low quality frequently ignite whatever little spark of creative talent slumbers in a student; their mediocrity cannot live up to our school system's standardized norms; and thus, in avoiding the schedule-prescribed rigid treatment, they involuntarily allow the student all the individuality and imagination his artistic development demands. And it is the reason for the failure of many decent composers to become useful teachers; their idealistic comprehension of music cannot submit to the prosaic yoke of schedule dictatorship.

If imagination is the agent that, over and above the acquirement of a reliable technique, ought to direct a future composer's instruction, we must accuse the majority of our teachers of a lack of this quality. They were brought up in a rigidly regulated system of exams, term papers, marks, and credits, and cannot think of any better method. Unacceptable to them is the irregular though sometimes successful way of the nonfitting teacher, but equally repulsive to them is the composer who without any pedagogic principle and regularity just lives an exemplary musical life which is more instructive to the students than all scholastic rules. It is the average teachers' unshakable belief in the stiff corset of schedules that is supposed to keep their pedagogic posture in shape, and they do not want to see that corsets are neither salutary nor fashionable. A superregulated bureaucracy, in our everyday life a mere ridiculous nuisance, grows into a disease with frequent fatal issue when applied to the arts and their instruction.

The teaching of music theory, intended to acquaint the student with the composer's working material and its treatment, has in our teaching system been degraded to a tedious educational by-product, which is presented without any relation to practical music and is accepted listlessly and practiced drearily. Students majoring in theory must, as a rule, be taken as the most deplorable products of our musical education. If you are totally ungifted for playing an instrument or singing, if you don't care for music history, even if you lack the least musical talent, there still is hope

for you as a theory major. You just fill several quires of staff paper
with dull harmonic progressions, sour counterpoints, and finally
some imitations of old motets and fugues, and in due time you
will receive your degree. By that time you have, of course,
learned how to pound simple harmony exercises on the piano,
and that is entirely sufficient for your future job.

What is such a fellow's future job? What else could he become
but a theory teacher? For him the corset of scholastic regulations
is not a mere support: it is, as in Poe's story of "the truly fine-
looking fellow, Brevet Brigadier-General John A. B. C. Smith"
(the man who without his artificial arm, bosom, eye, et cetera,
was just "a large and exceedingly odd-looking bundle of something"), the only means of keeping him upright. Hunting consecutive fifths is one of his favorite activities; with his beginners'
classes he reaches the six-four chord every year precisely on the
fifteenth of November; the species of Fux's counterpart are the
limits of his musical horizon; correctness is everything, live music
nothing. His ambition is to add to the wealth of old regulations
new ones; and meetings, conventions, and conferences with
other theory teachers, appointed for that very purpose, are to him
a godsent confirmation of his importance in our cultural setup.
Reaching mature age, he usually publishes his own textbook on
harmony, which is the thousandth rehash of the all-too-well-
known sterilized schoolbook rules.

We must admit that in spite of our criticism there are good
teachers of composition and theory who are aware of the debilities of our teaching system and try to reduce them and to improve
our methods by all the means in their power. They are the mi-
nority. The type here described is abundant; its representatives
are those who drive the intelligent student into the wilderness of
pseudomusical problems. Such a student cannot avoid seeing our
teaching system's sole purpose: the perpetuation of a composing
and teaching mediocrity, its leading up to a certain point of superficial traditional training and then, as an act of self-defense,
its refusal to give satisfactory answers to justified questions. For
the conservative teacher, nothing that could be analyzed and
systematically taught lies beyond this point, and for the more
liberal instructor there exist, for the most part, only decisions

based on vague aestheticisms, on stylistic preferences, on personal inclinations; in short, it is nothing but taste, good or bad, that is the guide through the vast regions not covered by traditional theories and teaching methods.

The situation is extremely unpleasant, both for the conscientious teacher and for the intelligent student. They need and want a better system of teaching theory and composition. For them no effort in establishing and introducing it must be spared. On the other side, the average teachers and those below average will always be opposed to improvements, because everything that disturbs their complacency is unwelcome, and furthermore they will never admit that they spent their life in working for something hopeless and fruitless. It is remarkable that people who are improving their households by buying the newest models of refrigerators, washing machines, television sets, and cars, are in their teaching profession clinging to old Goetschius and Kitson and many similarly antimusical textbooks which in an age of the aforementioned appliances are as outmoded as kerosene lamps.

If our system of teaching composition and theory has to be changed, we must not only get rid of the kerosene lamps but also of the anachronistic spirit that goes with them. A rejuvenation cannot start with changing the attitude of the students. They are young anyway, and the gifted ones usually know what education is supposed to give them. For the untalented crowd there need not be any serious professional instruction in composition and theory; for them a well-organized information service would suffice, and no jobs as composers or theory teachers should be made available for them. Our resolutions will never become materialized if we do not begin to remodel the viewpoints of our teachers. There is no hope for any improvement unless they abandon a trend which in pioneer times and their nonartistic life perhaps was a necessity, but in our time is an atrophying burden of musical education: the belief that a rigid scholastic regulation by marks, credits, and all the other frozen procedures of an outdated system can produce composers and theorists of a quality that our music-minded society has a right to demand.

# 10·

## BUSINESS MATTERS

A NEGATIVE photograph is necessary if we want to have the positive picture. The finished product in its convincing likeness to nature must go through a state of ugly reversion, in which light is shadow, white is black, right is wrong, and good is bad. Nevertheless, this reversion, useless as a picture in its own right and showing us the objects as we are never wont to see them with our own eyes, is just as real as the final reproduction. Without some experience the exact pictorial values of the positive cannot be clearly appreciated in the negative, yet even the untrained observer recognizes the inseparable union of the two pictorial forms.

The statements to be made in the present chapter need to be understood as such a picture with negative hues. They are not meant as a negative coming freshly out of the developer; rather, they are supposed to be one that has been used many times for copies. The reason for using the negative in this chapter is our more than sufficient knowledge of its positive form. It has been shown to us too many times, and in too many flattering finishes at that, its glossy, colored, magnified, and drastically retouched surface having absorbed all our attention and distracted our critical mind from the actual subject in question. Probing the basic facts of our musical existence, as we do in this book, we must not be satisfied with the superficial impression of a splendid reproduction that captivates the lay spectator's admiration: we must join the expert in his analysis of the negative, before he turns the copying-frame towards the light.

You have written a composition. Let us assume that its position in our musical setup, your own relation to your work, and your intention to secure a place for it in the actual process of supply and demand could be photographed, and let us evaluate the negative of the picture so obtained.

You will hardly think of your composition as a creation with an independent life, severed from its place of origin and going its own way; you rather like to look at it as a part of your own soul, belonging to you alone and to your joy and pain. On the other hand, involuntarily and immediately it grows into an object of realistic speculation. You have to take it as a manufactured product which must be brought into circulation and which has to reach its customer.

A musical work has this charming quality: unlike creations of the pictorial arts, where existence is established once and for all, it will, by the constant necessity of reproduction, always re-create in you and in others the original generative process. It will revive many times the sensations evoked by its growth from a mere notion through meditation and many technical operations to the finished form, thus soliciting to a higher degree than with the other arts the recipient's intellectual and emotional participation. This quality is invariably offset by the atmosphere of abject commercialism into which the musical composition inevitably plunges right after the moment of its release; there are involved in its reproduction too great a number of noncreative factors and persons, each with individual interests and demands that vulgarize every noblest effort. Unless you want to keep your work in a state of infertile, secluded inactivity, you must expel it into the jungles of our musical life; into regions governed by anything but artistic considerations; into operations too prosaic and trite for the distribution of other artistic products. The curse of which we spoke earlier, namely, the ability of a musical work to touch with eloquence both the highest human intellect and the lowest and haziest emotion is its companion throughout its existence. This curse cannot be eliminated by the artist's attitude towards his art. Neither can it be absorbed by the idealist's denial of worldly powers, nor will it be rendered innocuous by a realistic accord with its brutality.

In the blunt realities of our musical life, what are the factors that you as a composer of a prospective market product will have to take into account?

You need a performer. Most desirable, from the artistic point of view, would be the composer as performer. Not only is this combination time-hallowed, continuing the tradition of the great masters from Leonin to Brahms: it guarantees reproduction in the true spirit of the work. But the composer's labor, if pursued with conviction and with a desire to conquer all technical hurdles, must of necessity be a full-time job with only a little time left for keeping you fit as a player or singer and as a serious competitor of the professional performer, whose job is, again, a full-time occupation. Conducting, however, is an activity which, because of its comparatively limited technical requirements, can be achieved with less time and effort spent in practicing; and since you as composer know your score anyway (we hope!), your chances of being the best interpreter of your orchestral works are perhaps more promising than your other possible pursuits as a performer. Whether you will be given the opportunity of employing these chances is doubtful, if you are not respected as a decent conductor and your reputation as a composer has not risen far beyond the average. Even then, the regular conductor of an orchestra will cede his place only reluctantly, since he prefers to think of himself as the only authoritative performer of a new piece — a form of self-confidence which honors its possessor but which in many cases certainly is not warranted; besides, everyone thinks he has to do something for contemporary music, and even if the majority of pieces are not worth the pains spent in studying and performing them, who would miss the faint possibility of having first drawn into the limelight the great composer of the future? Players and singers follow similar considerations. Thus your first public steps as a fledgling composer are most likely taken under the intellectual, economic, musical, and moral sponsorship of a performer. This is like one of those strange cases of symbiosis, or rather, parasitism in plant or animal life, in which one organism dwells in complete dependence on another. Look at the host's pensioner! The immediate worries of life are removed from him, no dangerous fights for survival occur, there is no search for daily bread. The host keeps his companion alive, for perhaps the miserly fellow may in certain situations be of some advantage. He in his mollycoddled softness does not mind being kept in a state of indigence, and for the host he is not much of a burden anyway.

If you possess a strong creative talent and if you build up your musical world according to the blueprints shown in this book you will never become the partner of a symbiotic half-existence. You will be superior to your supposed benefactors. You may not go beyond them in their own specialized skill, but your musical activity will from the beginning surpass their ever-repetitious routine. You will be at home in regions which they in their inability to hurdle the fences of their petty vanity, officiousness, and jealousy will never enter. Do not expect to gain many friends among the performing specialists, once you reach this realm of quality, conviction, and independence. Be prepared for disrespect, boycott, and slander, but nevertheless trust in the strength of your work which, if it really bears all the hallmarks of genuine creation, has more chances of surviving than all the reproductions coming from keyboards, batons, strings, and tubes. And if by the adversity of circumstances your work is bound to disappear early, just as the performer's work disappears, should you not be comforted with the idea that yours was the creative talent which they so eagerly but vainly craved to own!

II

All this is well enough for the established and recognized creator. But as long as we are not sure that we belong to this rank, although potentialities and hope may boost our work and strengthen our ambitions, how can we fix our eyes on the far horizons if our next steps are on uncertain ground? And what if we feel within ourselves nothing more than a mere solid musicianship which in order to produce its best must not be strained to its limits — a gift that does not find its nourishment in deceptive promises of future glories but needs some friendly pampering?

We must face reality. Our compositions, although not of superior quality, have a right to be heard and we shall try everything possible in order to use the mechanisms of our society's musical system to our fullest advantage. After all, the world's — especially the democratic world's — institutions are made for people like ourselves, and the genius, being privileged in his field of talent, may see for himself how he is coming along. Let him proceed without compromise; we do not want to delay our successes.

We shall, as we always did, send our compositions to conductors, pianists, fiddlers, and singers. Letters of recommendation, written by prominent people who had to be pestered to write them, will be added. All our little achievements, the last singular performance will be mentioned, to prompt our prospective performers: do your duty, help struggling talent, foster our modern music, make your listeners acquainted with the new trends in our art! We do not want to be told that our scores are part of a heap of similar strugglers dumped on the far edge of our victim's writing desk and looked at with scornful ennui. A politely evasive rejection we shall not take as an expression of a routine that has grown from sympathetic disappointment to impatient disgust. A performance, appointed after painful hesitation and receiving neither acclaim nor a repetition elsewhere, we shall cherish as the just reward of our honest ambition and as progress towards the longed-for aim of our artistry, fame.

We want to go still further! All publicity shall be ours. Not only will we keep every Sunday issue of the local papers informed about our projects and their progress; the metropolitan papers also must not be left without a permanent trickle of news. We want to see our name appear in their columns as often as possible and we like to think of all other people as being possessed by the same passion on our behalf. Postal cards we send to one and all, announcing each instant spent in a nondescript performance of our products by any obscure radio station. Let us give interviews, let us have our picture taken, let us appear in radio and television. Now and then the stupendous wheeling of the publicity machine may produce a lone, less-than-average, and soon forgotten performance, but several such events will add up to a rather impressive sequence, they will blaze the trail for our future creations, and thus we will eventually, by sheer weight of numbers, receive our share of glory which our talent would never have earned.

We want our pieces to be spoken of. Reviews of their scattered performances of our pieces are of the utmost importance. Please do not tell us of the famous music critics' lack of time and interest to study our work seriously. Let us uphold our illusion of their being gifted with superhuman divination, musical knowledge, and unalterable good will. Let us on a ground of mutual toleration be satisfied with those many provincial critics' injudicious reviews which, with their important authors' picture added, do their best to spread musical ignorance among people otherwise willing and open-minded towards unknown music. Even bad and stupid reviews will make our name known, and for us middle-sized producers this is just what we want, not being gifted with the great musicians' impatience anyway and lacking the fighting spirit of superior artists of the past from the Renaissance to Wagner who frequently enough disposed of bad critics.

Of course we want our music to be printed and published. Since no publisher can afford the continuous printing and distribution of pieces that never will cover their expenses, and since few sales and scarce performances can never bring a piece out of the red, we shall always trust in certain beneficial funds for so-called cultural purposes that make publication possible. The cheapest kind of production, to be sure! Engraving of piano and chamber music pieces is too costly; it will be replaced by the reproduction of a copyist's more or less legible handwriting. Photostated copies of our own ill-written orchestral scores and parts will suffice for the few performances to be expected. No ambitions as to the looks of a publication! And never any financial returns to us, the composers. On the contrary, we may even consider paying part of the expenses.

We know of the other kind of publisher, the fellow who buys and sells compositions as other dealers handle potatoes. With him nothing counts but the supply and demand of the market; the composer he publishes is a mere provider of cheapest trash, his musical orientation oscillating between tin-pan alley and Broadway, and no business will be entered into that does not promise an immediate return of five or more dollars for each dollar spent. Here one can make his fortune as soon as he finds the tune that can be whistled by everyone. Needless to say, we are not the type of musician that fits into this scheme. Apart from the fact that nobody ever will whistle our tunes, we want to be understood as being the heirs of a great past. Ours is an idealistic belief in the nobleness of our art. (Frankly, it is a belief with a safety valve: there is always some hope that we will be counted among those rare writers in whose drudgery, mediocrity, and obscurity is hidden — perhaps unrecognized even by its owner — the divine fire of original creation, only to be discovered by later generations.)

### III

Well, if you don't want to be dragged into the simple and brutal system of musical commercialism, yet if the laurels of the great composer seem to be either temporarily or permanently unattainable, there are other ways and means not only of bolstering your ego but of leading you to a specific brand of fame. You merely need to use the word "American" constantly in respect to music, and particularly in respect to your own music. How many recommending facts about this kind of musician have we not been told! Some had ancestors among Leif Ericson's crew; others had no other musical education than listening to the horses' neighing on a midwestern farm, their birthplace; still others wrote their scores on the whitewashed walls of a county jail, and so forth. The fact that nobody has ever defined clearly what "American" actually means when referring to musical talent, technique, style, and taste, must not disturb you. You can never go wrong in betting on musical nationalism, for too many of our contemporaries are spellbound by it.

Let us look at the facts without mockery. It doubtless is encouraging to see in a country all native talent supported. Even a disproportionate support, if not driven to the extreme, is understandable and excusable. The exaggerated recognition of the native composer's works is far more sympathetic than the practice in some old-world countries with a long musical tradition, of treating the musical compatriot with suspicion and seeing in him a priori a musician with a comparatively minor talent. There it was the permanent overproduction of fairly high-ranking composers that made people snooty in their evaluation and caused them to always look beyond their countries' narrow boundary lines for new and stimulating talents. Musical nationalism was unknown; the nationality of the composer was taken for granted and was not used for an assessment of his artistic achievements.

Only during the last century was musical nationalism born and it had its cradle in countries without a tradition of art music. Nationalism was the simplest way of bringing their few and comparatively poorly equipped musicians to the fore, since everyone was willing, for a while at least, to enjoy national color, manners, and fashion instead of classical grandeur, mastery, and compelling seriousness. Today one knows the true rank of those figures who took shape only against a backdrop of national colors; and although new national composers, supported with all the fervor of their governments, continue to throw their pieces on the market, their glory usually is weak and short-lived. The golden age of musical nationalism seems to be gone.

It is all the more miraculous that the United States with an abundance of musical talent, hailing originally from all countries and being in the process of amalgamating into one homogeneous body of musical culture, has to resort to the petty nationalism of the musically half-cultured minor countries of the past century. If the epithet "American" were used as a plain and sober trademark similar to that accompanying bulldozers, razor blades, and nylons on their way to faraway places, nobody would object. But it is the sentimental display of an overwhelming and nationwide feeling of artistic inferiority compensated for by loudness that is so disturbing, the more so because it uses all the means of publicity, foreign relations, and economic superiority, to emphatically demand recognition for something which, like any other art, is for its production entirely independent from a nation's prosaic way of life. If up till now the recognition of this fact is in this country neither understood nor desired, because one prefers being lulled into a dream of easily achieved artistic glory, other countries have not been quite so ready to surrender unconditionally to the mass attacks of American musical importation. In spite of insistent pressure exerted on the rest of the world with the aid of economic and political influence, and in spite of many well-meaning assurances to the contrary, American compositions have not yet achieved an important or stable place in the world's concert programs, although certain American compositions can endure the stiffest competition with other countries' contemporary productions. In a spirit of well-meaning democracy, which, according to our former statements, is ineffective in the field of artistic creation, good American pieces were exported together and under the same label with a host of insignificant and sometimes revolting items, and the consumers, baffled by so disorganized a display, never gained a true impression of this country's abilities and potentialities. (The same democratic spirit could prove statistically such and such a number of performances of this or that piece, yet could hardly provide totals that match those of some of the contemporary standard works.)

Everyone knows a good car from a bad one. Composers obviously are not measured by a corresponding scale. They are leveled over by the term "American" like a hilly landscape in a blanket of snow. Suppressing superior talent in favor of a dime-a-dozen quality, this term has in place of its distinguishing meaning assumed an almost minimizing designation. It will be the duty of the more than average talent to live up to supernational standards, and by a detour via general and international acclaim of his work to restore the simple, honest, and honorable meaning of a term of proud distinction.

Don't misunderstand or misinterpret me. Nothing is said against a composer's national peculiarities; on the contrary. We all have our roots somewhere, and the more they are fastened in the native soil the more profitable it will be for our production. But I object to the misuse of a basically good thing, to its serving as a coverage for obvious debilities and as an excuse for a vulgar dilettantism, abundant here as elsewhere, to enjoy the same rights as the man who contributes with his work to the beautification of the world and the glorification of his native country.

It seems that the wishful thinking of an entire nation cannot breathe long-lasting life into a composition that simply is not endowed with vitality. The majority of new pieces, after having anemically overcome their *première*, hardly ever have enough stamina left to stagger along to a second performance. Some, especially chamber music pieces, appear sporadically, pushed into the foreground by the patriotic good will of a quartet society and its patient listeners. And in exceptional cases the presumptive national hero makes a dazzling appearance, shines for two or three seasons in utter brilliance, only to recede into darkest oblivion without ever again reappearing. The most fervent advocates of musical nationalism — conductors, players, and critics alike — after having praised a piece (mostly before its first hearing), will never undertake a second performance or a later revival, once it becomes clear that again a hope was shattered, a prophecy left unfulfilled. Of those other compositions which outlive several seasons and perhaps after decades will still be found going strong, we can assume that no faked nationalistic conjurations were delivered at their cradle.

IV

In branding musical nationalism as a superfluous, perhaps even pernicious, factor in our musical situation, our hopes of convincing other composers and their understanding sympathizers were not too strong. Theirs may be an unshakable belief in the beneficial influence of a chauvinist attitude on the production, reproduction, and reception of music, and if in replacing a high musical morality with cheap surrogates they feel their musical orbits completed, we can do nothing but deplore their bigotry and in our own relations to music limit ourselves to composers with a more genuinely musical conduct. The neutral bystander will probably find either attitude ridiculous, for the enjoyment music is supposed to provide is all he wants, and the professionals' specialized interests are something alien to this simple desire.

Once you decide in favor of nationalism, why don't you proceed further on the road of success-promising factors which are equally close to the exterior turmoil of musical life and equally far away from the genuine, quality-determining criteria of our own creed? There is the ever-pleasant hunt for prizes, awards, scholarships, and grants. By this I do not mean the aid lent you during your school years, nor do I hint at the meritorious artists and scientists who without considerable financial support could not complete important projects. What I mean is that form of organized laziness and evasion which young, unknown composers may enjoy if they have patience enough to write application after application and wait till the next award is granted. The chances for this are pretty good, since in this giant country, in which no ministry of cultural affairs takes care of the development of the arts and no coördinated system of distributing awards exists, the composer is almost in the same agreeable situation as his colleague in some of the tiny European states: with the money of numerous foundations available, one is bound to catch a prize sooner or later. You can develop your ability of winning prizes to a high degree. You just apply the glider technique of aviation: learn how to use the most favorable current of air. I know of quite a number of composers — mind you, not senile fellows but men in their prime — who lived on grants for twelve or more years here or in Europe, who, although having no fortune of their own, never faced the reality of earning their living in a normal musician's job. This would be right if their creations had turned out to be the fulfillment of a nation's expectations. Have we ever heard of such compositions? I doubt it.

You have heard my opinion. You, contrary-minded, may believe in your right to utilize every chance, disregarding its effect on your morale as a composer. And the neutral bystander, mentioned above, may, in his good-naturedness and his common bad conscience in respect to the arts, agree to any arrangement that frees him of obligations and gives the other fellow a chance, no matter how undeserved.

Now go ahead on your road of calculated successes to the next station. Enter one of the many clinics for composers, conducted every summer all over the country. You feel that in spite of your degree of master in music you are far from showing any mastery in your compositions, and a refresher course under clinical assistance would cure your ailments. Don't you see the fallacy of this idea? Those being supposedly in charge of your treatment are frequently in no better state of compositional health than the patients. They are by no means immune against the attacks of the morale-killing viruses of our musical life, and no doctor's license protects the health-seeking composer from quackery. Clinics are a continuation of our school system's tendency to release everyone from personal responsibility for failures. Your school teachers were entrenched behind a wall of marks and grades. They never developed a fairly accurate system of correspondences between grade numbers and the artistic and technical quality of musical exercises, yet they believe in their own arbitrary numerical deci-

sions as they do in celestial manifestations. It is never thought to
be the fault of a teacher or a teaching system if you leave school
insufficiently instructed, nor is it your lack of talent or your laziness or your aversion to the way in which the material is presented that makes you an unsuccessful student; you just "didn't
make the grades." In this purified paradise of numerical evaluation nobody will ever be responsible for his decisions. Individualities vanish behind numbers, and your college record as the
inevitable forerunner of your applications for jobs gives as clear
an indication of your intellectual and artistic capacities as your
portrait drawn by a baby would give of your physical constitution.

Sometimes in your studies of theory and composition, when
you felt that a particularly inspired and well-expressed phrase
received a bad mark, you probably became aware of this irresponsible system's incapacity to evaluate any artistic endeavors and
achievements. Due to its debilities it could not teach you what
you needed; yet here you are again in a clinic, undergoing the
same treatment, the difference being merely a shift of the inherent irresponsibility: since a great creative personality would
never be the curer or the cured in such a clinic, the members *in
toto* must, as an act of self-justification, refuse to acknowledge
the fruitlessness of any attempt at a collective treatment of the
most individualistic of all activities, artistic creation.

As a member of a composer's clinic you are in the exclusive
company of your fellow patients. A layman's opinion will not
penetrate the protecting wall of professionalism around your san-
itarium. This is good for you, because for the rest of his life he
probably would always see in a composer an incurable weakling.
But in one particular case of pseudo success you rely on the layman; in fact, you force him into a situation of complicity. This
is when you pronounce yourself a "composer in residence." We
know what you want to express with this term: I am giving you,
the layman, the honor of my presence in your community. The
layman, somewhat baffled, accepts the unexpected gift, since he
feels too uneasy to protest against the intrusion of a basically
harmless fellow. He does not feel competent enough to have a
definite opinion, and so does not object to a slightly possible

enrichment of his city's musical life, especially since no extra expenses are involved. Sometimes he may even go so far as to bestow on a composer the homely and inexpensive title, thus in his insecurity outdoing the destitute, shelter-seeking musical creator. If he was really sure of himself, he would most likely share our own opinion: namely, that the term "composer in residence" is the deplorable expression of a dissatisfied composer's desire to surround himself with an aura of faked importance as a compensation for his meaninglessness in an environment that is not at all concerned with his problems.

v

Finally, never forget to assert your modernity. The proclamation of one's modernity is the most efficient cover for a bad technique, unclear formulations, and the lack of personality. Not only that! Writing what is called modern music lifts you automatically into a world-wide society of composers with similar tendencies. The inevitable overweight of inefficiency in such a society must sooner or later tend towards the protection of the feeble composer and to an escape from the brutal selection of quality in the normal course of musical life. Thus a solitary, esoteric style will be the result, the well-known kind of secret language understandable only to the initiated, removed from any musical desires of an ordinary music lover and thriving under hothouse conditions. No wonder, then, that clashes occur whenever a piece of this kind appears in our commonplace concert life; that the situation is created which was described earlier in this book: The so-called modernist composer and the ordinary concert-goer, each following his own line of interest and totally disregarding the other's considerations, are drifting apart and the gap between them is widening with each further performance of an obscure piece.

If you want to follow the practice of most of your colleagues you will not ask what are the facts that caused this deplorable situation. Never will it occur to you that the composer may be guilty, that the consumers are not the only ones to be blamed. You rather accept the situation as an inalterable fact, grown out of historical necessity; as an unfavorable condition into which we are born. On this basis you will not cease to make your complaints heard: The neglect of our modern music is a burning disgrace; we shall not become the martyrs of the general conspiracy against our works! And then you meet with your fellow sufferers in international, national, and local societies for contemporary music; you arrange festivals, symposia, and anything else for the propaganda of your products and those of your fellow highbrows. In short, the entire machinery of promotion as shown in the preceding pages, is starting its noisy gyration.

Besides the fact that this bustling activity rather hampers the appreciation of contemporary compositions instead of helping it, the situation is not what you want us to believe. I think it would be quite impossible to find anywhere in this country a new composer who was not at least once given an opportunity of having a piece of his performed. Even if you want to hide yourself and wish your compositions kept away from a performance, somebody will snatch your manuscripts away and you cannot avoid hearing them broadcast over the nearest radio station. A first performance of a new composer's piece, no matter how good or bad it is, is almost unescapable; the undiscovered budding genius is a legendary figure of the past. Quite another matter is the step from the first to the second performance of a piece, or to the performance of a second piece. As repeatedly mentioned, many professed composers, perhaps the majority, never succeed here. It would be easy to accuse all those who arranged the very first performance of ungrateful forgetfulness. Might it not be that the composer actually did not live up to the expectations his erstwhile promoters and listeners nourished? It is risky for him not to take this possibility — or preferably, probability — into account. Better watch yourself and analyze the situation and also your composition's quality and position carefully before with hurt egotism you turn toward the world of sham successes I tried to depict.

# 11·

## ENVIRONMENT

THE negative picture, shown in the preceding chapter, must be converted to its positive form if a healthy influence on our musical situation is to be exerted by the combined efforts of our contemporary creators of music. How this can be done and what the auspices for such influence are will be discussed in the concluding paragraphs of the present chapter. Before we reach this point we must accompany a composition still further on its progress through its musical sphere of life.

With the nonrealistic, ideal form of this progress we have become acquainted in the earlier chapters of this book. The ethical and moral aspects of music, the participants' intellectual and emotional share in the audible realization of a composition, the principles governing the technique of constructing musical forms — all these factors are beyond the reach of our personal opinions and passions. Your manner of looking at those basic facts may differ from mine, conclusions we draw may not coincide, the greatest diversity may appear in their practical application; yet we have no power to change their eternal truth. The realistic part of the composition's course of life, on the other hand, is very much dependent on external circumstances, and the creative musician must, as we have seen, possess a navigator's sense and knowledge in order to steer his craft through barriers, high seas, and shoals — provided of course that it is seaworthy.

Now, as much as I like to assign a just part of the responsibility for success or lack of success to the composer himself, I do not ignore the existence of many hindering factors over which he has no control. There are many good pieces waiting for performances, and there are versatile composers who are unjustly denied the successes they desire and deserve. True, in most cases we can readily understand the reasons for this, though all our understanding cannot change the situation. In others we are entirely ignorant of the causes and have to accept the inconsiderate decisions of fate as final, since we are as powerless against the blind forces of life, growth, decay, and death in a composition's existence as we are in our own.

The form of appearance a musical work assumes may, in spite of all the good intentions of its creator, have no immediate appeal to the consumer. In sound, technique, and style unfamiliar arrangements may demand a long period of accustoming to be appreciated. The artistic attitude, the human quality of the composer, recognizable in his work, may remain inarticulate. The audible equivalent of his personal restraint may curtail the penetrating power of his work. And finally, a piece may demand means of performance which in prevailing circumstances are unavailable. One should be aware of these facts and not expect either improbable achievements of his works nor impossible reactions of the consumer. If the creative mind is incapable of lucid manifestations, the recipient cannot be expected to build his satisfaction on a ground of guesswork.

Then there are the fluctuations of the market, so to speak. Periods in which contemporary works of art are relatively highly esteemed alternate with others in which the general trend is averse to novelty. Sometimes a relapse into a period of predominant taste for traditional forms of expression may come as an understandable reaction against a forced cultivation of modernism. The reckless ambition of producers, the snobbishness of sponsors, the performers' hectic hunt for sensation may have caused an atmosphere of apparent prosperity in which modernism mushroomed indiscriminately, only to spoil the chances of the less spectacular, more solid product for a long time. Mostly, however, contemporary pieces play only a minor role in our musical life; we prefer to surround ourselves with the musical treasures of the past. Why that is so, nobody actually knows. The only plausible explanation seems to be modern man's tendency to escape from the irritating and insecure present into a world of rather firmly established values, the more so since this can be done (as in listening to music) without any noticeable exertion. Regrettable as the neglect of contemporary works may seem at first sight, it has the partly beneficial effect of a cruel selection: a composition's prospects of surviving are slim nowadays, and therefore we can be quite sure that a modern piece which has withstood its period of sensational success and is still played twenty-five years after its first appearance must have qualities that distinguish it in some way from others. I doubt whether the creative musician of today would be satisfied with the situation of former ages, when the life of a composition corresponded roughly with the life span of its creator. At that time the idea of music surviving the musician obviously was not appreciated. We, being accustomed to include in all our intellectual experiences the consideration of the past and expecting our successors to act similarly, like to regard our present deeds against a background of future developments, and it seems comforting to hope that once our individualities have passed from the scene, some surviving embodiment of our thoughts and feelings will for a while give evidence of our having been existent.

II

Diseaselike conditions may develop which prevent compositions from going through their proper circle of life. We will have to fight them if we care for health, dignity, and honesty in music. Some, like the aforementioned tendency towards sensation, can be cured by our determination not to submit to the demands of those providing or seeking sensation. Others need a subtler treatment.

There is one germ that has infected our musical life and has weakened it to an alarming degree. I am speaking of the inclination towards entertainment — a trend similar to the demand for sensation, but less violent and therefore more ruinous in the long run. By entertainment we mean not only the cheapest and most easily accessible satisfaction of a desire for sensual pleasure; we include in this term our entire complex system of distributing and receiving any kind of music up to superior compositions, if it is used for the sole aim of gratifying the listeners with the amenities of sound. Music as a science has been dead for centuries. Music as an agent of moral elevation seems to have lost its position; the ethic power of music is left unused. Music as a part of religious devotion has become an empty shell. Sound and its effect on our auditory nerves apparently is the only factor considered essential. What you read in criticisms, reports, books on music, after discarding the ephemeral facts of mere newsreel value, is hardly ever more than an endless concern with sonorities and how they are, or were, or ought to be produced. Symphony orchestras have degenerated into mere distributors of superrefined sounds, and the more sparkling and alluring the sounds appear, the higher is an orchestra's rating. Individual performers rarely cultivate any other virtues than an infallible virtuoso dexterity. Composers, too, have joined the dance around the golden calf of entertainment.

Technical perfection is the only positive gain that grows out of this basically unartistic attitude, but since it stimulates the receiving mind to demand more technical refinement, which demand in turn has to be satisfied with still greater technical skill on the part of the entertainers, the horrible senselessness of this submission to sound and its effects becomes more evident with every step towards ultimate excellence. It is the curse of virtuosity that it can beget nothing but virtuosity. A civilization that demands virtuosity for virtuosity's sake and neglects all higher aspects of musical activity is doomed sooner or later to produce a nation-wide musical dementia, an effect similar to that of a universal and excessive use of narcotics.

We must not object to musical entertainment in general. Like the other enjoyments of this world it has its rightful place in our mental diet and therefore we included it in our philosophical approach to music. But even school children nowadays know about the harmful effects of unrestricted addiction to delectations. We must remain the masters; the weakening results of a permanent enjoyment of audible luxuries should never be permitted to get the upper hand. On the other side, we need not go so far in castigating ourselves as some purists do, who feel they are dwelling in mud and sin if occasionally and unexpectedly a phrase in their carefully selected musical fare has a plainly pleasant effect on their recondite souls.

It is the musicians' vanity, their reckless hankering for success and fame, no matter how enticingly disguised by a fraudulent human magnanimity, that created and maintains this unsavory state of affairs. Hand in hand goes the critics' saturation with sonority, their failure to see and proclaim nobler objectives. And if all this is not enough, an army of music-alien concert managers, agents, and talent scouts will do their utmost to extinguish the last decrepit longing for artistic sublimation. We cannot condemn the music-consuming public for having little resistance to the incessant administration of musical opiates. The audiences in this country as in any other country with public distribution of music are well-meaning and have the best intentions in respect to music, but they are weak, undetermined, and playful like children. They need, and joyfully accept, understanding leadership. Whatever the above-mentioned group of selfish usufructuaries may say in disparaging the public's tendencies and glorifying their own deeds, a congenial education is always appreciated, and the professional can do nothing better than to reach a mutual understanding with the consumers on their inarticulate desires and his ability of wisely and honestly satisfying them.

The general good will of the sum total of listeners taken for granted, we must not forget that in an audience composed of attentive listeners, there will always be an infinite number of gradations in attention, ranging from the lowest extreme of superficial perception by those whom we may call playful seekers of entertainment, up to the highest level of a cultured appreciation. But whatever mental energy the listener invests in his attention, whatever his quality as a listener, the mere fact that he is attentive has to be recognized by the musician as a positive factor even if it is nothing but a very small step towards the ideal artistic cooperation of artist and listener. As long as an effort is made at all, the listener has a moral right of existence, and there is a gradual, but not an essential difference between the man who considers which first-class concert he is going to attend and the music fan who contemplates the prospective charm of his musical selection before inserting a coin in the nickelodeon — provided, of course, that after inserting his nickel he listens. If artists or those interested in artistic culture do not like to see the majority of attentive listeners devoted to nickelodeons and other music-spitting devices as the people's main source of musical enjoyment and education, they will have to find means of information and conviction which will convert those devotees into more important and more qualified consumers of music. Nowadays the actual number of attentive listeners counted all over a country is infinitely larger than ever before, and even in single places of performance, such as concert halls, stadiums, and so forth, we see more listeners assembled than there could formerly have been in all the concert halls together of a fair-sized country. Nevertheless, we can be sure that the percentage of cultured listeners in our audiences is considerably lower. Millions may be attentive listeners to a symphony concert — counting those actually present at the performance and all the others who tune in on their radios — but among these millions we may find scarcely more than several thousands who are participating in a sense of moral elevation. A music performance in aristocratic Vienna in the nineteenth century, or in the music-loving circles of eighteenth-century London, doubtless showed a greater proportion of such participants. An optimistic observer may take the actual number of several thousands as a wonderful symbol of progress in musical appreciation, while a pessimist will be discouraged by the low percentage. I think there is no reason either for enthusiasm or for dejection. In our state of musical development a tremendous influx of new listeners has occurred, and we cannot blame these countless newcomers if they need a long time to develop among themselves a higher percentage of proficient participants. We must even be lenient with our producers and reproducers if in the face of so new a situation they do not know how to properly satisfy the appetites of those masses, and try to retain as long as possible our traditional means and standards of composing and performing, and to accommodate them to conditions never known before. As long as they do so with idealism and with a consciousness of their mission, they must be given every chance at improvement. But if, as has happened in our time, those new innocents are caught in the nets of unscrupulous wholesalers of low-grade entertainment, it becomes time for serious writers, performers, distributors and teachers of music to save what can be saved, if something that with some conviction can be called musical culture is to follow our present chaos.

## III

Let us now contemplate a kind of listener who by his very nature can never be reached by any sincere endeavor of a musician; a listener who never existed in earlier times, who is the exclusive product of our system of musical mass-distribution carried on by radios, Muzaks, and other relentlessly running music-faucets; a listener of the most degenerate type, who is surrounded by music every minute of his daily life. When he first came in touch with this continuous stream of music, he enjoyed it as a musical treat. Then he got used to the permanent outpour of sound, and now he does not listen at all. Yet he wants to have this lulling noise, and the only time he feels uncomfortable is when by some mechanical defect his sound distributor ceases to emit its gifts. There is no question of quality, of characteristic expression, of ethical aims, of moral effects. Everything else disappears, if the one condition is accepted: a nonstop flow of faceless sound.

There is no way of escape. If our hands are dirty, we can wash them; if we are not hungry, nobody can force us to eat; if we don't like to look at something, we can close our eyes. But against this musical pestilence nothing can be done. It is poured out on us, we cannot wash it off; it does not stop when we are replete; we cannot shut off our ears. Those who apparently cannot live without this idiotic accompaniment to their daily routine permit their minds to be treated as they would never treat their car. Even the simplest jalopy gets some cleaning and polishing now and then, but those so-called listeners swim up to their necks in the morass of sound and let themselves get besmirched with ever-renewed dirty coats of noise and do not feel the desire for any cleansing. They are in respect to music worse than a habitual drunkard, because in the drunkard's behavior there is at least some faint suggestion of a motion made after a decision formed by his own free will — although for the minimum motion to get his liquids the following reward seems to be disproportionately great. Our musical drunkard's only meaningful move is to turn the faucet on in the morning and shut it off at night.

Perhaps it is understandable that with the complete lack of any protective sanitary instruction in this field people simply do not have the consciousness and courage to resist, much less fight, an ever-present inundation of sound. But it is surprising that no department of health, no school, no police, no government ever recognized its demoralizing effect. On the contrary, noted educators who probably would object to ruining a youngster's body by permitting him to eat an endless amount of candy, frequently enough praise the pedagogic value of the permanently sounding loud-speaker, thus agreeing to the mental equivalent of a chronic stomach disease. It is not so much the fact that music has lost all its dignity, all its artistic and ethic value, which is so depressing; it is the degradation of the human mind, the violation of man's right to self-determination, his being inseparably chained to something that normally is used only as a kind of stimulus. We went to war to fight dictators and dictatorships, but here at home we permit ourselves to be the slaves of the lowest kind of subjugation: to yield to a dope that weakens the addict's character, removes his power of resistance, and makes him an irresolute prey of any seduction that comes along.

In the eyes of the army of managers who operate this tremendous sewage system of sound, man seems to belong on the same level of intelligence as chickens or cows, whose egg and milk production is said to be favorably influenced by constantly flowing music. I have my doubts. I am sure that after several generations of hens and cows exposed to crooning, jazz, and hillbilly, eggs will deteriorate into something uneatable, and the milk and meat of cows will turn poisonous. Probably not until some of these nutriments have killed a few customers will people see that something was wrong.

One thing surprises me: that this exasperating outpour of music has never been used for grandiose anticapitalistic propaganda. "Look here," they could say, "the labor slaves of the capitalistic state can be kept working only when their brains are put into a permanent stupor by being filled to the brim with musiclike noises." This propaganda probably was left unutilized merely because the noncapitalistic governments in their notorious inclination towards everything gigantesque outdid the feeble-minded West by mounting ten loud-speakers where in those backward capitalist countries a single one is provided.

It is said that one of the most horrid tortures inflicted on captured political enemies of Nazidom's tyrant was the incessant gramophone playing of patriotic songs; this drove the victims to the verge of insanity. Compare this fact with the answer given by the owner of a delightful little hotel when asked why the otherwise pleasant atmosphere of his lobby had to be marred by a daily and nightly groaning loud-speaker. He said: "Have you ever felt how horrifying silence is?" Silence, one of the most merciful gifts of heaven in this noisy world! Silence, the horizon against which alone music assumes contour and meaning!

It is our era that has had the privilege of adding to those old disgraceful blemishes on mankind's record — political dictatorship, slave labor, prostitution, racial prejudice — the modern complement, the "captive audience." We may have some hope that this plague of bastard music, like others that scourged the human race, such as cholera and scurvy, will wane and be reduced to a bearable minimum, simply because there has been too much of it.

IV

Even if we admit that the consumer of music in his most abject form as captive auditor is so low that he should not be counted as having any relation to music at all — despite the fact that he may by the weight of numbers and the amount of pseudomusic provided for him eventually ruin the world's serious musical achievements — we cannot deny that the listener in general has reached an appalling level of degeneration. Artists, managers, agents, catering maliciously to his ever-ready tendency towards the least resistance instead of trying to raise his musical ambitions, do their best to support the decline of music and musicians: they neglect entirely any genuine artistic considerations and orient everything musical towards the one goal, entertainment. It is their fault that the craving for entertainment has a grip on our musical life like a cancerous growth, and they will see to it that a state of health is simulated. Anyone will be calumniated who dares utter the slightest doubts about our allegedly ideal musical situation. Yet, one can, if he cares to listen, hear in ever growing insistence the voices of those who are profoundly distressed.

Doubtless they will in due time be followed by crusaders against the pestilence, who will fight the idolatry of virtuosity, sonority, and glamorous emptiness.

If the producer of serious music loses his listeners to the grip of never-ending entertainment, he loses the most important outlet for his products. Writing exclusively for the specialized demands of the professional musician is not enough, since the field is too small to be sufficiently rewarding for the composer; nor can remarkable improvements for music in general grow out of so restricted an artistry. Therefore a further loss of competent listeners must be prevented, and the man who writes music must do his just share. To be sure, a plague cannot be treated by applying local plasters or by sipping medicated drops. More powerful remedies must be used. If the totality of listeners have in themselves lost the ability of regeneration, and if our performing and managing providers of audible entertainment are not willing to tackle the problem, the task of finding a cure for the evil will be left with the creative musician. His most efficient means of accomplishing this will be to write music for the singing and playing amateur. Such activity may also aid him in his own striving for an adjustment of his craft in its present-day forlornness and misesteem.

Let us have a closer look at the amateur. In former times the broad phalanx of those participating in music consisted predominantly of a vast middle field of amateurs: people who made music their hobby in the form of singing and playing but did not practice it professionally. At their right wing there was a relatively small group of professionals, and at the left, an equally small number of mere listeners. The amateur, having always been a considerable factor in musical life, reached the climax of his importance in the eighteenth and nineteenth centuries. Our classical literature is unthinkable without the amateur in the background. He played in the orchestras together with the professional, he sang in the choirs, and for him all chamber music was written. Haydn's, Mozart's and Beethoven's quartets, even Brahms's chamber music counted mostly on the amateur.

Today, with the number of participants in musical performances swollen from thousands to millions, their make-up has changed considerably. The right wing, the group of professional performers, has gained in numbers, but lost in percentage. The left wing, the listeners, now covers almost the entire area, and the middle field has dwindled to almost nothing. If we assume that the former distribution of listeners, amateurs, and professionals was, expressed in per cent, about 5, 90, and 5, respectively, we can for our modern times take 95, 1, and 4 as a fair estimate. We cannot think of a musician who would not see in this remarkable change of powers a turn toward shallowness. The reason for it is the general change in our social set-up, combined with the evolution of our musical tastes and habits. A change in the percentage distribution of the three music-participating groups in favor of the musical amateur would be a most commendable first step towards recovery.

Of course, we still have amateur musicians. Although their percentage is low, their actual number is higher than ever. Think of all the high school and university orchestras and bands, the glee clubs and choral groups. The trouble with them is that usually they provide musical activity for the youth only. Boys and girls, having played an instrument during their school years, may hardly ever look at it again, once they enter professional life or marry; in exceptional cases only do they join amateur orchestras or choruses; and usually they prefer to increase the army of listeners, drown in musical laziness, and lose their function of circulating life blood in the musical body. They degenerate to unproductive consumers. The goods they consume can be and are easily produced by a small number of musical trusts, consisting of a few leading orchestras, conductors, and soloists, and consisting of those concert agents who with their packaged delivery of complete New-Yorkized concert seasons to provincial towns kill all local initiative and paralyze the cities' own musical endeavors. In economic life men knew how to break the neck of antisocial trusts, by introducing antitrust laws, but in music the dictatorship of trusts seems to be accepted as inevitable and even pleasant, although it lowers musical taste and knowledge, promotes artistic inertia, and in addition, ruins hundreds of musical careers every year and drives thousands of musicians and intelligent listeners into dissatisfaction.

Our school system, if it was capable of any imaginative and

creative action, could devote the major part of its activities to the production of teachers whose task it would be to augment the one per cent of amateurs to a more respectable size. Instead, our musical education is almost exclusively concerned with the professionals' four per cent. Teachers' colleges seem to be an exception, but as their graduates are spreading music among the school and college student crowd only, which, as said before, ends up in the anonymous multitude of listeners, the picture remains the same.

## V

Would not the situation be improved, if we could encourage those singers and players in high schools and universities to keep up their singing and playing? Of course, one would have to make their efforts worth while, would have to provide rehearsals, concerts, literature, and instruction of a kind that interests the layman and convinces him that he gets more out of musical community work musically and morally than from The Famous Conductor being broadcast between commercials of tooth paste and crunchy crackers. Teachers, as we produce them nowadays, cannot do this job, because they are trained for other purposes. They would infallibly teach the amateur their own professional musical attitude, and who wants to have other people's professional attitudes if he has the desire to get something for his own benefit, and something that he is able to love wholeheartedly at that?

It certainly will not be easy to gear the educational system to such an entirely new task, since replacing the musical trusts with something useful for the amateur will tax the power and conviction of many musicians. Both the experts of music education and those profiting by the trust system will tell us that it cannot be done. Many problems will turn up which thus far in our musical life have been entirely unknown. I do not want to dwell in hypotheses and predictions, but I want to draw your attention to only one of the new points of view in a new educational setup. Piano playing, keyboard playing in general is of no use for the amateur. Amateurs' music is essentially community music. Not only does a piano forbid any community of players — except in the professional's or semiprofessional's playing of quartets and

quintets; it isolates the amateur pianist psychologically. Whatever your ability as an amateur pianist is, you never will enjoy it
fully. You will always be dissatisfied, because you know how the
pieces you are playing are supposed to sound and you never have
enough technique to play them with perfection — if you have,
you are as good as a professional and cannot be counted among
the amateurs with their peculiar desires and enjoyments. On the
other hand, though you may be the worst fiddle player in the
world, there will always be a seat for you in the second violin
section, where you can play your few scratching tones with
full enthusiasm, can improve from session to session, and will
not be looked at with scorn and contempt. On the contrary, once
you join an amateur group, you are a member of a great frater-
nity, whose purpose is the most dignified one you can imagine:
to inspire one another and unite in building up a creation that is
greater than one individual's deeds. Amateurs of this kind, when
listening to music, will not be the stupid receivers, the targets of
virtuosity, the idle gourmands of which our audiences predominantly consist. They cannot merely be fed with music of a conductor's or a concert agent's choice. They know what they
want, and they intend to get it.

It is here that the composer comes in. He would have to provide
the music needed and appreciated by the amateur; music written
in the professionals' concert style would not serve the purpose.
He would have to search for a new technical and stylistic approach — a new human approach, too! Until through years of
work and the concerted devotion of many like-minded musicians
such technique and style are developed and many listeners have
been converted, the work will frequently enough be similar to
that of the boy at the dike, when he checked with his hand a
trickle of water, preventing the dike from ultimate collapse. We
know, the boy did it!

Could not the detour through the amateur's musical domain
reopen another source of musical regeneration which today is
entirely dried up? The musical life of the family, not in the well-
known form of a television screen with the mute array from
grandma down to the toddler, but as a singing and playing community — could it not be revived? True, we cannot hitch the cart

before the horse, and if family life in the old solid, intelligent, and stimulating manner has been lost, music may not be the medium that will be victorious over all unfavorable factors. But once a broad rank of amateurs has been won over, their musical activities may readily extend their beneficial influence into the family, and the road from there to a creative writer's devoting his imagination towards the provision of suitable music for them should not be too difficult to find.

A German proverb says: *Böse Menschen haben keine Lieder* (bad men don't sing). It is not impossible that out of a tremendous movement of amateur community music a peace movement could spread over the world. Could it not be supported by our high dignitaries? Instead of the president of the United States solitarily playing the piano in Washington and the ruler of the Russians strumming his balalaika (or whatever he strums) in Moscow, could they not, together with their respective governments, join once a week in an orchestra or chorus, thus giving the world an example of common enterprises towards a lofty goal? People who make music together cannot be enemies, at least not while the music lasts.

## VI

Our analysis of the environment the contemporary composer lives in acquainted us with conditions hardly gratifying to the man who allegedly adorns the world with his creations. The universal overestimation of the performer at the expense of the creative musician which is one of the prevalent trends in our era's evaluation of the arts may be justified in respect to the writer of worthless music, but it places the real creative mind in a position deprived of dignity. Although it has happened at all times and in all places, that great geniuses lived and died unrecognized, musical creation as such was formerly revered as the most precious gift a musician (and through him a musical culture) could possess. Never before was there a time when compositions were regarded merely as vehicles for the performers' selfish deeds. How desirable it would be for the world of music if the old confidence could be restored, and if the producer of music himself could do it. It is, however, questionable whether a constant and all-out fight against that evil of our musical industrialism would produce more than tactical successes with limited results. Besides, such a fight requires the full strength and the full fury of a man, and so does composing. The man who writes music will by the very nature of his profession hardly have enough aggressive spirit and endurance to fight until he is the winner. Yet, his physical inefficiency need not be an excuse for a retreat into monkish seclusion. No evasion of the brutalities of musical reality is commended.

What should be aspired to is a life which induces action. In the preceding pages I tried to show at least one method by which the composer, in addition to the mere technical practice of his craft, could be the helper and even the spiritual leader in a search for a more salubrious musical world: it should be his main objective to lift the consumer to a higher level by convincing him of the harm a constant yearning for entertainment produces; and as a means to this end the writing of suitable music for the amateur was recommended. Certainly, writing such music will not be the only means, but it will be the form in which the desire for replacing external brilliancy with genuine musical values finds its clearest expression. Once a writer's technique and style is organized in this direction, so that music which satisfies the amateur's wishes can be created, his approach to his entire work will inevitably undergo a radical change: the emphasis on moral aspects will now become recognizable also in his works written for the concertizing professional, and now he will talk with a different spirit to the general audience, which, in its basic benevolence, will be ready to accept his leadership towards better goals.

Of the many other possible paths leading to the same objective some are, due to the present chaotic musical situation, either hard to find or blocked by too many obstacles. Others yield only to a more ferocious pioneer spirit than is good for the production of serious music, and still others are made inaccessible by adversaries. Whatever means of ennobling music is used in individual instances, it seems clear that before any action can be entered into, a thoroughgoing mental self-examination of the musician must take place, in which he must find an accord between his aims and the labor to be invested in their achievement.

Such preparatory examination will, as the first ray of a dawning illumination, doubtless lead to a revocation of everything that we branded as negative a while ago. Now our musician will decide not to enter serfdom in the form of obeying the performers' orders; begging for their condescension will be below his dignity; no blaring publicity for publicity's sake will be his ambition. The opinion of short-sighted critics, be it bad or flattering, will not touch him; publishers will have no chance of pushing him around. He will refuse to build his fame on a ground of musical chauvinism, and he will not belong to cliques the only purpose of which is mutual featherbedding of their members. The ceaseless hunt for sinecures masked as scholarships, ever-renewed instruction, and plain payment for laziness will appear to him what it really is: an enervating excuse for a meager output.

His choice is honest and hard work, and with this he turns our negative picture into its positive form, in which the arrangement of light and shadow is correct and artistically most satisfactory. If we then ask what the auspices of his work are, the answer will be: he has entered the inner circle of veritable artistic creation, and if his talent permits, he may well be on his way to producing a musical masterpiece.

We know this way. We have outlined it elaborately in our chapters on basic musical facts. In them beacons can be found that will lead our aspirant to truth and perfection. He will then know about musical inspiration and how to touch validly the intellectual and emotional depths of our soul. All the ethic power of music will be at his command and he will use it with a sense of severest moral responsibility. His further guides will be an inspiring creative ideal and the search for its realization; an unshakable conviction in the loftiness of our art; a power to evoke convincing and exalting forms and to address us with the language of purity. A life following such rules is bound to exemplarily persuade others to become associated. This life in and with music, being essentially a victory over external forces and a final allegiance to spiritual sovereignty, can only be a life of humility, of giving one's best to one's fellow men. This gift will not be like the alms passed on to the beggar: it will be the sharing of a man's every possession with his friend.

The ultimate reason for this humility will be the musician's conviction that beyond all the rational knowledge he has amassed and all his dexterity as a craftsman there is a region of visionary irrationality in which the veiled secrets of art dwell, sensed but not understood, implored but not commanded, imparting but not yielding. He cannot enter this region, he can only pray to be elected one of its messengers. If his prayers are granted and he, armed with wisdom and gifted with reverence for the unknowable, is the man whom heaven has blessed with the genius of creation, we may see in him the donor of the precious present we all long for: the great music of our time.